# THE BLACK MUSLIMS IN AMERICA

# THE BLACK MUSLIMS
# IN AMERICA

REVISED EDITION

# C. ERIC LINCOLN

FOREWORD BY GORDON W. ALLPORT

Published simultaneously in hardcover and paperback editions

Beacon Press books are published under the auspices of the Unitarian Universalist Association

9  8  7  6  5  4  3

Library of Congress Cataloging in Publication Data

Lincoln, Charles Eric.

The Black Muslims in America.
Originally presented as the author's thesis, Boston University.

1. Black Muslims.    I. Title.

E185.61.L56   1973      301.45′29′77073      72-6234

ISBN 0-8070-0512-6
ISBN 0-8070-0513-4 (pbk.)

*This book originated as a dissertation submitted in partial fulfillment of the requirements for the degree of Doctor of Philosophy in the Graduate School of Boston University*

ACKNOWLEDGMENTS

The author wishes to acknowledge with thanks use of material from the following sources: E. D. Beynon, "The Voodoo Cult Among Negro Migrants in Detroit," *American Journal of Sociology* (July 1937-May 1938); A. E. Fauset, "Moorish Temple Science in America," in J. M. Yinger's *Religion, Society, and the Individual,* Macmillan; E. Hoffer, *The True Believer,* New American Library; Mike Wallace and Louis Lomax, "The Hate That Hate Produced," *Newsbeat* (WNTA-TV); *Sepia,* November 1959.

To

Cecil, Joyce, Hilary, and Less Charles

# Contents

# Preface

In the autumn of 1956, I was teaching courses in religion and philosophy at Clark College in Atlanta, Georgia. This study of the Black Muslims began when I read the following appraisal of Christianity in a term paper submitted to me by a senior student:

> The Christian religion is incompatible with the Negro's aspirations for dignity and equality in America. It has hindered where it might have helped; it has been evasive when it was morally bound to be forthright; it has separated believers on the basis of color although it has declared its mission to be a universal brotherhood under Jesus Christ. Christian love is the white man's love for himself and for his race. For the man who is not white, Islam is the hope for justice and equality in the world we must build tomorrow.

Inquiry revealed that the writer, a sensitive and gifted young man, had come under the influence of the local Muslim minister, as had a few other students at the college. Despite their Christian backgrounds, and despite the fact that they were even then attending a church-related college, these young men had despaired of Christianity as a way of life capable of affording them the respect and dignity they sought and deserved.

I did not share those sentiments, and I do not share them today; but the challenge to study the alternative proposed in the term paper was irresistible.

This study of the Black Muslims has been an interesting and fascinating adventure, full of surprises and of social and religious inconformities. I soon discovered, for example, that these were no ordinary Moslems, nor did they wish to be taken as such. To distinguish themselves from the small Moslem enclaves that have existed in a few American cities for generations, they chose the spelling "Muslim" rather than the more familiar "Moslem." Further, these Muslims emphasize that they

are "Black Men," *black* as the antithesis of white. <u>They do not sub-</u>
<u>scribe to the familiar Moslem doctrine that a common submission to</u>
<u>Allah erases and transcends all racial awareness.</u> On the contrary, they
do not conceive the white man as capable of being a Muslim. "By
nature he is incapable!"

The racial emphases peculiar to this rapidly growing, Chicago-cen-
tered movement suggested the descriptive phrase "Black Muslims,"
which I coined in 1956 and which has been widely used since to desig-
nate this group. Theretofore they had been variously known as the
<u>"Temple People," "the Muhammadans," "the Muslims," "the Voodoo</u>
<u>Cult" and "the Nation of Islam."</u>[1]

The study of the Black Muslims has taken me to many cities across
the country, and it has provided unusual opportunities for me to sense
directly the several pulses of America's Negro community, which is now
making a determined struggle for a creative and meaningful existence.
To most Negroes the teachings of the Black Muslim leader, Elijah
Muhammad, are intellectually repugnant, but one is uncomfortably
conscious of an emotional ambivalence towards the attraction and the
power of a doctrine which promises an "escape into freedom" after so
many years and so many forms of bondage. The rational self rebels
against racism in any form and from any quarter, but the emotional self
resists the contemplation of a reversal of fortune only with great effort.

This study is in no sense complete. At best it presents a partial
perspective of the dark and serious problems of racial tension—problems which confront responsible men in this country and throughout
the world. We need more studies about the voiceless people who want
to be heard in the councils of the world. We need more action in terms
of the truths that are already known. We shall have to hurry, I think, if
we hope to pass on to our children a world in which there is reasonable
hope for creative survival.

Many individuals and institutions have lent encouragement or support to the study during the years it was in progress. It would be
impossible to name them all, but I wish to express my thanks and
appreciation to every person who has in any way participated in bringing this piece of research to its present stage. First of all, I would
express my thanks to Albert and Jessie Danielsen of Wellesley Hills,
Massachusetts, whose comfortable home and warm friendship have provided a haven of refuge at periods when the day-to-day pressures have
demanded respite.

I am particularly indebted to Professor Gordon Allport of Harvard University and to Professor Harold Isaacs of the Center for International Relations at the Massachusetts Institute of Technology for their encouragement and advice at critical periods of research and writing.

Dr. Kenneth Benne, Director of the Boston University Human Relations Center, and Mr. Frank Hurwitz, Executive Secretary of the Center, not only placed the facilities of the Center at my disposal but also relieved me of the normal responsibilites incident to being a Human Relations Fellow, thus permitting me to give full time to research on the Black Muslims. Professor Robert Chin at the Center has been of invaluable help and encouragement in helping to structure the research and in criticizing my methods of procedure and investigation.

I wish also to express my thanks to Mr. Elijah Muhammad, the "Spiritual Head of the Muslims in the West," for his cooperation in certain phases of the study. I am especially indebted to Minister Malcolm X of New York City and to Minister Louis X of Boston for the unusual degree of cooperation I have received from them during the course of the investigation. While we have not always agreed on certain premises incident to the Movement, these gentlemen have always welcomed me with courtesy, respect, and a spirit of cooperation.

The *Pittsburgh Courier* made its files available to me, an important courtesy for which I am very grateful indeed.

To President James P. Brawley and Dean A. A. McPheeters of Clark College, I would express my appreciation for their continued encouragement, and for the extended leave of absence which made it possible for me to complete the research, the dissertation, and this manuscript before returning to my post as Professor of Social Philosophy at Clark.

It would be difficult indeed for me to adequately express my gratitude to Dean Walter G. Muelder and Associate Professor Paul Deats, Jr., of the Boston University School of Theology. Nominally the professors directing my graduate studies, they have in fact been friends and counselors through three long and crucial years. I cannot hope to repay them for their guidance and confidence—and for their abiding friendship, which has always been a dimension external to the professor-student relationship.

I wish to express my indebtedness to Miss Sylvia Lafargue, Miss Hester W. Price, and Mrs. Bertha S. Mintz, whose expert typing turned my original notes into an acceptable manuscript.

This has been an expensive undertaking, and it could not have been accomplished without generous support from several sources. The initial investigation was unsupported; but three years of study and research at Boston University were supported by grants and fellowships from the John Hay Whitney Foundation, The Crusade Scholarships of the Methodist Church, the Lilly Foundation, the Boston University Human Relations Center, the Society for the Psychological Study of Social Issues, and the Anti-Defamation League of B'nai B'rith.

Professor Lyman V. Cady, head of the Department of Religion and Philosophy during my graduate studies at Fisk University, very graciously interrupted his summer vacation to read portions of the manuscript and to make suggestions for its improvement; so also did Alex Haley, who has himself been an observer and interpreter of the Movement, and Dr. J. T. Wright, former director of the Staten Island Mental Health Association. All three are wise and perceptive friends and critics. Whatever inadequacies may persist in this study can but reflect my own inability to employ effectively the prudent judgments available to me.

Finally, it should be acknowledged that the real sacrifice making this study possible has been borne by those most dear to me, who have had to carry on in my absence longer than it was reasonable to ask. I only hope that in some way this effort has been worth their patience and deprivation.

C. ERIC LINCOLN

Boston, Massachusetts
December 1960

# Foreword

One century after the Emancipation Proclamation we are still trying in our country to repair the moral ravages of slavery. Our progress is slow and sluggish. It is this sluggishness that has given rise to the melodramatic Black Muslim Movement.

Dr. C. Eric Lincoln gives us a clear, moving, balanced account of the origins and rationale of this movement. His book makes fascinating reading. It is also one of the best technical case studies in the whole literature of social science. From it we learn that while the tenets of this strange Moslem sect are fantastic and unbelievable, yet at the same time the movement as a whole makes good sense and has functional value for its numerous adherents. Oppression evolves a logic of its own. An ideology, though weird, often means more than it says.

The Black Muslim believes that the day of the white man has passed—or soon will. Peaceful integration is not the Negro's goal, for "why integrate with a dying man?" What the Negro requires is a new morale, economic self-sufficiency, a high code of personal morals, and a return to the pristine glory of his race. He needs to free himself from all remnants of slave mentality and from Christianity which has too long kept him doped in subservience to the white man. These are the underlying propositions upon which the movement rests. It has a Nietzschean flavor. But since abstractions require concrete symbolization in order to motivate, Elijah Muhammad, the leader, has evolved a heady array of myths, rituals, styles of greeting, to provide the effective scaffolding of imagery needed by his less educated followers. The tie to Islam is, of course, an historical monstrosity, but this fact does not trouble minds innocent of theological antiquity.

The entire movement rests upon an absolute and inflexible dichotomy of white-Negro, or, more accurately, white-nonwhite. White is evil; nonwhite is good. Here are a few key phrases: "There is no white man a Muslim can trust." If you say the movement rests on hate, it is "the hate that hate produced." Even the impartial reader concludes that much Elijah Muhammad says about the white man is "true enough to be embarrasing."

Thus the reader himself easily slips into a spurious black-white frame of mind. Like the Black Muslim he may find himself exalting race, "man's most dangerous myth," to the position of a final fixed truth.

Biologically speaking, color is a trivial fact. It leads none the less to coarse and dangerous misclassifications when it is applied to relationships within the human family. Some white men say that nonwhites (all of them) are inferior. They are, of course, wrong. The only true statement would be that in *some* respects *some* of them are inferior, *many* are not. Similarly, the Black Muslim says "the white man" is responsible for all the disprivilege suffered by the nonwhite. The truth is that *some* white men under *some* conditions are responsible for *some* of the disadvantages of colored people. Overgeneralization is the very essence of prejudice. Hence such dogmas as these follow the line of bigotry rather than logic.

Most of us believe that improvement in group relations will come about when—by education and exhortation, by law and law-enforcement—fewer and fewer whites are led to behave in ways injurious to nonwhites. But the Black Muslin does not agree. For him the case is closed: it is nonwhite *versus* white. All people are fatally typed by skin color forever. Human beings are not mixtures of good and bad, wise and stupid, friendly and unfriendly, just and unjust, trustworthy and untrustworthy. Rather they are white and nonwhite, the one group, by its essence, incarnates evil qualities, the other virtues. This erroneous slicing marks the thought of all racists—of Hitler, of the White Citizens Council, of the Black Muslims.

Why do I feel it necessary here to refute the haunting irrelevancy of race? I confess it is because in reading these pages I found myself at times carried away by the persuasiveness of Elijah Muhammad and his ministers. I succumbed to Dr. Lincoln's deeply understanding and sympathetic account. Even though he writes as a social scientist his penetration of the topic forces me to wrestle with both the pros and cons of the case.

The author properly notes the ambiguity with which the leaders shroud the ultimate objectives of the movement. Its implications for the future are in a sense frightening, even though for the present one must admit there are gains for its devotees in heightened morality, economic improvement, and in hopeful outlook.

Further developments will bear close watching—by government authorities and also by social scientists. Will the sect continue to spread or will it wane? Will the fantastic legends on which it is based lose their appeal as the educational level of Negroes rises? Or, to the contrary, will educated Negroes find it possible to subscribe to an absurd ideology as did many German intellectuals under Hitler? And what other changes will occur over time? It is not enough to dismiss the movement as a lurid anomaly. It has deep roots in protest and is puzzling in portent.

Many of us live with false but cozy illusions concerning our relationships with other racial, ethnic, and national groups. We are not aware that a present battle rages between enlightened and fanatic solutions of our family problems. The situation in the United States, in South Africa, in Asia shows this to be the case. By deepening our insight Dr. Lincoln strengthens the hand of enlightenment. For only if we face the realities of race relations with accurate knowledge can we hope to find a sensible issue out of our predicament. We do well, therefore, to ponder closely the case of the Black Muslims.

GORDON W. ALLPORT

# Introduction to the Revised Edition
## The Black Muslims and
## Social Protest

Social protest is the corporate instrument of social change, and the social movement called the "Black Muslims" is symptomatic of the anxiety and unrest which characterizes the contemporary world situation. It has its counterparts in Asia, in Africa, in South America, in Europe, and wherever the peoples of the world are striving for a realignment of power and position. Such conditions of social anxiety generally follow in the wake of major disturbances in the power equilibrium, or in anticipation of such disturbances. Wars ("hot" or "cold"), major political changes, in short, whatever is perceived as a threat to the continued existence of the group, or to the values without which the group would interpret existence as meaningless, contributes to a condition of anxiety which may well be reflected in various forms of conflict—of which the protest movement is one.

We may restate our thesis in another way: Whenever there is an actual or a felt discrepancy in the power relations of discrete systems or subsystems, a condition of social anxiety will emerge.

A protest movement is an expression of the pervasive anxiety and discontent of a group in negative reaction to what is perceived as a discrepancy of power. Power is the control over decisions. The protest movement is a reaction protesting that control, or the character of its expression.

Conflict may also derive from a persistent inequity in the distribution of scarce values within a society. By scarce values I mean such tangibles as jobs, food, houses, and recreational facilities (*resource scarcity*); and such intangibles as status, recognition, respect, and acceptance (*position scarcity*).[1]

Such conflict may exist at one of several possible levels: It may be (1) *latent,* with the subordinated group unorganized in the recognized presence of a vastly superior power. The conflict may be (2) *nascent,* a situation in which an organization for conflict is in existence or under development, but the conflict has not yet become overt. Or, conflict may be (3) *ritualized* by the contending parties, thereby assuming a nonviolent expression. Very often conflict is (4) *suppressed,* by proscription of the organization of the subordinated group, or by force or the threat of force. In extreme circumstances conflict becomes (5) *violent,* resulting in the destruction of life and property.[2]

The Black Muslims are a symbol and a product of social conflict. They represent a point at the extreme edge of a spectrum of protest organizations and movements which involves, directly or indirectly, probably every Blackamerican. The spectrum of protest begins on the near side with the conservative churches, then shades progressively into the relatively more militant congregations, the Urban League, the NAACP, the SCLC, the SNCC, CORE, and finally into the unknown number of black nationalist organizations of which the Black Muslim movement is the largest and the best known. The organizations mentioned do not exhaust the roster of protest by any means. Some of the protest movements have sizable memberships in spite of their amorphous character. Some have no more than ten or twelve members. Some do not even have names.

But almost every church, every social club, sorority, or fraternity, every business or civic association doubles as a protest organization. The effort is total, or very nearly total. In some cities the protest membership is quite fluid, with individuals moving freely from group to group within a defined range as they become more activist oriented, or perhaps less certain of the final efficacy of the action groups. The wide range of affiliative possibilities is both functional and dysfunctional to the protest interests. Because there are many organizations, there is greater opportunity for a wider variety of personal expression than was possible when the Urban League and the NAACP had the field to themselves. However, the supply of leadership material has not kept pace with the proliferation of movements and organizations. The most effective leadership remains concentrated in a few organizations, while the energies and enthusiasms of a good number of the lesser-known protest groups are dissipated for want of planning and direction. Theirs is an inarticulate protest—unknown and ineffective.

The Black Muslims are among the best organized and most articulate of the protest movements. In terms of their immediate internal objectives, they have a highly effective leadership, some of which has been recruited from the Christian churches and retained by Elijah Muhammad to serve the cause of Black Islam. Their newspapers and magazines are superior in layout and technical quality to much of the black press; and their financial support of the movement is probably higher in proportion to income than that of any similar group.

Yet, the Black Muslims are not generally acceptable to the spirit of protest which has won universal respect and frequent admiration for some other members of the Blackamerican spectrum of protest. To understand why this is so, it will be fruitful to offer some analysis of the circumstances out of which the movement was born, the character of its membership, and the nature of its goals.

The psychological heritage of the Black Muslim movement, in common with that of all other Blackamerican protest organizations, is at least as old as the institution of slavery in America. Protest has been a distinctive although frequently a subdued thread widely distributed across the whole fabric of white-black relations throughout the history of white and black contact in America. The successive roles of masters and bondsmen, masters and slaves, white men and freedmen, majority and minority groups have been successive arrangements of hegemony and subordination in which the Black Man's role *vis à vis* that of the white man has not changed. From time to time, especially since the Second World War, there have been varying degrees of adjustment *within the system of arrangements,* but the power relationship has remained constant. Hence, the capacity of Blacks to affect decisions relating to themselves and the system of values they hold to be important is not appreciable.

Even the Black Man's limited capacity to affect decisions and produce change depends primarily upon the conscience and the convenience of the white man, rather than upon any existing corpus of power possessed by Blacks. Indeed, it is unlikely that the Blackamerican will ever have a dependable share in the control of the decision-making apparatus of his country until he either controls a significant segment of the economy, or a much larger percentage of the vote than he does at present. His inordinate dependence upon "protest" derives precisely from his failure to achieve the more dependable protection for his interests that comes from sharing the white man's power rather than appealing to the white man's conscience.

A protest movement is an aggressive expression of a subordinated group. It is the organization of the resources of the subordinated group to resist the coercive power of the dominant group, or to challenge the morality or the justice of the expression of that power. The Black Man did not wait until he was delivered in America to begin his protestation of the white man's concept of the Black Man's "place" in the caste system to be established here. Available records show that no fewer than fifty-five slave revolts occurred at sea between 1700 and 1845. During the height of the slave period—the two hundred years from 1664 to 1864—there are recorded accounts of at least 109 slave insurrections which occurred within the continental United States. Since it was customary to suppress all news and information concerning revolts lest they become infectious, it is reasonable to assume that the reported cases were of some magnitude, that very many cases were not reported, and that some cases which were reported have not yet been made available to research.

Protest was not limited to armed insurrection. The rate of infanticide was high. Suicide became a problem of such magnitude as to require the slave owners to devise "the strongest arguments possible" (supported by religious and social taboos) to reduce the rate of self-destruction. Sabotage of livestock, machinery, and agricultural produce was not unknown. "Taking" (from the white man, as distinct from "stealing" from each other) was routine. Running away was a form of protest so common as to have been considered a disease. Southern physicians described its symptoms in the journals of the period and gave it the name monomania—"a disease [it was said] to which the Negro is peculiarly subject."[3]

As slavery became increasingly profitable, the slavocracy became concerned to offer a moral justification for its peculiar institution. At the same time, it sought to inculcate the illiterate slaves (as it sought later to indoctrinate the freedmen and their abolitionist friends), with an image of the Black Man shrewdly designed to discourage protest and to encourage resignation and accommodation. This was the "Myth of the Magnolias," so called because it was usually accompanied by a fantasy of banjo-strumming darkies lounging peacefully under the sweet-scented magnolias behind the big house—happy and contented in their station, and forever loyal to the kindhearted master and his arrangements for their mutual felicities. The Magnolia myth explained the Black's condition in terms of "his *natural docility*, his *instinctive servility*, and his *inherent imbecility.*" It alleged that the Black Man's "docile nature" led to his willing acceptance of his condition of bondage, and that his "instinctive servility" made him an ideal slave—a being equipped psychologically to submit his will completely to that of another; who sensed his own inferiority, and who willed that his body be at the complete disposal of the more sophisticated will of his master. His alleged "imbecility" derived, it was argued, from an inherent incapacity to be creative, or to learn at a level beyond the simple abilities of a child. This was a principal intent of the Magnolia myth—to perpetuate an image of the Black Man as being inherently intellectually inferior, and therefore incapable of mastering the complex requirements of adult citizenship and self-determination. The Black Man was a child who could never grow up. He would never be "ready." This was the image the world was asked to accept.

The historians, the novelists, the politicians, and a varied assortment of other mythmakers have done America a great disservice. Each repetition of the myth makes it more difficult for those segments of the white majority who believe it, to understand the behavior of black people; and each repetition of the myth increases the determination of the black minority to belie it. Both science and history have discredited the Magnolia Myth, but the protest movements provide the most dramatic refutation. There are, for example, no docile Muslims. There are no servile student revolutionaries. And considering its success before our highest tribunal, it is hard to believe that the legal staff of the NAACP is a council of imbeciles.

The Magnolia Myth with local modifications remains a pervasive influence in our society. Our information media have done little to refute it. The editors of the texts we use to educate our children have done even less. It has remained then to the Blackamerican to destroy the myth himself. The Black Muslims have gone a step further and have created for themselves a countermyth, *the myth of black supremacy.*

The Black Muslim movement had its beginning in the black ghetto of Detroit. The time was 1930. It was the first year of the Great Depression—a time of hunger, confusion, disillusionment, despair, and discontent. It was a period of widespread fear and anxiety. Between 1900 and 1930 two-and-a-quarter-million Blackamericans left the farms and plantations of the South. Most of them emigrated to selected urban areas of the North—New York, Philadelphia, Chicago, and Detroit being among the most popular destinations. The black population of Detroit, for example, increased 611 per cent during the ten years of

1910 to 1920. During the same period, the total black population in the North increased from a mere 75,000 to 3000,000, an increase of 400 per cent.

Floods, crop failures, boll weevils, and the revival of the Ku Klux Klan all served to hasten the Blackamerican's departure from the South. One hundred Blackamericans were lynched during the first year of the twentieth century. By the outbreak of the First World War in 1914, the number stood at 1,100. When the war was over, the practice was resumed—28 Blacks were burned alive between 1918 and 1921. Scores of others were hanged dragged behind automobiles, shot, drowned, or hacked to death.

The Blacks who left the South were temporarily welcomed in the North, although the congenialities of the North have always been of a most impersonal sort. Many industries sent agents into the South to lure the Blacks north with promises of good jobs. But the Black Man was soon to find that it was his labor, not his presence, that was wanted. It was a common practice for the agents to purchase tickets for whole families and to move them *en masse* for resettlement in the great industrial cities. The war had drained away the white manpower needed to build the ships, work the steel, pack the meat, and man the machines; and it had also cut off the normal supply of immigrant labor from Europe.

After the war was over, the Black Man's welcome wore thin. It became increasingly hard for black people to get jobs except as strike-breakers. Soon there were not enough jobs to go around, and thousands of Blacks were fired and replaced with white men. There was not enough housing, and most Blacks were crowded into the black ghettos in the most deteriorated part of the inner city. Landlords and law-enforcement agencies alike were unsympathetic. But still the Blacks came out of the South. Few had skills; many were illiterate. All were filled with hope for something better than what they had left. Soon there was hunger and crime and delinquency—and trouble with the police. The bright promise of the North had failed. Hope turned to desperation. In desperation is the onset of anxiety.

It is an interesting historical phenomenon that when a people reach the precipice of despair, there is so often waiting in the wings a savior—a messiah to snatch them back from the edge of the abyss. So it was that in Detroit there appeared in the black ghetto a mysterious Mullah who called himself W. D. Farad Muhammad. He had come, he told the handful of Blacks who gathered to hear him, from the holy city of Mecca. His mission, as he described it, was "to wake the 'Dead Nation in the West';[4] to teach [them] the truth about the white man, and to prepare [them] for the Armageddon." The Armageddon? What did the apocalyptic concept have to do with the problems of the Black Man in America? Farad was explicit on the point: In the Book of Revelation it is promised that there will be a final battle between good and evil, and that this decisive battle will take place at Har-Magedon, "the Mountain of Megiddo," in the Great Plain of Esdraelon in Asia Minor.[5] But the Bible has a cryptic message for the initiated of Black Islam (even as it has for more familiar sects). The forces of "good and evil" are the forces of "black and white." "The Valley of Esdraelon" symbolizes "the Wilderness of North America." The Battle of Armageddon is to be the Black Man's final confrontation of the race which has so long oppressed him.

At first Farad (who was at the time thought to be a prophet, but who was after his departure recognized as Allah himself) met from house to house with small groups of Blacks. He want about his mission as unobtrusively as possible, listening to the problems of the destitute Blacks, sharing whatever they had to offer him.

The fame of the Prophet spread and he soon established in Detroit the first of the Temples of Islam. As his following increased he grew more bold in his attacks upon the habits and the culture symbols black people in America had always taken for granted. In the first place, he taught his followers that they were not "Negroes," but "Black Men." The word "Negro" was alleged to be an invention of the white man designed to identify his victims better and to separate them from their Asian and African borthers. Further, the so-called Negro was not an American, but an "Asiatic," for his forefathers had been stolen from the Afro-Asian continent by the white slavemasters who came in the name of Jesus. Christianity, the Prophet taught, was a white man's religion, a contrivance designed for the enslavement of nonwhite peoples. Wherever Christianity has gone, he declared, men have lost their liberty and their freedom. Islam was declared to be "the natural religion of the Black Man." Only in Islam could the so-called Negroes find freedom, justice, and equality.

In the troubled times of the early 1930s, men and women everywhere were looking for some panacea to save them from the desperate circumstances of the Depression. Large numbers of people found that they could not cope rationally with the excruciating anxiety—the uncertainties with which they were confronted from day to day. Some escapists leaped from the rooftops of the very buildings which were symbols of more stable times. Some clairvoyants, who thought they could discern the wave of the future in Marxist philosophy, found their panacea in the Communist party. Black escapism tended to be of a more practical nature. Instead of taking the long route to heaven, they built "heavens" here on earth in the cults of Father Divine and Daddy Grace.

The followers of Farad were both escapists and clairvoyants. Farad himself was the messiah who had come to lead the so-called Negroes into the millennium which was to follow the Battle of Armageddon. He was the Prophet who had foreseen and foretold the Golden Age that would be theirs when the Black Nation in the West had thrown off the yoke of the white slavemasters. But soon Farad had disappeared.

Under Elijah Muhammad, the new "Messenger of Islam," the movement spread from the initial temple in Detroit to almost every major city in the country where there is a sizable black population. In most of these cities there is a temple; in others, where the movement is less strong, there are missions. Where there are no missions there are likely to be representatives of the movement who are in contact with the Muslim leadership in nearby cities.

The black ghetto is the principal source of Muslim recruitment. There, in the dirty streets and crowded tenements where life is cheap and hope is minimal, where isolation from the common values of society and from the common privileges of citizenship is most acute, the voice of the Messenger does not fall upon deaf ears. So often, his is the only message directed to the pimps, the prostitutes, the conmen, the prisoners, the ex-cons, the alcoholics, the addicts, the unemployed, whom the responsible society has forgotten. It is a voice challenging them to recover their self-respect, urging them to repudiate the white man's religion and the white man's culture, daring them to believe in black supremacy, offering them a Black God and a Black Nation, promising them that the day will come when "we will be masters . . ."

Such is the challenge of Elijah Muhammad who is hailed by his ministers as "the most fearless black man in America." His followers are, with few exceptions, from America's most underprivileged class. They are denizens of the black ghetto. To them, the voice of Elijah Muhammad is a voice raised against injustice—real or imagined. Muhammad is a paladin who has taken up the cudgel against the "devil" who is responsible for all of their miseries and their failures. The resentments and the hostilities that breed in the ghetto are finally brought to focus upon a single object—*the white man.* Outside the black ghetto there are Muslim units in many of the state and federal prisons across the country. Here the movement finds its audiences ready made and highly receptive, for the racial character of the law-enforcement agencies, the courts, and the custodial personnel is a key factor in sharpening the black prisoner's resentments and his sense of persecution.

Generally speaking, the Black Muslim Movement has been a protest directed at the whole value-construct of the white Christian society—a society in which the Black Muslims feel themselves (as Blacks) an isolated and unappreciated appendage. Hence, the burden of their protest is against their "retention" in a society where they are not wanted. This is the soft side of the "Armageddon complex" which looks to the removal of the source of their discomfiture (i.e., the white man) rather than to going anywhere themselves. Mr. Muhammad teaches that "the white man's home is in Europe," and that "there will be no peace until every man is in his own country."

In every issue of the Muslim newspaper, *Muhammad Speaks,* the Muslims state their protest in the form of the following ten propositions:

1. We want freedom. We want a full and complete freedom.
2. We want justice. Equal justice under the law. We want justice applied equally to all, regardless of creed or class or color.
3. We want equality of opportunity. We want equal membership in society with the best in civilized society.
4. We want our people in America, whose parents or grandparents were descendants from slaves, to be allowed to establish a separate state or territory of their own. . . .
5. We want freedom for all Believers of Islam now held in federal prisons. We want freedom for all black men and women now under death sentence in innumerable prisons in the North as well as the South.

We want every black man and woman to have the freedom to accept or reject being separated from the slavemaster's children and establish a land of their own. . . .

6. We want an immediate end to the police brutality and mob attacks against the so-called Negro throughout the United States.

7. As long as we are not allowed to establish a state or territory of our own, we demand not only equal justice under the laws of the United States, but equal employment opportunities— NOW!. . . .

8. We want the government of the United States to exempt our people from ALL taxation as long as we are deprived of equal justice under the laws of the land.

9. We want equal education—but separate schools up to 16 for boys and 18 for girls on the condition that the girls be sent to women's colleges and universities. We want all black children educated, taught without hindrance or suppression.

10. We believe that intermarriage or race mixing should be prohibited. We want the religion of Islam taught without hindrance or suppression.

These are some of the things that we, the Muslims, want for our people in North America.[6]

Some of the proposals of the Muslims are obviously unrealistic, and we need not discuss them here. Other tests and demands of the Black Muslims as stated in the foregoing propositions do not seem unreasonable. I do not know any Americans who do not want freedom, for example. Justice under the law, equality of opportunity, and freedom of worship are all approved values in our society, and they find their sanctions in the American creed. Further, these are objectives which are implicit in the programs of all other movements within the black spectrum of protest. What, then, are the factors which qualify the Muslim protest movement and make it unacceptable to the general American public?

The fundamental differences between the attitudes, the behavior, and the goals of the Black Muslims as compared to other black protest organizations may be explained in terms of their differing degrees of dissociation deriving from the unusual anxiety and frustration incident to their status in the American social arrangement. Blackamericans, as a caste, are *all* outside the assimilative process, and they exhibit from time to time the frustrations which are the corollaries of their marginality. However, the dissociation of the Muslim membership from the larger society, and even from the general black subgroup (which ordinarily seeks to identify itself with the American mainstream), may be considered extreme. In reacting to the unique pressures of their day-to-day experiences as low-caste Blacks in a white-oriented society, the Muslims have abandoned the fundamental principles of the American creed and have substituted in its place a new system of values perceived as more consistent with the realities of their circumstances.

It is meaningless to label the Muslims as "unAmerican," for the American creed is not a legal or constitutional document against which the political loyalty of a group may be measured.[7] The American creed is a common set of beliefs and values in which all Americans have normally found consensus. It is a body of ideals, a social philosophy which affirms the basic dignity of every individual and the existence of certain inalienable rights without reference to race, creed, or color. The roots of the American creed are deep in the equalitarian doctrines of the eighteenth-century Enlightenment, Protestant Christianity, and English law. For most of us, it has been the cultural matrix within which all discordant sociopolitical attitudes converge, and from which derives the great diversity of social and political interpretations which makes democracy possible in a society of widely variant populations.

The Black Muslims, by the nature of certain of their goals and institutions, have excepted themselves from the aegis of the American creed. The Black Muslims repudiate American citizenship in favor of a somewhat dubious membership in a mystical "Asiatic" confraternity, and they are violently opposed to Christianity, the principles of which are fundamental to our understanding of the democratic ideal. Not only do they resist assimilation and avoid interracial participation in the life of the community, but the Muslim creed assigns all nonBlacks to the subhuman status of "devils" (and promises to treat them as such); the sustaining philosophy is one of black supremacy nurtured by a careful incalculation of suspicions of the white man and his characteristic institutions. By their own choice the Black Muslims exclude themselves from the body of principles and the system of values within the framework of which Americans have customarily sought to negotiate their grievances.

Other groups advocate white supremacy, resist the assimilation of

Blacks and others, and practice suspicion and hatred rather than love, yet they retain an idealistic loyalty to the principles of the American creed. The point is that although the creed is violated constantly in practice, it remains an *ideal* to which all give their asseveration—in which all believe, and from which we continue to derive our laws and our moral values in spite of our failures to honor them completely.

The Black Muslim Movement does not conceive itself to be in violation of the principles and values of the American creed. Rather, the movement views itself as having substituted new principles, new values, and a new creed based on a radically different interpretation of history from that expressed in the American creed. Muhammad promises a new order based on the primacy of a nation of black men with a manifest destiny under a Black God. His is an ideology radically different from those now determining the shape of the existing American society. In spite of the fact that the Black Muslim movement shares at some points the immediate goals of some other black protest movements, its oppugnance to traditional values limits its general acceptability as a protest organization. However, the action impact of the movement on the general black community has been considerable. Considering the fact that most of America's black millions live under conditions considerably more iniquitous than those which at other times and places have been productive of the gravest social consequences, we have probably been lucky. Very lucky. The Blacks in the black ghettos are certainly aware of the Black Muslims, and there is open admiration for their militant, nonaccommodative stance against the traditional aggressions of the white man.

Nevertheless, the tenacity of the Blackamerican's commitment to the democratic procedures implicit in the American creed has operated successfully to contain the Muslim movement—while at once realizing and appreciating its potential for alternative means of protest. But the Black Muslims remain a somber symbol of the social callousness that is possible even in an equalitarian democracy. Such movements do not "just happen." The Muslims are the most insistent symptoms of the failure of the society to meet effectively the minimum needs of one-tenth of its population to find a meaningful level of participation in the significant social values most white Americans take for granted.

The Muslims represent that segment of the black subculture who, being most deprived of traditional incentives, have finally turned to search for alternatives outside the commonly accepted value structure. They are the products of social anxiety—people who are repeatedly frustrated in their attempts to make satisfactory adjustments in a society unaware of their existence except as the faceless subjects of statistical data. As "Negroes," their future was unpromising. As Black Muslims, their creed is uncompromising. As Americans, the responsibility for what they are, or what they will become, is our own.

C. ERIC LINCOLN

Kumasi Farms, Gardiner, N.Y.
June 1972

# THE BLACK MUSLIMS
# IN AMERICA

# 1  The Verdict Is "Guilty"—
## The Sentence Is "Death"

A slightly built, light-skinned youth paused casually before twelve grave-faced black men and women sitting in a jury box at Boston's John Hancock Hall. There was an air of gentle friendliness about him, and he hardly looked the part of a prosecuting attorney. Slowly he turned and looked at a red-faced, tow-haired white man slumped disconsolately in the dock and flanked by two grim and alert black policemen. The prosecutor's eyes hardened. His jaw stiffened, and the veins stood out clearly about his temples. His right arm shot out like a rapier and froze—the index finger pointing at the figure in the dock like a javelin momentarily suspended in flight. The white man cringed in his chair and was hauled erect by the officers. Some two thousand black people in the audience sat petrified with the novelty and daring of it as the young Bostonian delivered his indictment against the white man on behalf of the Black Nation of Islam:

I charge the white man with being the greatest liar on earth! I charge the white man with being the greatest drunkard on earth. . . . I charge the white man with being the greatest gambler on earth. I charge the white man, ladies and gentlemen of the jury, with being the greatest peace-breaker on earth. I charge the white man with being the greatest adulterer on earth. I charge the white man with being the greatest robber on earth. I charge the white man with being the greatest deceiver on earth. I charge the white man with being the greatest trouble-maker on earth. So, therefore, ladies and gentlemen of the jury, I ask you, bring back a verdict of guilty as charged![1]

The foreman polled the jury in the box. Within seconds he rose and read the verdict:

"We find the defendant guilty—as charged."

The sentence pronounced was "death," and the frightened defendant was dragged away, loudly protesting his innocence and enumerating all he had "done for the Nigra people."

The audience thundered its approval of the play. Its repeated ovations required several curtain calls by the players.


What was behind it all? Who were these people clamoring for the death of the white man? They were, for the most part, Black Muslims—followers of Elijah Muhammad, "Spiritual Head of the Muslims in the West." The drama they had just witnessed was written and produced by members of the Movement,[2] and it has been staged in many of the major cities across America.[3]

The Black Muslims are probably America's foremost black nationalist movement. Thousands of the faithful await the day when the white man in America will be "treated as he ought to be treated." Exactly how many Black Muslims there are is unknown, but in December 1960, there were sixty-nine temples or missions in twenty-seven states, from California to Massachusetts. Since then the Movement has had its ups and downs, but it retains a solid following in the black ghettos of white America. In 1972 there were still at least fifty mosques with viable congregations. Under the leadership of Elijah Muhammad, who has been hailed by thousands inside and outside the Movement as "the most fearless Black Man in America," the Black Muslims get a hearing from a significant element of the black community. Their ultimate demand—that black men be allowed to set up a separate state within the United States, occupying as much as one-fifth of the nation's territory—commands attention among non-Muslims and the lashing indictment of the white man that supports the demand strikes a responsive chord in many Blackamerican hearts.

The Black Muslims are neither pacifists nor aggressors. They pay zealous attention to the requirements of the letter of the law regarding peace and order. They engage in no "sit-ins," test no segregation statutes, participate in no "marches on Washington" or anywhere else. But they do believe in keeping the scores even, and they have warned all America that "an eye for an eye and a tooth for a tooth" is the only effective way to settle racial differences. The late Minister Malcolm X of the New York temple explained in a Boston address:

We are never aggressors. We will not attack *anyone*. We strive for peaceful relationships with everyone. BUT—[we teach our people that] if anyone attacks you, *lay down your life!* Every Muslim is taught never to [initiate a] fight. Respect another man's rights whether he is white, black, brown, yellow, or what-not! Respect him as a man. "Do unto others as you would have them do unto you!" Never be the aggressor, never look for trouble. *But if any man molests you, may Allah bless you!*[4]

Tense situations involving the Muslims and the civil authorities have occasionally developed and violence has been associated with the Movement from time to time. The Black Muslim image is such that an eventual eruption of violence seems always anticipated. The police in many communities maintain constant alerts, and the news media which cooperate with the local police avoid publicizing the Movement. In the seething black ghettos the police openly worry about "what it's going to take to light the fuse."[5] The leaders of the sect are under constant surveillance by the FBI, and most of their important meetings are probably monitored by informers, a fact which may on occasion produce through fear and misinformation a self-fulfilling prophecy. A bloody clash between the Los Angeles police and local Muslims in 1965, for example, was reported by an informer to have occurred because "the police department came to the conclusion that the Black Muslims were getting too big, too powerful." The informer says that he "was instructed to make a phone call to the police precinct saying that there were guns going in and out of the Muslim Mosque."[6] The police raided the mosque.

In January of 1972, a deadly shootout between an alleged group of Black Muslims and the police of Baton Rouge, Louisiana, was reported in the Sunday edition of the *New York Times:*

On they came in a ragged phalanx, their black shoes drumming on the rain-lacquered street, kicking rubble and refuse from their path. On they marched, orange slickers whipped by the wind, weapons held firmly across the chest, plastic face shields blunting their features into anonymity beneath the helmets.

The riot squad of two Baton Rouge police agencies moved implacably down the center of a shabby street called North Boulevard in the city's black section, destined for one of the bloodiest clashes in the turbulent history of Southern race relations. And one of the most bizarre.

Facing the advancing line of policemen and sheriff's deputies last Monday noon was a new presence on troubled Southern streets. A line of 18 black men, dressed almost as if for a wedding in plain business suits, dress shirts, and floppy bow ties, stood like a wall in front of a Cadillac that had been used to block the street for a morning rally. On the sidewalks and in the storefronts facing the street, a more threadbare crowd of about 200 black men, most in their late teens and 20's, watched the opposite walls of men in the street engage, hesitate and then crumble in violence.

It only lasted about 90 seconds, but by the time the last shots had been fired, two of the black men in the floppy bow ties and two sheriff's deputies lay dying on North Boulevard, their blood mingling on the rainy asphalt. In addition, 31 others had been injured, most by gunfire, including 10 wounded police officers.

The aftermath brought outraged cries from city and state officials. W. W. Duman, the Mayor, said the blacks were Black Muslims from Chicago who had boasted they were taking over Baton Rouge;[7]

Elijah Muhammad disclaimed any knowledge of the young Blacks involved in the Baton Rouge fracas. They were not, he said, "on our registry as good Muslims. If they were . . . good Muslims, we would try to do the best we could to uphold their goodness."[8] Despite such disclaimers, the expectation of an eventual racial clash involving the Muslims is widespread among whites who fear the Movement, and among Blacks who project upon it their own fantasies for revenge against the white oppressor. The perspective of a New York youth is typical of the latter:

Man, I don't care what those [Muslim] cats say *out loud*—that's just a hype they're putting down for The Man [i.e., the white man]. Let me tell you—they've got some stuff for The Man even the Mau Mau didn't have! If he tries to crowd *them* like he's been used to doing the rest of us all the time, they're going to lay it on him from here to Little Rock! I grew up with some of the cats in that temple—

went to school with them; ran around with them. Man, those cats
have changed. They ain't for no light playing. Those cats are for
real, and you'd better believe it![9]

How did it all begin? What is the meaning of the Black Muslim
Movement? What kind of people belong to it, and just what are its
aims? All observers agree that its influence is already a significant factor
in the black community, and that it is increasing. The Muslim mosques,
though reduced in number from the peak they reached in the early
sixties, are well attended, and the ever-hustling Ministers who serve Elijah Muhammad command the admiration and respect of many who
accept Elijah but eschew his discipline.[10] Just what are the Black Muslims after? And what are their chances of achieving it?

To answer these questions, we shall have to look at the sociological
drama of contemporary America, especially at the Blackamerican's increasing dissatisfaction with the "bit" role he has been permitted to
play. As one Muslim minister put it in the early days of the Movement:
"We've just had a 'walk-on' part. We've been nothing but background
scenery for everybody else. Now we've got something to say, and we're
going to say it loud enough for the whole world to hear." Could he
have been portentous of the "Say it real loud, I'm black and I'm
proud" syndrome of the late sixties? Certainly the Muslims played a
major part in the development of black pride and black self-confidence.

### The End of the Second-Class Ride

How different [was the tolerant spirit of the medieval Western
Christian] from the spirit in which the white-skinned Western Protestant of modern times regards his black-skinned convert. The convert may have found spiritual salvation in the White Man's faith; he
may have acquired the White Man's culture and learnt to speak his
language with the tongue of an angel; he may have become an adept
in the White Man's economic technique, and yet it profits him
nothing so long as he has not changed his skin.[11]

Thus observes Professor Arnold Toynbee: in Western Protestant societies, at least, the first credential for acceptance is a white skin. A man
who happens to be born with a different skin color cannot hope to be
accepted, whatever his spiritual or intellectual merit.

This observation, from the perspective of world history, is on solid sociological ground. In his famous "Yankee City" studies, W. Lloyd Warner writes:

The ethnic group carries a divergent set of cultural traits which are evaluated by the host as inferior. . . . The racial groups are divergent biologically rather than culturally. . . . Such physical attributes as dark skin, the epicanthic fold, or kinky hair become symbols of status and automatically consign their possessors to inferior status. . . . The cultural traits of the ethnic group, which have become symbols of inferior status, can be and are changed in time; but the physical traits which have become symbols of inferior status are permanent.[12]

The data of sociology derive, of course, from observable human relationships. Every intelligent Blackamerican experiences a feeling of quarantine when he ponders his future and the avenues of creative existence open to him. The late Malcom X, the "angriest Muslim," protested loudly and at length: "When you say 'Negro,' you're trapped right there. Makes no difference who you are nor how many degrees you have from Harvard; if you're a Negro, you're trapped. If you're black, the doors close." And the Muslims are not unique in these sentiments. No less distinguished a person than Dr. Anna Hedgman, former administrative aide to the Federal Security Administration and an administrative assistant to New York's Mayor Wagner, complained bitterly to a television audience: "I don't know why white people are so absolutely wound up on this business, but [you] have to be white. If you could manage it, you ought to be white with blue eyes and blond hair." America, she charged, "has so bottled up the Negro" as to render him completely frustrated and defiant.[13] And one of the symptoms of his frustration and defiance is his fervid desire to be rid of the term "Negro" with all its pejorative stereotypes. "Negro" has become a bitter symbol of American apartheid in the minds of almost all Blackamericans.

The "school case" decision which the United States Supreme Court handed down in May 1954 was instrumental in focusing extraordinary attention upon this major racial dichotomy in the American society. It is unlikely that any single event since the Emancipation Proclamation of 1863 has produced so disturbing an effect, or has been so portentous of the possibility of extensive social change.[14] People throughout the world acclaimed the new promise of broadened opportunity for the expression of human creativity implicit in the decision and were encouraged by it.[15] Yet, in practice, the shift from "segregation" to "integration" has been very long in coming in education, and the political and social consequences (not to mention the psychological and learning consequences for children, or the economic consequences for black teachers) have yet to be realistically assessed.

There have been other scattered but hopefu. indices of change in black-white relations since 1954. Much encouragement for change has come from the courts. Segregated seating in interstate transportation no longer has legal sanction, and in most areas black citizens now enjoy the unrestricted use of parks, beaches, and other public recreational facilities. These and similar public advances have given impetus and encouragement to improvements in some private institutions which, by their nature, cannot be the subject of litigation aimed at desegregation. This has been particularly true of some churches and church-related schools, which have admitted Blacks although under no legal compulsion to do so.

In the economic sphere, the picture is less bright. Race remains a determining criterion for employment throughout the South and generally elsewhere in the country, and job restriction is a formidable barrier to the black citizen's fulfillment of his creative potential. In spite of federal executive orders and state and municipal legislation,[16] discrimination in employment remains the rule rather than the exception.[17] In 1971 there were twice as many black people unemployed (percentagewise) as there were whites. An even larger percentage of black workers were underemployed.

In political affairs the black involvement has been dramatic in some instances, but Blackamericans still lack sufficient power to affect major decisions in the government with any consistency. The old barriers are crumbling. For example, in the late 1950s in Fayette County in west Tennessee Blacks were "starved out" for wanting to vote. For months it was impossible for black citizens to buy oil or gasoline for their tractors and other machinery. Bank credit for crop loans—indispensable in this rural county—had been stopped. No Blacks could buy food or household necessities in the local white stores, and wholesale houses refused to supply black businesses.[18] Why? Because 450 Blacks insisted on registering to vote, as did 3,000 white citizens. Blacks constitute a majority in the county, but they were not permitted even a single voice in its government.

It is against this backdrop that one must come to grips with the persistence of the Black Muslim Movement. The horror of prison life, the danger of being killed while under arrest,[19] the unevenness and uncertainty of justice in the courts, poverty and hunger, the continuing problem of simply finding a decent place to live—all are contributory to the making of a Muslim and to the propagation of a mass movement of protest.

Perhaps the nearest parallel to the Black Muslim Movement was the Garvey movement of the post-World War I era. The social conditions which made Garveyism possible were similar to those obtaining at the present time, if not quite the same. We have had "Little Rock" and "Selma," and more recently we have had Attica, but there has been no wholesale murder of black people such as occurred during the infamous "Red Summer" of 1919. There have been improvements in the Black-american's total status since Garvey's day—a little here, a little there. There have been some important breaches in the high, white wall of segregation. But for Blacks in general, and for the Black Muslims in particular, these isolated improvements in the Blackamerican's total status are not enough. The tradition of disprivilege and the continuing formidable opposition to first-class citizenship are the discouraging elements that contribute most to the "Muslim mood."

Yet we cannot dismiss the Black Muslim Movement as simply another reaction against the traditional expressions of American race-consciousness. The history of the Black Man in America is per se a bi-story of race-consciousness and its consequences,[20] but American history has not heretofore produced an archetype of the Black Muslim Movement.

The new and most challenging factor, of course, is the expansion of the Blackamerican's political horizon from the national to the international scene. World War II saw the practical end of European colonialism, at least that was our hope, and the rapid demise of colonialistic philosophy has been a significant feature of postwar international relations. The determination to be free is the characteristic mood of the hundreds of millions of people whose destinies have not for centuries been self-determined; and for the most part, the colonial powers have seen and heeded the signs of the times. In an address before the United

Nations as the world community welcomed the newly independent Cameroons into membership, French delegate Armand Berard called pointed attention to the fact that "independence need not come as the result of conquest and violence."[21] Seventeen African states achieved more or less peaceful independence in 1960. "Everywhere the Dark Continent is emerging into the news spotlight. It is demanding attention—and getting it. Some observers are calling 1960 'Africa Year.' "[22]

M. Berard's optimism has not been completely justified. More than a decade has passed since "Africa Year," but the true African jubilee is still far off. Fifteen million Africans still smart under a hateful system of "apartheid" imposed by Europeans in South Africa; the Portuguese are still in Angola and Mozambique; and in Rhodesia, 250,000 whites have undertaken to steal a country from five million Africans through political chicanery and intimidation.

The emergence of Africa is a vitally significant factor in the aggressive impatience of the American Blacks. Most of the colonial peoples of the past three centuries have been non-white and under white domination, and American Blacks have understandably felt some identification with them. The independence of India, Indonesia, the Philippines, and other nonwhite Asian nations stirred applause, though little hope, in the breasts of America's largest minority. With Africa, the parallel strikes painfully close. Many Blacks for whom Africa once seemed as remote as the planet Jupiter now find themselves exhilarated and encouraged by the emergence of black national states in what American textbooks had always referred to as "the dark continent." Suddenly, the "dark continent" became "the Motherland," and identification with Africa and the African peoples became the trademark of the liberated Blackamerican. The embrace of Africa was not without its precedents. Some Blackamericans have always been uncertain about how they ought to feel about Africa and Africans, and at various times in our history the pros and cons of the issue have been hotly debated as various back-to-Africa schemes or movements gained or lost prominence in the Black Man's effort to solve the practical problems of his day-to-day existence in white America. But in all times previous, Africa herself was under the dominion, or at the mercy, of the white man. Now Africa was free, or was about to be. So there was a difference.

One difference quickly recognized by the more sensitive Blackamericans was that freedom for the Africans left the Blacks in America the only "colonized" peoples in the world (assuming—prematurely, it turned out—that in those halcyon days of decolonization and black liberation the gentle winds of freedom loosed by the British and the French would also stir the consciences of the South Africans and the Portuguese. Another difference was that the newly liberated Africans tended to look upon themselves as their own liberators, and to wonder why the Blacks in America had not done as well. The Blackamericans saw themselves as better educated, better experienced in the arts of government; they were Christian and had higher standards of living; in short, by all the standards of Western civilization they were better fitted for freedom than any of the African states who had suddenly acquired it. Now it began to look as though Western virtues notwithstanding, the Blacks in America were destined to be the last remaining symbols of racial inferiority left in the world. They were still "colonized." They were still not free. All the world seemed to be waiting to see if they were fit to be counted as men, whether they could have political and social autonomy. Whether there would emerge a national state for the free Black Men in America.

### The Stranger in Detroit

Sometime in the midsummer of 1930, an amiable but faintly mysterious peddler suddenly appeared in the black ghetto of Detroit. He was <u>thought to be an Arab</u>,[23] although his racial and national identity still remains undocumented. He was welcomed into the homes of the culture-hungry Blacks who were eager to purchase his silks and artifacts, which he claimed were like those black people wore in their homeland across the sea.

> He came first to our houses selling raincoats, and then afterwards, silks. In this way he could get into the people's houses, for every woman was eager to see the nice things the peddlers had for sale. He told us that the silks he carried were the same kind that our people used in their home country, and that he was from there. So we asked him to tell us about our own country.[24]

His customers were so anxious to learn of their own past and the country from which they came that the peddler soon began holding meetings from house to house throughout the community.

At first, the "prophet," as he came to be known, confined his teachings to a recitation of his experiences in foreign lands, admonitions against certain foods, and suggestions for improving his listeners' physical health. He was kind, friendly, unassuming, and patient.

> . . . he would eat whatever we had on the table, but after the meal he began to talk. "Now don't eat this food, it is poison for you. The people in your own country do not eat it. Since they eat the right kind of food they have the best health all the time. If you would just live like the people in your home country, you would never be sick any more." So we all wanted him to tell us about ourselves and about our home country and about how we could be free from rheumatism, aches, and pains.[25]

He also used the Bible as a textbook to teach them about their true religion—not Christianity, but the religion of the Black Men of Asia and Africa. He used the Bible because it was the only religious book his followers knew. It was not the proper book for the Black Nation; but, carefully interpreted, it could be made to serve until they were introduced to the Holy Qur'an (or Quran).

Eventually the stranger's teachings took the form of increasingly bitter denouncements against the white race; and as his prestige grew, he "began to attack the teachings of the Bible in such a way as to shock his hearers and bring them to an emotional crisis."[26] People experienced sudden conversions and became his followers.

> Up to that day I always went to the Baptist church. After I heard the sermon from the prophet, I was turned around completely. When I went home and heard that dinner was ready, I said: "I don't want to eat dinner. I just want to go back to the meeting." I wouldn't eat any meals but I [went] back that night, and I went to every meeting after that.

Before long, the house-to-house meetings were inadequate to accommodate all those who wished to hear the prophet. The solution was obvious: they hired a hall, which they named the Temple of Islam. Thus the movement which has become known as the Black Muslims was born.

No one knew very much about the founder of this first temple.

Usually he referred to himself as Mr. Farrad Mohammad or Mr. F. Mohammad Ali. He was also known as Professor Ford, Mr. Wali Farrad and W. D. Fard. One of his earliest converts recalls that, on one occasion, the prophet said:

> My name is W. D. Fard, and I come from the Holy City of Mecca. More about myself I will not tell you yet, for the time has not yet come. I am your brother. You have not yet seen me in my royal robes.[28]

Inevitably, there was a proliferation of legends about so mysterious a figure. One such legend is that Fard was a black Jamaican whose father was a Syrian Moslem. Another describes him as a Palestinian Arab who had participated in various racial agitations in India, South Africa, and London before moving on to Detroit. Some of his followers believed him to be the son of wealthy parents of the tribe of Koreish—the tribe of Mohammed, founder of classical Islam.[29] Others say that he was educated at a London university in preparation for a diplomatic career in the service of the kingdom of Hejaz, but that he sacrificed his personal future "to bring 'freedom, justice, and equality' to the 'black men in the wilderness of North America, surrounded and robbed completely by the Cave Man.' "[30] Fard announced himself to the Detroit police as "the Supreme Ruler of the Universe," and at least some of his followers seem to have considered him divine. At the other extreme, a Chicago newspaper investigating the Black Muslim Movement refers to Fard as "a Turkish-born Nazi agent [who] worked for Hitler in World War II."[31]

Fard described himself to his followers as having been sent to wake his "uncle"—that is, the Black Nation—to the full range of the Black Man's possibilities in a world temporarily dominated by the "blue-eyed devils." The illiterate Blacks who heard his heady talk were awed by his apparent fearlessness (as were to be the thousands who pledged themselves to follow his successor a generation later). They became increasingly alert to the subtle discriminations they faced in the North. For the North was no Promised Land: it was the South all over again, with the worst features of racial prejudice thinly camouflaged by "sweet talk about equality."

The fact that the country was in the throes of the great Depression did not help the situation. The starving, overcrowded Blacks living in the slums of Detroit (as in other Northern cities) became increasingly bitter toward the whites who seemed to control their lives. Policemen, who are the ever-present reminder of the white man's power; white workers, who displaced Blacks as jobs became more scarce, or who retained their jobs as thousands of Blacks were being laid off; even the welfare workers, who insulted the Blacks and made them wait long hours before passing out the pitiful supplies of flour and lard—all these became the symbolic targets of a virulent hatred of the white man growing in the breasts of Fard's Black Nation. One extreme example:

> An Asiatic trend among Negro dole recipients of the Elmwood district, noted at the time as a passing whim . . . came back with horror to two women welfare workers on learning that the fanatical [Black Muslim] Robert Harris had intended them for human sacrifice as infidels. . . . Harris stated to the police that each of these was a "no-good Christian," and that they would have been sacrificed if he knew where he could have found them.[3 2]

At first the contact between the Blacks in the ghetto and Fard was casual and informal. After a temple had been secured, however, the house-to-house meetings were discontinued, and a tightly knit organization replaced the informal gatherings. Members were examined before acceptance and were then registered, and a hierarchy was established. At this point, some of the followers of the late Noble Drew Ali began to pledge themselves to Fard.

Fard continued to teach his followers about the deceptive character of the white man and to help them relive, at least in fantasy, the glorious history of black Afro-Asia. An unusually resourceful teacher, he was able to utilize such varied literature as the writings of Joseph F. "Judge" Rutherford, then leader of the Jehovah's Witnesses, Van Loon's *Story of Mankind*, Breasted's *The Conquest of Civilization*, the Quran, the Bible and certain of the literature of Freemasonry to bring his people to "a knowledge of self." Some of the illiterate were taught to read so that they could learn firsthand about the past greatness of their race. All were encouraged to purchase radios so that they could hear the addresses of Rutherford and of Frank Norris, the Baptist fundamentalist.

The white man's words were not to be taken literally, for he was considered incapable of telling the truth. His writings were symbolic and needed interpretation, and this was Fard's mission to his "uncle" in the West. So, having taught his followers to read, he then interpreted for them what they read—interpreted it in the name of the one true God, "whose right and proper name is Allah." Thus, he explained, the white man served as a tool in the hands of Allah through which the Black Man could learn the secrets of his own past and prepare himself for the role history would demand of him.

To supplement the "symbolic" literature of the white man, Fard himself wrote two manuals for the Movement. *The Secret Ritual of the Nation of Islam* was (and still is) transmitted orally; it is memorized verbatim by the students at the Movement's parochial schools and has become an oral tradition. *Teaching for the Lost Found Nation of Islam in a Mathematical Way*, though it was printed and given to registered Muslims, was written in Fard's own "symbolic language" and required his interpretation.

Within three years, Fard had developed an organization so effective that he was able to withdraw almost entirely from active leadership. He had not only set up the temple and established its ritual and worship but also founded a University of Islam (actually, a combined elementary and secondary school), dedicated to "higher mathematics," astronomy, and the "ending of the spook civilization." He had created the Muslim Girls Training Class, which taught young Muslim women the principles of home economics and how to be a proper wife and mother. Finally, "fear of trouble with unbelievers, especially with the police, led to the founding of the Fruit of Islam—a military organization for the men who were drilled by captains and taught tactics and the use of firearms."[33] A Minister of Islam was now appointed to run the entire organization, aided by a staff of assistant ministers. Each of these men was selected and trained personally by Fard, who gradually stopped his public appearances and eventually disappeared from view.

One of the earliest officers in the Movement under Fard was Elijah Muhammad, who was born Elijah Poole. Poole and his family migrated from Georgia in the 1920s; and after Fard's appearance, several of them were soon identified with the Nation of Islam. An interesting mishap occurred at the time of Poole's initiation into the Movement. Under Fard, each proselyte was required to write a letter asking for his "original" (Islamic) name; when he received this name, the "slave name" given his ancestors by the white man was discarded. When the three Poole brothers applied for names, they neglected to mention that they were blood brothers, and "despite his omniscience, the prophet gave [them] the surnames of Sharrieff, Karriem and Muhammad." When the mistake became apparent, Fard explained that he had "divine knowledge" of the proper names of the three brothers.[34]

Elijah Muhammad devoted himself wholeheartedly to Fard and to the Movement. Though opposed by moderates in the hierarchy, he became Fard's most trusted lieutenant. At his initiation he had been given the "original" surname Karriem, but Fard now acknowledged his higher status by renaming him Elijah Muhammad. When a chief Minister of Islam was named to preside over the organization, Fard chose Muhammad, and the choice proved a wise one. Elijah Muhammad was almost singlehandedly responsible for the deification of Fard and for the perpetuation of his teachings in the early years after Fard disappeared.

The Prophet's disappearance occurred in June 1934. Shortly after Muhammad was named Minister of Islam, Fard vanished as mysteriously as he had arrived. Even the police seem to have been baffled. A report that he was last seen "aboard a ship bound for Europe" is unsubstantiated; so also are reports that he met with foul play at the hands of either the Detroit police or some of his dissident followers. It is certain that many of those who heard Fard were openly hostile to his anti-white diatribes and resented his attacks on the Christian church.[35] But any link between these antipathies and his strange disappearance remains in the realm of undocumented conjecture.

Some of Muhammad's critics hint darkly at the coincidence of Fard's disappearance at the moment of Muhammad's rise to power. But Muhammad's rise was neither sudden nor unchallenged, and Fard himself had had to struggle to retain leadership after the Movement began to grow. Muhammad simply cast his lot on the side that eventually prevailed.

The very nature of the Prophet's teachings made schism and factionalism inevitable. Quite early in the life of the Movement, Abdul Muhammad, another of Fard's trusted officers, withdrew and organized a competing temple. Fard had consistently taught that his followers were not Americans and that they owed no allegiance to the American

flag. It was stupid, he argued, to pledge allegiance to a flag that offered
no protection against "the depravities of the white devils [who] by
their tricknology . . . keep our peoples illiterate to use as tools and
slaves." Abdul Muhammad's splinter group, in contrast, was founded on
the principle of complete loyalty to the American Constitution and to
the nation's flag. This splinter group, however, did not survive.

As early as 1932 the Communist party attempted to infiltrate the
Black Muslim organization and take it over. It was followed by the
Japanese, who sought to establish a fifth-column beachhead in the
group under the direction of the wily Major Takahashi. The major tried
to persuade the Muslims to swear allegiance to the Mikado, and he
succeeded in splitting off some members of the Movement.[36] Nor were
these the only international interests seeking to cultivate the Muslims.
By 1934 even the Ethiopians developed a sudden interest in "the Black
Nation in the West"; one Wyxzewixard S.J. Challouehliczilczese sought
to use the Movement to promote various financial schemes in the interest of his native land. Closer to home, America's "union-busting" interests did not hesitate to take advantage of the hunger and poverty of the
unsophisticated Blacks in a war against the CIO. All these efforts failed,
but the struggle against them drained much of the vitality of the Movement.

After Fard's disappearance, the Muslims soon lost their aggressiveness; and th.¹ Movement, to which Fard had drawn eight thousand
adherents, began to decline in size and in power. Quarrels broke to the
surface, and the relatively lethargic moderates drove Elijah Muhammad
from Detroit to Temple No. 2 in Chicago, which had been established
as the Southside Mosque two years earlier. There he set up new headquarters and began to reshape the Movement under his own highly
militant leadership. Fard became identified with Allah; having been
thus deified, he was worshipped with prayer and sacrifice. Muhammad,
who had served "Allah," naturally assumed the mantle of "Prophet,"
which "Allah" had worn during his mission in Detroit. Today Muhammad is referred to both as the Prophet and, more often, as the Messenger of Allah.

The Black Muslims have come far under Muhammad. He has given
them temples and schools, apartment houses and grocery stores, restaurants and farms. Most important of all, he has given them a new
sense of dignity, a conviction that they are more than the equals of the

white man whose "tricknology" is a constant threat to their well-being. "The Divine Wisdom, Knowledge and Understanding administered by our Dear Leader and Teacher," writes Edna Mae 2X Vaughn of Flint, Michigan, "save his Beloved people from perplexities encountered in white America's corrupt ways of life." Another follower reports with equal confidence: "The devil [i.e., white man] cannot fool a Muslim, for the God of Truth has raised us up; a divinely appointed, divinely prepared Black Leader, Messenger Elijah Muhammad." "The Messenger," the faithful say reverently, "has taught us knowledge of ourselves; and this is the knowledge that makes it possible for us to obtain freedom, justice, and equality in the world, no matter what the white man thinks, no matter what the white man does." This is not a passive belief: Muhammad has promised to "do something for my beautiful Black Nation," and the Muslims are certain that he will. "That's right! That's right!" they say fervently, and swear to lay down their lives if it should be his will.

The Muslims seem duly grateful for Muhammad and for his leadership:

"My heart went out to the Honorable Elijah Muhammad . . . He was subjected to prison for the sake of his people."

"You say 'Plato says,' or 'Mao says,' or 'Fanon says,' . . . but none of these men are my teacher. The Honorable Elijah Muhammad is my teacher: should not I say, 'Muhammad says?' "

"Muhammad's voice is a voice totally blending with and echoing accurately the will of the Divine Supreme Being; the voice of a man who loves us more than we love ourselves."

"The Most Honorable Elijah Muhammad has exalted the women who follow him to the heights we are unable to measure [enabling] her to be extremely intelligent, submissive, refined and well cultured."

"I am a Puerto Rican. . . . But I am an Original [Black Man]. To the Young Lords I say Right On! . . . right on to Muhammad's Mosque. There you will find the solution to our problems."

"I know you love us all, Dear Holy Apostle, and I love you too. And I thank Allah for sending you to us." Sister Marquita X (Third Grade)

". . . one of the luckiest students in the world . . . to have knowledge of myself through the Most Honorable Elijah Muhammad." Elbert X (Level 1)

*Economic and Political Power*

The Black Muslims are an intensely dedicated, tightly disciplined
organization of black men convinced that they have learned the ultimate truth and ready to make any sacrifice it may demand of them.
Theirs is not a "Sunday religion": the Muslim temples hold frequent
meetings, and every Muslim is required to attend two (and often more)
meetings a week. Nor is it is a religion that spares the billfold. The mass
of Muslims are from the black lower class, with relatively low incomes,
and they are encouraged to live respectably and provide for their families. The men are urged to hold steady jobs; and all Muslims are forbidden to gamble, smoke, drink liquor, overeat, indulge in fripperies, or
buy on credit. As a result most Muslims enjoy a healthy standard of
living and still have enough cash left over to support the Movement.

Every Muslim is expected to give a fixed percentage of his income
to the Movement each year. This percentage was set at one-third of all
earnings; but the figure is probably not always so high. In addition, the
temples collect contributions for a variety of funds, many for local
purposes, and at least six for the use of the national headquarters at
Temple No. 2 in Chicago. Of the six known national funds, four are
earmarked for real estate, public relations, official travel, and new cars;
one is an annual collection on the anniversary of Fard's birthday, February 26th, with no purpose designated; and one is a discretionary
fund, the "No. 2 Treasury and Central Point Fund," for Muhammad to
use as he sees fit.

The Muslims' power to influence the general American community
is significant, not only because of their increasing financial resources,
but also because they can be mobilized to act in unswerving unison on
any matter designated by the leadership. Should they ever vote, for
example, assuredly they will vote as Muhammad tells them to vote and
buy where he tells them to buy . A Muslim bloc, therefore, even in a
large city, could be the determining factor in the balance of political
and economic power.

It was once said in Harlem that Malcolm X, then minister of the
large Temple 7 and Muhammad's chief lieutenant, could decide the
election of U.S. Representative Adam Clayton Powell's successor. This
issue was mooted by Malcolm's death, but the deference shown him—
and his successor—by the political powers in Harlem is impressive. Even

more impressive evidence of the Muslims' political weight is the fact that Fidel Castro, during his dramatic sojourn in Harlem in the autumn of 1960, invited Malcolm X to a private conference which lasted some two hours. Malcolm had earlier been invited, along with other important Blackamericans, to visit Castro in Cuba. That the invitation was not accepted—or that acceptance was delayed—can be attributed in part to Muhammad's distaste for communism as a white ideology and in part to his doubt whether Castro is a black man or a "blue-eyed devil" hiding behind a slogan and a sword.

Muhammed has not yet seen fit to use the potential power of the Black Muslim vote as a lever to pry concessions from the white or the non-Muslim black community. From the start, Muslims have generally preferred not to vote at all. This has been due partly to their self-identification with Afro-Asia, partly to their belief that America is already corrupt and doomed, and partly to their sense of futility in electing any white man to office. Malcolm X noted that "Roosevelt promised, Truman promised, Eisenhower promised. Blacks are still knocking on the door begging for civil rights. . . . Do you mean to tell me that in a powerful country like this, a so-called *Christian* country, that a handful of men from the South can prevent the North, the West, the Central States, and the East from giving Negroes the rights the Constitution says they already have? No! I don't believe that and neither do you. No white man really wants the Black Man to have his rights, or he'd have them. The United States does everything else it wants to do."[3][7]

The Muslims have also refrained from voting in an effort to keep their strength a secret. "If you don't vote, nobody knows what you can accomplish when you do," and so far there has been no issue worth a real display of strength. Muhammad admonishes those Blacks who do vote to simply "go to the polls with your eyes and ears open, and remember that it is not necessary for you to go seeking justice for anyone but yourselves. . . . The white people of America already have their freedom, justice and equal rights.[3][8]

The time may come, however, when more than an undefined "justice" will be at stake. The Muslim leadership may one day feel ready to issue specific demands on local, state, and national political bodies. Then, even at the national level, they can expect to be heard with respect. Recent elections seem to have demonstrated that a party, to win, must control the large industrial cities of the North, in which the black vote is potentially pivotal. But Blacks do not vote as a bloc; they split their votes between the two major parties. Anyone who could amass and "deliver" a significant number of black votes in these cities, therefore, would lead from strength in dealing with the national party organizations. It is precisely in these cities that the Black Muslim Movement is now flourishing. And, as the late Malcolm X said, "You can be sure of one thing. Every single Muslim man and woman will vote the way Mr. Muhammad tells him to vote."

The Black Muslims' political power is ominous but, for the moment, latent. It is reckoned with seriously at the local and state level in many states, but Muhammad is not seeking political alignments even there, and he is unlikely to attempt a national power-play for some years to come. The Muslims' economic power, on the other hand, is already being felt in the black community. There is no organized boycott of white merchants, but every Muslim is expected to "buy black"— that is, to trade with his own kind in preference to "spending your money where you can't work and can't sit down." The Muslims were vocal in their contempt for the sit-in movement, in which black men "went out of their way to force the white man to let them spend more money with him," rather than contribute to the establishment of businesses run by and for black men.

The Muslims demand an entirely separate black economy, arguing that not until the Blackamerican is economically independent will he be, in any real sense, free. The total annual income of the black community, they point out, is greater than the total income of Canada and greater than that of several European states. Such a purchasing power, if spent among black businessmen and invested in black enterprises, would earn the respect of every nation in the world. The Muslims concede that the white man has, for the moment, an edge on technical and commercial know-how. The Black Man must learn whatever the white man can teach him and then outstrip the white man in productivity and trade.

### The Believers . . .

Who are these faithful, these true believers, these Black Muslims? Most simply, a Black Muslim is a Blackamerican who is a follower of Elijah Muhammad, "Spiritual Leader of the Lost-Found Nation in the West." Black Muslims are distinguished from orthodox Moslems not in the mere spelling of the word (strictly speaking, either form is correct), but in their belief that their leader, the Honorable Elijah Muhammad, is the Messenger of Allah, directly commissioned by Allah himself, who came in person (under the name of Fard) to wake the sleeping Black Nation and rid them of the white man's age-old domination.

A survey taken in Detroit during the early years of the Movement (1930-1934) showed that the overwhelming majority of Muslims—all but half a dozen or so of the two hundred families interviewed— were recent migrants from the rural South. The majority had come to industrial Detroit from small communities in Virginia, South Carolina, Georgia, Alabama, and Mississippi. Investigations by the Wayne County Prosecutor's office indicated the same origin.[39]

Those attracted to the early Movement were not only recent migrants, but they had typically visited their old homes in the South one or more times before becoming Muslims. The limited freedom they had experienced in the North made them acutely conscious of the extreme subordination of Blacks in the South—a realization which sharpened their hostilities and increased their sense of frustration.

> Through these visits they had become more conscious of race discrimination on the part of the Caucasians. After their brief sojourn in the North they tended to reinterpret with sinister implications incidents of race contact in the South. They began to realize that lynchings and the indignities of the Jim Crow system were perpetuated by Caucasians who worshipped the same God as they did and worshipped Him in the same way.[40]

Finally, most of those who joined the early temples were, one can fairly assume, functionally illiterate.

At first the pattern of membership remained generally stable, but the disproportion of recent, rural migrants in the movement has steadily leveled off in recent years. Several factors may be responsible. In the first place, the proportion of Blacks in the North and East is now much greater than it was in the depression years 1930-1934, and they have been there longer. The Muslims can thus proselytize a more established population. Secondly, although there is a continuing stream of migrants from the South, many of the current migrants are from Southern cities and towns, or at least have had some urban experience before pushing on to the North. Again, the Black Muslim Movement is no longer limited to the industrial cities of the North. Its temples are scattered from New England to San Diego and from San Francisco to Miami.[41] At least a dozen cities in the South have temples or missions.

Thus, while the vast majority of Muslims still belong to the most disprivileged class, they are no longer necessarily recent, rural migrants from the South, nor are they predominantly functionally illiterate. A poll taken of 460 Muslims in Atlanta, Chicago, Boston, and New York[42] revealed that more than half had lived in their present city longer than five years. Fifteen per cent had lived in the city for at least ten years, and 5½ per cent were born there. Forty-six per cent of the group sampled claimed to have had at least a sixth-grade education, and only 2 per cent admitted to less than a fourth-grade education.

But we must not lean too heavily upon this sampling. Muslims are extremely wary about giving *any* information about themselves or the Movement unless such information is of obvious propaganda value. The typical Muslim will talk freely about the teachings of the Messenger or the treacheries of the white man, but he will seldom provide information subject to statistical analysis. If he does not evade factual questions entirely, the Muslim brother politely refers them to his minister, who in turn invokes Elijah Muhammad.

Critical observation and informal interviews have, therefore, been the best tools available for determining the constituency of the Movement. My observations and experiences with Muslims in several cities suggest the following:

1. *The membership is young.* Up to 80 per cent of a typical congregation is between the ages of seventeen and thirty-five. This pattern has been noted again and again in temples across the country. In the newer temples, youth is even more pronounced; in some, fully three-quarters of the membership is under thirty years of age. About the same proportion of the ministers are under thirty-five.

The reason for such a concentration of youth is clear. This is an activist movement, and the appeal is *directed* to youth. Large, young families are eagerly sought, and least attention is paid to older people reared as Christians. Older people have a certain security in their familiar religious orientation, and they do not readily shift to a position so unfamiliar and radical as that preached by the Muslims.

The older people who do belong to the movement, especially in the Northern cities, are for the most part ex-Garveyites or ex-Moorish Science Moslems, or they have belonged to some of the more esoteric cults flourishing in Harlem, Detroit, or Chicago. Many of these older "nationalists" consider Muhammad a natural successor to both Garvey and Noble Drew Ali, and they have had little difficulty in making the transition. Muhammad himself professes "a very high opinion" of both Garvey and Noble Drew Ali; he refers to them as "fine Muslims" and calls upon their sympathizers to "follow me and cooperate in our work because we are only trying to finish up what those before us started."[43]

*2. The membership is predominantly male.* Unlike the typical Christian church, the Muslim temples attract many more men than women, and men assume the full management of temple affairs. Women are honored, and they perform important functions within a defined role; they are not in any sense considered mere "property," as has sometimes been the case in classical Islam. However, they do not constitute the organizational foundation through which the Movement functions, either in service or in finance. They work alongside the men in the various business enterprises owned by the temples, and they share in the affairs of the temples themselves, but almost always in roles not in conflict with the male assumption of primary responsibility.

*3. The membership is essentially lower class.* A generation ago Erdman Beynon could report:

At the time of their first contact with the prophet, practically all of the members of the cult were recipients of public welfare, unemployed, and living in the most deteriorated areas of Negro settlement in Detroit.[44]

That was in the early 1930s—the worst of the depression years. By 1937, however, Beynon observed:

At the present time, there is no known case of unemployment among these people. Practically all of them are working in the automobile and other factories. They live no longer in the slum section ... but rent homes in some of the best economic areas in which Negroes have settled. They tend to purchase more expensive furniture, automobiles, and clothes than do their neighbors even in these areas of higher-class residence.[45]

The socioeconomic pattern today is a fusion of these two trends. Muslims are fully employed, yet they live and meet in the most deteriorated areas of the slums, but not exclusively. The "Protestant Ethic" is not abandoned in black Islam. The visible evidences of Muslim prosperity are increasingly noticeable in the best neighborhoods occupied by middle-class Blackamericans.

Recruitment for the Movement is still predominantly from among low-income groups at the lower end of the educational scale. It has attracted a few intellectuals, an increasing number of college students, and a scattering of business and professional men; but a majority of the membership of any given temple is composed of domestic and factory workers, common laborers and the like.[46] An increasing number of the men, however, are skilled and semiskilled craftsmen; the businesses owned by the group are usually housed in buildings renovated by the Muslims themselves—from the plumbing to the electric signs that mark the entrances. The Muslims are justifiably proud of the "technicians" who operate their sound and recording equipment, and of their expert stenographers and secretaries. They have a corps of excellent photographers, who make film records of every important event; the photographic mural on the wall of their Temple 7 Restaurant in New York is a display of their professional skill. Their newspaper has the best coverage and the largest circulation of any black paper in the country.

Many Muslims have come into the movement from various levels of extralegal activity. Some are ex-convicts—or even convicts. Some temples are behind prison walls. Some have come into the Movement as dope addicts and alcoholics, or from careers as pimps and prostitutes, pool sharks, and gamblers. But all who remain in the Movement are rehabilitated and put to work. The members' claim that they are able to secure work much more easily than other ghetto Blacks[47] appears valid. There are no idle Muslims; and delinquency, juvenile or adult, is almost unheard of.

Today's Muslims, however, despite their new economic leverage, do not typically identify with the strivers of the black middle class. They tend to live comfortably, but frugally. The Movement continues to emphasize its affiliation with the working class. There are exceptions: Elijah Muhammad lives in a nineteen-room mansion in a quiet neighborhood near the University of Chicago. But the Messenger has an unusually large family (seven children); his offices occupy part of the building; and several rooms are set aside for the use of his many guests—ministers called to Chicago for consultation and, often, visitors from abroad. Even in this mansion there is no ostentation in furnishings or appointments, and few of Muhammad's ministers and followers have elected to abandon the slums. However, there were public rumblings when it was announced that Muhammad intended to build a "retirement" mansion for himself in Chicago at a cost of about a half-million dollars.

The Muslim leaders tend to live and to build their temples and businesses in the areas from which they draw their major support—the heart of the black ghetto. This ghetto houses the most dissident and disinherited, the people who wake up to society's kick in the teeth each morning and fall exhausted with a parting kick each night. These are the people who are ready for revolution—any kind of revolution—and Muhammad astutely builds his temples in their midst. Furthermore, in the segregated black ghetto, the illusion of a "Black Nation" within a surrounding and hostile "white nation" takes on a semblance of reality. The only whites around are the hated shopkeepers who "suck my people blind." These white tradesmen are ready-made symbols—representatives of the impersonal white oppressor who has "penned us up like sheep, the better to drink our blood."

4. *The membership is almost wholly American—Blackamerican.* The Garvey movement was built around a hard core of West Indians, who, sharing his nationality and cultural experiences, were most readily attracted to his program. American Blacks gave Garvey little attention until he had already attracted a large following of West Indian immigrants.[48] But the Muslim leadership has not especially welcomed the West Indians in this country, possibly because the West Indian habit of making distinctions among themselves in terms of color could jeopardize the Muslim appeal for a united black front.

There may have been some Japanese "advisors" connected with the Movement in its early days, when Major Takahashi was active in Detroit. The Muslims consider all nonwhites to be black men, whatever their skin color, and it is worth noting that Muhammad was indicted for pro-Japanese sympathies in the first year of World War II.[49] But no significant Oriental influence is apparent in the Movement today.

At one time, Muhammad's chief minister was a Haitian, Theodore Rozier. More recently, a number of Arab nationals have been associated with the movement in teaching or advisory capacities. Shaikh Diab, a Palestinian Arab, for example, taught Arabic at the (Chicago) University of Islam—a combined elementary and secondary school—for several years. A number of Egyptian nationals are friendly to the Movement and its leadership, but whether they hold membership in the temples is not known. A Nigerian graduate student also taught at the (Chicago) University of Islam, and foreign students from all parts of Asia and Africa frequently attend the local temples, which are found in nearly all cities having large universities.

These foreign contacts are highly prized, yet the Movement itself remains distinctively Blackamerican. Other Moslems have been welcomed as visitors, but they have not been encouraged to seek membership.

5. *Finally, the membership is predominantly ex-Christian.* American Blacks have always been a religious people; and until very recent times, religion has for them meant Protestant Christianity. Except for the Moorish-Americans and a few hundred ex-cultists of varying past proclivities, most of the Muslims seem to be drawn from Protestant families or traditions, although there are significant numbers of ex-Catholics in the Movement. Many Muslims have come from revivalistic sects, but most have held active membership in the established denominations, and some of the Muslim ministers are former Christian preachers.

The younger Muslims, especially those under twenty, have usually had no strong Christian convictions, but almost without exception they come from Christian homes. All too often, their conversion reflects a serious inadequacy in their religious environment. One parent whose son had "gone Muslim" turned to his minister in anguish. "Now," said the minister, "he expects me to save his son from the Muslims when I haven't a single handle to grab him by. The parents come here four or five times a year, and the boy doesn't come at all. No wonder the Muslims got him; he was looking for something."

### . . . And Why They Become Believers

The fundamental attraction of the Black Muslim Movement is its passion for group solidarity, its exaggerated sense of consciousness-of-kind. What matters above all is that men acknowledge themselves as black or white, and that all black men work together to accomplish their group aims. These aims have been summed up by a Muslim minister as:

> To get the white man's foot off my neck, his hand out of my pocket and his carcass off my back. To sleep in my own bed without fear, and to look straight into his cold blue eyes and call him a liar every time he parts his lips.[50]

The ultimate appeal of the Movement, therefore, is the chance to become identified with a power strong enough to overcome the domination of the white man—and perhaps even to subordinate him in turn.

In this context, although the Black Muslims call their Movement a religion, religious values are of secondary importance. They are not part of the Movement's basic appeal, except to the extent that they foster and strengthen the sense of group solidarity.

The Muslims make no secret of the fact that they count themselves a part of the growing alliance of nonwhite peoples, which they expect eventually to inundate the white race, washing away the hated supremacy that that race has so long enjoyed. Years ago, Dr. Buell Gallagher warned about orthodox Islam:

> There are signs that the Pan-Islamic movement may harden into a new political nationalism, based on race, which may replace the Islam of an international and interracial brotherhood. This Pan-Islamic spirit which appears about to come to full fruition in a union of the entire Muslim world against the rest of the globe is one of tomorrow's imponderables. . . [51]

Gallagher did not refer to, or even contemplate, the Black Muslims; yet his words are pertinent to them. The Muslims are not recognized by orthodox Moslems in this country, but they consider themselves Moslems and are apparently so considered by the many Moslem countries in Africa and the Middle East who have welcomed and honored their leaders. Certainly, to the extent that the Pan-Islamic goal is a power structure forged out of anti-white sentiment, these goals are shared by the Black Muslims in America.

The anti-Christian tone of much of the Muslim teaching also has a strong attraction for some Blacks. Occasionally this attraction is personal, as with the youth rebelling against a parental authority which has been symbolized by enforced church attendance. But increasing numbers of black people are disillusioned by the continuation of racial segregation in the church and are coming to identify the church with social apathy and racial subordination. To these disaffected Christians the Muslims make a shrewd appeal. On the one hand, aware that the Christian tradition rejects hatred, they proclaim a positive slogan: "Not anti-white, just pro-black. We're so pro-black we haven't time to be anti *anything!*" But at the same time, they insist on the close link between the Christian church and white supremacy.

Your Christian countries, if I am correct, are the countries of Europe and North and South America. Predominantly, this is where you find Christianity, or at least people who represent themselves as Christians. Whether they practice what Jesus taught is something we won't go into. The Christian world is what we usually call the Western world. . . . The colonization of the dark people in the rest of the world was done by Christian powers. The number one problem that most people face in the world today is how to get freedom from Christians. Wherever you find nonwhite people today they are trying to get back their freedom from people who represent themselves as Christians, and if you ask these [subject] people their picture of a Christian, they will tell you "a white man—a Slavemaster."[52]

The appeal works—with individuals and with groups. One minister in Richmond, Virginia, discouraged by his denominations's posture on the racial issues in that state, led his entire congregation out of the Christian church and into the local Muslim temple, where he eventually became the new Muslim minister. His congregation is said to have doubled since in numbers and vitality.

Because Christianity is "the white man's religion," the repudiation of Christianity is an overt act of aggression against the white man. To be identified with a movement that openly rejects the fundamental values of the powerful majority is to increase vastly one's self-esteem and one's stature among one's peers. This social incentive to defiance is not limited to the Muslims; among black intellectuals generally, a deviation from the white man's way of doing things has come to be called "independent thinking," and reaps its rewards. The difference between the intellectual and the Muslim in this regard is simply one of degree: the intellectual's defiance is carefully calculated; the Muslim's is wholehearted and absolute. Thus the intellectual will not become a Muslim, but he will embrace Bahai. Both men are repudiating an identity to which they are hypersensitive in the presence of the white man, and both are chiding Christianity for its racism. But the intellectual astutely remains within the orbit of the white man's culture, while the Muslims set themselves completely adrift.

The challenge of an ascetic ideal, balanced by the absence of social barriers to affiliation and service, have brought thousands under the banner of Muhammad. Probably in no other religious organization are alcoholics, ex-convicts, pimps, prostitutes, and narcotic addicts welcomed so sincerely. The Christian church is, in most instances, careful to take none to its bosom until they are cleansed. The Muslims welcome the most unregenerate and then set about to rehabilitate them. They have stern rules of conduct, but no man is condemned for what he was—only for what he refuses to be.

They say a man should never be condemned or tried twice for the same crime once he has paid the penalty. Yet when a man goes to prison and pays his debt to society, when he comes out he is still looked upon as a criminal. . . . Well, Mr. Muhammad has succeeded there where Western Christianity has failed. When a man becomes a Muslim, it doesn't make any difference what he was [doing] before as long as he has stopped doing this. He is looked upon with honor and respect and is not judged for what he was doing yesterday. And this, I think, explains why we have so many men who were in prison following Mr. Muhammad today.[53]

The stress upon—and the outward manifestation of—fraternal responsibility is a strong attraction for many Blacks whose social and civil insecurity is often extreme. The Blackamerican has often been characterized as a ready "joiner," and more often than not this characterization has been justified. He is compelled to join in order to escape the isolation and sense of helplessness he experiences as a social outcast. He joins for recreation when public recreation is not available to him, and for security against sickness and want. He joins for consolation and companionship—the attempt at flight of an earthbound black man in a white man's world.

All of these elements are present, to some degree, in the appeal of Muslim membership. But the appeal goes deeper: every Muslim holds himself ready to die for his brother, and more especially for his sister.[54] This extreme solidarity attracts not only those in search of security but also those in search of a *cause*—a focus for the free-floating hostility that racial oppression always breeds. A Muslim was arrested in New York City (on a false identification, as it turned out). Within an hour, several hundred of his brothers turned up at the precinct station in a quiet show of fraternal solidarity to insist that "justice be done." They waited patiently and quietly until the wrongly accused man was released; then they took him away with them. Membership in the local temple immediately spiraled. Their show of solidarity had won what the black community interpreted as an important victory.

The intensity of this sense of unity makes unnecessary the usual trappings of organizations which emphasize group solidarity. It is unrealistic (though at least one black leader has done so) to dismiss the Movement as "another mutual admiration cult—another opportunity for people who aren't going anywhere to hang out the signs to prove it." The usual signs of social status associated with lower-class black organizations are fanciful titles and flamboyant uniforms. Among the Black Muslims, however, there are no phony "doctors" or specious "saints," no uniforms and no prestige offices. The only titles are those given to Muhammad and to the hierarchy of the secret military organization, the Fruit of Islam. To be called a "brother" or a "sister" is the highest compliment a Muslim can be paid, for as New York Minister Farrakhan put it, "we were brothers before we were ministers." Christians, of course, also call each other "brother" and "sister" at times, but one senses that the Muslims are appealing to something beyond ordinary religious courtesy.

Another aspect of the Movement that has strong appeal value is its emphasis upon youth and masculinity. The ministers are young and personable; some have been entertainers or have otherwise had public followings. All Muslim men are clean-shaven, close-cropped, and well-dressed in conservative clothes whenever they appear in public. Inside the temples there is a constant movement of young men with military bearing; they move quietly but with an unexaggerated dignity and the inescapable suggestion of latent force. They wear no uniforms or insignia except for a small star-and-crescent button in their lapels. Polite and self-assured, they seem alert to the demands of the present and confident of the future. Their attitude toward black Christians is not quite one of condescension, nor yet one of toleration. It is more a kind of patient amazement that intelligent people could be unimpressed with the Messenger's dicta or could still find it possible to want to live in the world of the white man.

These are the "Young Blacks" who will usher in the Black Nation of Islam. "We are not looking for crumbs," said Malcolm X:

In America today, where the so-called Negro is concerned, you have a high degree of dissatisfaction. It is hard for me to believe that the white man, as intelligent as he is, cannot realize the degree of dissatisfaction in the minds of the young generation of Black Men. The old generation forgets. . . . It is on its way out. . . . What you [whites] have to know now is what the man is thinking [whom] you will have to deal with in the future.[55]

A surprising number of young people are attracted by the Muslims' redefinition of the roles men and women should play in the home and in the religious life of the sect. There is a strong emphasis on the equality of individuals irrespective of sex, but each sex is assigned a role considered proper to itself. The trend in our larger society today seems to be toward blurring the distinct line between the traditional social roles of men and women. The Muslims, on the other hand, claim to have restored the woman to a place of dignity and respect, while restoring to the man his traditional responsibilities as head of the family. Muslim women seem to welcome the security and protection implicit in this arrangement and the men seem to exhibit a deeper sense of responsibility than is common to others of the working class. Children seem to profit the most, for among Muslim children, delinquency is unheard of.

In her weekly column in *Muhammad Speaks,* Magary Hassain declares:

Messenger Muhammad teaches The Woman in Islam that Allah

taught him that the Woman is the greatest pleasure that the man has.
Nothing pleases man more than woman. . . . The Bible verifies this
truth (Gen. 2:18). . . . Black Man, the Original Man is the God, and
after He made Himself, He was not satisfied alone and then He
made Woman. . . . ALL PRAISES ARE DUE TO ALLAH! Messenger Muhammad teaches us . . . that Man made Women for the purpose of his pleasure. He did not need the woman to put one star in
the heavens. He wanted the woman for love and companionship.
She is the field to produce a nation. . . . ALL PRAISES ARE DUE
TO ALLAH [for] this divine message.[56]

Finally, the parochial schools maintained by the Muslims have attracted many followers. If, as is planned, the Muslims establish schools
in most of the larger cities where they have temples, their numbers will
probably increase proportionately. One Chicago domestic, who was not
a Muslim, was asked whether she sent her children to the Muslim school
in her neighborhood. "Well, no, sir," she replied with some hesitation.
"But my husband, he's been talking about it. Whatever *he* says. They
teach the children how to behave up there, and they teach them something about ourselves, too—all about what the black people have done
in the world, not just the white. You ought to know something about
your own people, don't you think? Especially if you're going to live in
a free country."

Few if any children of the middle- or upper-class black families
attend the Muslim schools, for not many of their parents are in the
Movement. Yet there is a widespread sympathy for the Muslim curriculum emphasis on the history of the Black Man in America and on the
black African civilizations of the pre-Colonial era. This is often expressed obliquely by resentment of the completely white-oriented training given to almost all black children. Said one Nashville intellectual:
"They grow up, and they don't know *who* the hell they are. They
aren't white, and white rejects them. But white is all they know about.
And you talk about adjustment! It's a wonder any of us survive!"

# 2 The Dynamics of Black Nationalism

he Black Muslims are not an isolated phenomenon. They are rooted in the whole structure of racial tension. In New York City alone, a score or more organizations operate in the name of black solidarity. Their central theme is always the glorification of black civilization and the deprecation of the white man's culture, which, whenever it has been adopted by the Black Man, has reduced him to impotence and ignominy.

In the South, where resentment of the white man has until recently been less overt, black nationalism has expressed itself in lodges and fraternal societies, in which tens of thousands of Blacks learn various "ancient rites" of supposed Afro-Asian origin. Every black community in the South has its multitude of legends illustrating Blacks' superior physical strength, sexual prowess, and moral integrity. "Mr. Charlie" is never a match for the cunning of "Ol' John." And "Miss Ann," though she is "as good a ol' white woman" as can be found anywhere, remains in the mind of the black Southerner a *white* woman and, therefore, a legitimate target for the machinations of her black servant "Annie Mae." In the last decade, the lines have hardened and the legends have gone out of style. "Mr. Charlie" and "Miss Ann" are both dead—swept away by the new dignity of black ethnicity. "Annie Mae" is gone too (although she lingers on in the cultural limbo of the television screen as "Geraldine"). "Ol' John" has become "Mr. Blackman," at least in his own perception of the way things are—or ought to be.

Most Blacks nowadays spend most of their time thinking black. But no part of life is wholly free of this defensive offensive. A defensive kind of black nationalism used to find occasional expression in the quarrels of black children: "Black is honest," they cried out, and "the blacker the berry, the sweeter the juice." Even the black churches were often tinged with nationalism. An obscure African slave who rescued the prophet Jeremiah from a cistern into which he had been thrown by his enemies has long been exalted as a symbol of righteousness and fearlessness in the service of God. And the biblical promise that Ethiopia shall soon "stretch out her hands" has for generations been taken as a divine pledge that black sovereignty will be restored.

From the soil of repression and hostility grow bitter fruits, and black nationalism is one of the most bitter. It feeds on the prejudices, stereotypes, and discriminations which tend to characterize relations between whites and blacks in America. It accepts the white man's allegation that there are "inherent differences" between people who have different colored skins. But it inverts the values: it worships what it cannot change. It forges a weapon of vengeance for the Black Man out of the very attributes for which he is held to be inferior. Black children aren't concerned to justify their blackness anymore. It speaks for itself. A tentative black biblicism in the churches has given way to a full-blown black theology. Never mind the color of some obscure slave in Hebrew history; God himself is black and on the side of the oppressed. This is Christian black nationalism possibly following a lead the Muslims recognize as their own.

The Black Muslims have made a science of black nationalism. They have made *black* the ideal, the ultimate value; they have proclaimed the Black Man to be the primogenitor of all civilization, the Chosen of Allah, "the rightful ruler of the Planet Earth." And their extreme doctrine has attracted more than a hundred thousand adherents—a vivid warning of the deep resentment American Blacks harbor for their status in our society and of the futility they feel about the likelihood of a genuine and peaceful change.

## I. BITTER SOIL AND BITTER FRUITS

### Group Consciousness

An interesting phenomenon found in every society in which discrete groups live side by side is known as *consciousness of kind*, that state of mind in which a man is vividly aware of himself as a member of a group different from other groups—as a black, a white man, an Irish Catholic, an Anglo-Saxon Protestant, a Jew.

Consciousness of kind usually operates as a defense mechanism for a minority group which is seeking to preserve its identity or its most cherished values. But group consciousness may also be aroused in a *majority* group when a minority is seeking to merge with and lose itself in the larger, more powerful or otherwise preeminent group. In such a case, the majority may feel that some of its prized values are threatened; its social status, racial purity, religious cohesion—or even its economic security or physical survival. Majority group consciousness is an almost instinctive defense against such a real or imagined threat.

The group consciousness of a minority is, of course, increased by acts of discrimination directed against it by an effective majority. An effective majority need not be a numerical majority: 250,000 Europeans constitute an effective majority in the African state of Rhodesia, which they share with five million Africans and 3½ million Europeans are an effective majority in South Africa, a country of fifteen million Blacks.

An effective majority, whatever its size, holds the main concentration of power. Its power may be *actual*, as in the military superiority of a contingent of soldiers armed with modern weapons and garrisoned in a native village; it may be *potential*, as when a pair of patrolmen walk the streets of a tough neighborhood; or it may be *imaginary,* as is the power of the cult of priests or magicians in a primitive society. When it enjoys actual power backed by a massive numerical superiority—as does the white majority in the United States—the group consciousness of the minority can be very sharp indeed.

For any minority group, faced with a constant environment of prejudice and discrimination, three basic types of response are possible. These responses are *avoidance, acceptance* and *aggression.*

### Avoidance

Group consciousness is a form of consolation derived from a shared sense of discrimination; it is often expressed in ambivalence and self-hatred. Such an acrid consolation is not for every taste. Many individuals would rather not be identified with a minority; they would prefer not to have a personal awareness of its existence or its claim on them as members. Such persons may seek to avoid entirely their identification with their group.

Avoidance may also be motivated by a haunting concern for per-

sonal security, physical or psychological. In this case, while acknowledging themselves as members of a group, individuals may seek to avoid
the *meaning* of that identity in a wider context. Many black people, for
example, avoid contact with whites by doing business with black businesses wherever possible; if they find it necessary to deal with white
businesses, they order goods and pay their bills by mail. In this way,
they minimize the likelihood of being insulted or otherwise humiliated
by whites. Such avoidance also reduces the possibility of an inadvertent
breach of the highly complex "etiquette" of race relations which, in
many parts of the South, could readily incur physical harm or even
death.

For those individuals who wish to avoid their identification with a
minority group, the most complete form of avoidance is to withdraw
entirely by "passing" into the dominant group. But such passing is
often hindered by distinctive names, accents, or other cultural signs
associated with the minority group. Black people encounter a far more
immediate obstacle: their distinctive color or "visibility," which is an
unrelenting barrier to total acceptability in white America. Thousands
of fair-skinned Blacks do pass as white, however, and some dark-
skinned Blacks pass as Filipinos, Spaniards, Italians, or Mexicans.

In the past, light-skinned Blacks often passed in order to shop at
certain stores or to use such facilities as libraries, toilets, theaters, and
hotels. In Memphis, one family of light-skinned Blacks regularly attended white churches. "This way," they explained, "we get to hear
speakers not otherwise available to us, and the children have a chance
to hear the great music and see the pageants performed on festival
occasions." In Boston, at least two black businessmen passing as white
operate businesses in white neighborhoods and because of their loca-
tions, cater almost exclusively to whites. In Birmingham, a fair-skinned
Blackamerican lunches occasionally at the best downtown hotels "just
to look at the other side from time to time." In New Jersey, a black
man passing as white and married to a white woman holds a major
executive position in a nationally known drug firm. Such examples
could be multiplied a thousandfold.

A second kind of avoidance is often exhibited by upper-class members of the black minority, especially those in the business or professional groups who are not dependent upon the white majority for a
livelihood. These individuals often seek to insulate themselves from

contact with lower-class Blacks as well as from the whites, and they do not identify themselves with the common problems of their group. They become a society unto themselves, "asking the white man for nothing" and sharing nothing with the Blacks from whom they derive their status and wealth. They form themselves into tight little cliques which play at being part of the white society from which they are excluded.

For those individuals who wish to avoid the social *meaning* of their minority-group status, avoidance may take the form of developing towns or communities composed principally of members of their own group. Even when such residential segregation is initiated and enforced by the dominant group, minority-group members may actually *prefer* to live in the ghettos, rather than contend with the constant harassment incident to living in the larger community. But no ghetto, forced or voluntary, can really ward off the consequences of prejudice and discrimination; and the mere fact of its existence is a constant reminder of the lack of a more healthful and harmonious relationship.

Finally, avoidance may take the form of escape from feelings of inferiority and futility while maintaining contact with the dominant group. Those who choose this path attempt to obliterate the meaning of their minority-group status by emphasizing and enhancing their status as individuals. The result may be clearly beneficial—a determined self-improvement in order to meet the approved values of the dominant group in such areas as education and professional skill.

But the attendant marginality, the confusion of not really belonging anywhere, may be more than enough to offset the sense of achievement, or may make that achievement the very symbol of rejection and nonidentity. The danger is an attempt to escape into a world of make-believe, where fantasies of wealth, power, or position in "society" shut out the realities of humiliating and frustrating day-to-day existence. Black people of wealth and education, whose only barrier to unrestricted participation in the complete life of the community is the fact that they *are* black probably constitute the largest single class of social neurotics. Often their relationship to their white social counterparts is tenuous and marginal, but they can no longer find a place acceptable to their heightened sense of personal worth within the black community out of which they emerged. In their frustration, the creative talent which pushed them to the top and set them off from the masses is often dissipated in attention-oriented behavior which belies the security of their achievements.

### Acceptance

Some minority-group members feel that it is sensible to accept what cannot be changed or avoided: "You don't like it, but what can you do?" This attitude of conscious resignation or futility is the most common form of acceptance, but it is not the whole story. At the other extreme is the wholehearted acceptance of disparate social conditions characteristic of a caste society such as pre-Gandhian India. In such a society every group—high or low, favored or scorned—is felt to have a divinely ordained place in the sun. Social discrimination is no more than obedience to the divine order of the universe, and resentment against it would be as unthinkable as resentment of God. This attitude comes naturally, of course, to many white men in America; but there is some evidence that it was also widely held among American Blacks in times of unusual repression. Vestiges of this kind of adjustment behavior are probably retained among some Blacks living in isolated rural areas and among certain family retainers who identify closely with their employers.

Few Blackamericans today exhibit this wholehearted acceptance of discrimination and special privilege for white people, but many will consciously defer in specific situations in which inferiority is implied. Some Blacks accept Jim-Crow, for example, when no other means of accommodation or transportation is available; and a black servant may accept the epithet "boy" or "girl" because to reject it would mean the loss of employment and the possibility of livelihood. But, in both instances, the individuals involved may privately reject the whole status pattern and its implications. They reason that survival is the first order of reality.

These outward accommodations to specific situations of discrimination or prejudice are often misinterpreted as a wholehearted acceptance of inferior role or status. Such an assumption is, of course, illogical, and it can only be made by a mind which brings to the situation a serious misconception of black intelligence. No healthy mind assumes that another healthy mind will welcome an inferior status or its degrading concomitants.

Prejudice has been called "the refuge of a sick mind, and a method of transferring that sickness to others." Certainly anyone who *welcomes* the kind of social subordination imposed upon black people in America may be considered to be quite ill. No more can be said for those who practice it.

### Aggression

Aggression is an act or a pattern of behavior which aims to discomfort, injure, or destroy a person or his values. As an individual response among American Blacks, it may express itself in very different forms. To be a "race man"—that is, a professional champion of the in-group, speaking or writing in its defense, or agitating for its rights—is a common expression of direct aggression, especially among the upper classes but increasingly among all classes. Boycott; inefficiency and sloppy work done for white employers; ostentation, such as expensive automobiles or homes; refusal to observe the customary forms of etiquette—all these are direct means of expressing personal hostility. Some physical attacks also take place, especially against the police, who are recognized as often as not as the "strong arm" unit of white oppression. Traditionally, Blacks have avoided physical attacks against whites, but there is less hesitation now to return violence for violence, whatever the cost.

Literature, art, and humor are readily available vehicles of direct aggression, and they are widely used as such. The Black press is well known for its explicit posture against prejudice and discrimination, but countless individual black poets and novelists have also used their talents to express their resentment of and hostility toward the white man.

Not all aggression, however, is overt and outspoken. Silence or absolute immobility may also be aggressive, as, for example, when a black man fails to respond to what he considers a degrading epithet or refuses to enter into what he considers meaningless "dialogue" with whites over issues he thinks have already been decided.

Even certain postures of meekness and deference may be expressions of aggression, as with the apparent humility and self-effacement often displayed in situations of great dependence or where intimidation is present. The suffering then experienced is accepted as a means to ultimate victory for, from the suffering, power is derived. Again, meekness is a Christian virtue, and through its expression the humble Black may assert his moral superiority to the arrogant white. Aggressive meek-ness is also a common device for ridiculing the white man; while he egotistically accepts the meek behavior at face value, the Black Man may be laughing at him secretly for his gullibility.

So sensitive are white men to any challenge to their position that even a *possibility* that aggression *might* be expressed is considered dan-gerous. A black man in North Carolina was arrested and charged with "assault" because he *looked* at a white woman; and in Georgia, a parade featuring a high school band and the usual corps of majorettes was stopped and disbanded because Blacks joined other citizens in standing along the street to watch. In the southern part of the United States and in South Africa, even a suspicion that a black might want to strike back can cost that black his freedom or his life.

But aggression can also be misdirected. Hurt and angry, yet too frightened to act against his powerful tormentor, the Blackamerican sometimes thrashes about, seeking a target for his hostility. Often un-consciously, he displaces his aggression onto other minority groups—Jews, for example, who are highly visible as merchants in the black ghettos. All too often, the aggression is simply inverted: Blacks turn their rage against other Blacks or against themselves. The result is spora-dic intragroup violence and a general splintering of group solidarity, a disastrous development in the world unsympathetic to the dignity of powerless individuals or groups.

Even responsible and controlled aggression, as a response to offen-ses against one's human dignity, is a dangerous undertaking, and it is shrouded in moral and ethical ambivalence. Many individuals prefer the paths of avoidance and acceptance. In every minority, however, there will always be people who are willing to confront directly the source of their oppression and who will seek to remove, moderate, deflect, or destroy it. Such groups as the Black Panthers and the Black Liberation Army may be considered examples of this kind of response, the Pan-thers operating boldly and defiantly within the law, the Black Libera-tion Army claiming indiscriminate tactics.

## II. BLACK NATIONALISM, U.S.A.

### Stereotype and Identity

Aggression as an actual and continuing expression of black protest is usually underestimated in America. An image of the Negro as casual, passive, and content with his lot was fabricated during the days of slavery. Manifestly spurious, it found ready acceptance and has persisted into modern times. Such a picture has done little to prepare Americans to live together in peace and mutual respect.

Historians have contributed to the confusion by stereotyping the black slave as a docile, devoted, contented servant, or else by ignoring him altogether. The Blackamerican's active protests to the condition of slavery imposed upon him by a comparatively infinite power do not commonly appear in America's textbooks. Knowledge of the numerous slave revolts and insurrections, for example, was until recent times available only to the scholor who had the facilities for laborious research.

The problem is intensified by the racial segregation which prevents knowledgeable contact between whites and educated Blacks. Incredible as it seems, many Americans are surprised to learn that black people love and hate, accept and reject, with all the intensity of feeling common to human nature. Or perhaps it is not so incredible: he who would systematically degrade his fellow man must defend himself against reprisals. Since this cannot be done empirically, one way to gain a comforting sense of invulnerability is to pretend that the problem does not exist. If the Black Man does not feel *anything*, you don't have to be concerned about what you do to him.

Aggressive leaders will arise, however. Since they threaten the protective fantasy, the most militant of them must be discounted and isolated from the masses. By dismissing them as "Communists" or "radicals" (or whatever is beyond the pale at any given moment), we can keep our fantasy of the contented Negro pure. But the Blackamerican is not contented, and he will be heard. If his moderate leaders are dismissed as radical, then movements which are *in fact* radical will become more and more extreme, if only to get on ground where the white man will acknowledge their existence.

We are mired in complacency. The majority of unsuspecting whites are still shocked with disbelief and chagrin by the Blackamerican's insistent repudiation of the stereotype of good-natured, uncomplaining docility, which they have always accepted as true. When the Negro they thought they "knew" so well steps out of the role in which he has been cast, it seems to many like an act of treason. For example, when Marcus Garvey announced in 1920 that "the white man need expect no more Negro blood shed on his behalf" and that "the dying to be done by the black man in the future . . . will be done to make himself free," the speech was sufficiently alarming to be cited as sedition.[1] And when, forty years later, black people insisted upon being served at the lunch counters of stores which readily accepted their money in every other department, no less a person than ex-President Harry Truman—a man who had done much during his administration to remove racial barriers—cried out in outrage.

It is incredible that such expressions against the system should be viewed with surprise. It would be logically more surprising if resentment and hostility were *not* felt by a people who conceive themselves as oppressed and who can identify their oppressors. But this is precisely the tragedy of America, that she is oblivious of the smoldering resentments of millions for whom the American Creed is often a mockery. This "ignorance about the Negro is not, it must be stressed, just lack of interest and knowledge. It is a tense and high-strung restriction and distortion of knowledge, and it indicates much deeper dislocations within the minds of Southern whites"[2]—and, to a lesser extent, of the entire white community.

This convenient ignorance[3] of white people compounds the frustrations of the black minority, which now more than ever before is determined to be heard—or at least seen. The conspicuous consumption; the overemphasis on titles; the preoccupation with such values as academic degrees, foreign travel, and unique professional appointments; and the increasing activity of organized protest—all these add up to an open rejection of racial anonymity and the traditional stereotype.

Every important aspect of the Blackamerican's behavior is likely to have a race angle, though he himself is not always conscious of that fact.

To the Negro himself, the Negro problem is all-important. A Negro probably seldom talks to a white man . . . without consciousness of this problem. Even in a mixed white and Negro group of closest friends in Northern intellectual circles, and probably even in an all-Negro group, the Negro problem constantly looms in the background. It steers the jokes and allusions if it is not one of the dominant topics of conversation.

The Negro leader, the Negro social scientist, the Negro man of arts and letters is likely to view all social, economic, political, indeed, even aesthetic and philosophical issues from the Negro angle. What is more, he is expected to do so. He would seem entirely out of place if he spoke simply as a member of a community, a citizen of America. . . . In the existing American civilization he can attain some degree of distinction, but always as a representative of "his people," not as an ordinary American. . . . The Negro genius is imprisoned in the Negro problem.[4]

### Black Nationalism

Under the circumstances confronting him, the Blackamerican is required to be *black* before—and sometimes to the exclusion of—anything else. At some point, therefore, he will inevitably be tempted to glorify that from which he cannot escape. He may repudiate the white man's stereotype, turn his eyes from the painful reality, and substitute for them an idealized self-image. Drawing on the political parallel, in which each nationality considers itself distinct from and superior to its neighbors, this attitude has come to be known as *black nationalism.*

It would be absurd to say, of course, that all black race pride is only a rationalized form of acceptance. It is often a simple and spontaneous awareness of one's human dignity. Such, for example, was the pride of Denmark Vesey, an ex-slave who engineered an elaborate insurrection in Charleston in 1822:

Even whilst walking through the streets in company with another, he was not idle; for if his companion bowed to a white person he would rebuke him, and observe that all men were born equal, and that he was surprised that any one would degrade himself by such conduct; that he would never cringe to the whites, nor ought any one who had the feelings of a man. When answered, "We are slaves," he would sarcastically and indignantly reply, "You deserve to remain slaves."[5]

Vesey was hanged, along with thirty-four confederates, for leading the insurrection; but he died as he had lived, with courage and conviction, acknowledging no man his inherent superior.

Black nationalism is more than courage and rebellion; it is a way of life. It is an implicit rejection of the "alien" white culture and an explicit rejection of the symbols of that culture, balanced by an exaggerated and undiluted pride in "black" culture. It involves a drastic reappraisal not only of present realities but also of the past and future. The black nationalist revises history (or corrects it, as he would say) to establish that today's black men are descended from glorious ancestors, from powerful and enlightened rulers and conquerors. This reconstruction of history may reach ridiculous extremes; and it can never be accepted by white men, who, to bolster their own security, must perceive history as a record of *white* men's achievements. But a proud history is essential to the black nationalist's self-respect. Essential, too, is the certainty of a brilliant future, in which the inherent superiority of his race will triumph and he will again rule the world.

In any conventional sense, of course, it is inaccurate to speak of Blackamericans as black nationalists, for that term implies that they are—politically, culturally, ethnically, or racially—a distinct group. But this is emphatically not true. Politically they are Americans, as American as one can be (with the sole exception of the American Indian). Culturally they reflect the American mainstream; as Lloyd Warner observes, they are "culturally more like the white 'old American' than [are] any other sub-groups in America."[6] Nor are they ethnically separated from other Americans, holding allegiance to an earlier shared culture. On the contrary:

> The conspicuous feature of the Negro in America is *that his aboriginal culture was smashed*. . . . The importance of this basic fact for the Negro in America cannot be overestimated. It means in effect that the old types of social organization and all their derivations could not continue, but a new type of emergent adjustment derived from the new conditions would have to be established.[7]

Nor, finally, are they racially distinct. "Race" is at best a nebulous term.[8] There are no pure races, and it would be especially inappropriate to apply the term to the American Blacks, for they are at once African and Anglo-Saxon, Indian and French, Portuguese, Spanish, German, and Italian—a composite of every major "racial stock"[9] and every nationality of Western Europe and Western Africa.[10]

W. E. B. Du Bois observes that a common suffering, rather than a common biology or ethnic identity, has been the important factor uniting the Blackamerican in what is usually referred to as "nationalism."

> The so-called American Negro group . . . while it is in no sense absolutely set off physically from its fellow Americans, has nevertheless a strong, hereditary cultural unity born of slavery, of common suffering, prolonged proscription, and curtailment of political and civil rights. . . . Prolonged policies of segregation and discrimination have involuntarily welded the mass almost into a nation within a nation. . . .[11]

The times and the goals have changed since Du Bois. The nationalism of the Blackamerican is often prompted by a desire to set himself apart in order to preserve some cultural values. It is first a defensive response to external forces—hostile forces which threaten his creative existence. But it is a response born of the wish to conserve *and* to *escape* a set of conditions. It is the black response to white nationalism.

Black nationalism seizes the conditions of disprivilege and turns them to advantage as a tool for eliminating the disprivilege. It challenges the supercilious attitude of the majority group by glorifying the unique symbols of the Blacks—symbols which the whites consider repugnant. Some sociologists have labeled this behavior "negritude":

> . . . an exaltation of African-Negro specificity, a "kind of highly elaborated counterracism." . . . It involves a "particularly intense racial awareness," not uncoupled to political activity and demands. It is a term descriptive, also, of an appreciation of a new black unity experienced by its adherents, a consciousness of sharing in a past and in the making of the future. . . .[12]

Nationalism is ordinarily political; it refers to common values arising out of the existence of a state. Black nationalism addresses itself not to an existent state but to a state of mind.[13] But if there is no past or present black nation, what is to prevent the projection of a Black Nation of the future?

To the extent that it is couched in political terms—and this varies from movement to movement—black nationalism envisions and works toward the creation of such a state. In the creed of some movements, this political goal is relatively insignificant, a potentiality which the Black Man may or may not choose to realize. For the Black Muslims, however, the goal of a black nation is of consuming importance. The Muslims do not rest content with any concept of black nationalism that is not expressed in concrete economic and political terms. They want, they say, "some of this good earth," a prime prerequisite for any nation ready to "go for self."

### Black Nationalism and Social Class

In contemporary America hardly anyone wants to be a "Negro." There are Blacks who seek to identify themselves with the white society; others prefer to identify themselves with any group *except* the whites in order to escape the danger and humiliation of white capriciousness. A few Blacks are still willing to call themselves Negroes and, at the same time, to seek an accommodation with the white society. Black nationalism, with its repudiation of both Negro identity and white culture, sinks its roots deepest in the lower class and finds its greatest strength among the young.

Some Blackamericans are not black by choice. Some who have obvious strains of white ancestry are often at great pains to dissociate themselves from those who do not, and they are remarkably oblivious of the implications of their whiteness. Dark-skinned Blacks who were sensitive about their color used to make pointed references to their "Indian ancestry" lest they be mistaken for full-blooded Africans—an intolerable possibility.

The discovery that "black is beautiful" has changed all that. Still, some Blackamericans remain committed to the idea that America's racial dilemma will be resolved when the Black Man loses his distinctiveness, social and biological. They would prefer to become so thoroughly assimilated into the American mainstream as to be *biologically* indistinct, so as to avoid the possibility of exposure and rejection at the whimsy of the white majority. The ultimate security in living among a white majority is to be white. But this security is impossible to achieve in view of the general disdain for miscegenation. The barrier is circular; unqualified social acceptance is the only gateway to racial anonymity, which in turn is the only gateway to unqualified social acceptance.

Today's black masses do not worry overmuch about the white man's social acceptance. (The upper-class Blacks who do worry about it appear to be willing to settle for that degree of assimilation which will make them socially and economically indistinct from their counterparts in education and professional attainment.) They may not venerate all that is white and western, but they see themselves as part of this tradition, and they resent the irrationality which permits the color of their skins to obscure the more fundamental aspects of their identity.

The members of the young middle class are not too concerned about such issues. They ridicule the upper class as "neurotic sub-marginals" who make themselves ridiculous in trying to attract the white man's attention. Nor can they see the importance of having white ancestry, since almost all Blackamericans share this trait to some degree. Besides, white ancestry is not a criterion of the white man's judgment when he erects barriers to set himself apart from all others. Segregation is directed at a *class,* not at members within it; and all Blackamericans, whatever their names, ancestry, or skin color, belong by definition to the segregated class.

The black middle class is ambivalent about black nationalism. The black nationalists' emphasis on a united struggle against subordination has a certain appeal but the summary rejection of American identity and the search for cultural roots in Afro-Asian tradition seems unnecessary to many, and threatening to some. Despite the handicaps, those who have "made it" have done so in America. That is the one thing of which they are certain, and for many, that is enough. The middle-class Blackamerican feels no need to be either "Asiatic" or "European." He accepts the designation Blackamerican with no particular sense of opprobrium, and often with a certain pride, for he thus identifies himself with America's most important minority—a minority which overcame the terrible handicap of slavery, and in a brief span of history has distinguished itself and the nation of which it is a part, far beyond the wildest hopes of many. And the credits are not all in.

The self-image of the black middle class is one of ability and militancy, uncontaminated by either sycophancy or hatred for the white man. The middle class is not obsessed with status pretensions, as is the upper class, nor does it suffer the abject despair of the masses. As a result, it seldom displays the kind of insecurity that needs to search for ancestral pegs upon which to hang a claim for present status and acceptance.

The main appeal of all black nationalist movements, then, is to the lower class. Here resentment is crystallized and hardened. The mass man has long despaired of the white man's justice and of the trustworthiness of the "acceptable" black leaders who court the white man's favor. Moreover, he is already at the bottom of the ladder, so his economic and social position is not vulnerable. An indiscreet word, an admission of hostility, or an identification with "radical" or "extremist" groups can cost him nothing. What has he to lose if the purveyors of black nationalism fan his resentment into hatred, openly expressed in defiance of all white men and their compliant black lackeys?

The mass man lives in a no man's land between two alien worlds, both of which he spurns. Unlike his upper-class brother, he has no conscious desire to be white or even "like the whites," whom he identifies with most of his misfortunes. But neither will he accept the implications of being "Negro"—a white man's word, which he sees as an epithet of contempt. He recognizes that his race has a rich cultural heritage, extending thousands of years into the past; but the Black Men who were torn from their homes and shipped to the New World in chains were carefully isolated from that heritage. The history of the "Negro" begins in the torments and degradation of slavery in America. That is not the sum of *his* history; rather, that is the distortion of history. To him, "Negro" means humiliation, inferiority, and perpetual contingency. He is ripe for the challenge of black nationalism. He is anxious to rediscover himself as a black man linked to the ancient civilizations of Mother Africa. He is grateful for a mystique, especially a dignified religious mystique which rationalizes his resentments and his hatreds and makes them spiritual virtues in a cosmic war of good against evil. And he is jubilant at his new vision of the future—a future not of racial equality, for which he believes the white man has shown himself to be unfit, but of the return of black ascendency in a world returned to freedom, justice, and equality for all men through a black hegemony.

Many counterpressures exist, of course, to restrain the mass man from active participation in black nationalist movements. The Christian church is still powerful, though its traditional authority has been seriously eroded. Personal friendships with white men, where they exist, make the absolute generalizations of black nationalism difficult to accept. Some Blacks, like some white men, find a certain comfort and security in being considered inferior; they cling to the status in which all their personal failures are overlooked and nothing much is expected of them. Others are so conditioned to the status quo that they never dream. Above all, the mass man is a decent and responsible human being, loath to give his life over to hatred and vengeance. He will not do so unless forced to the wall by a smug and callous society intent on his dehumanization.

# 3 Black Nationalism: The Minor Leagues

ll black nationalist movements have in common three characteristics: a disparagement of the white man and his culture, a repudiation of Negro identity, and a concomitant search for and commitment to the Black (African) heritage. Within this framework, however, they take shape in a remarkable variety of creeds and organizations. The smallest groups range in temperament from the innocuous United African Nationalist Movement, with its New York City street-corner evangelism, to the ultramilitant secret society of the Ras Tafarians. The Ras Tafarians are based in the West Indies, but operate in New York as well.

The more influential black nationalist movements also seize upon varying interests as focal points for group identification or as vehicles of counteraggression against the white majority. One favorite focus is religion; another is political or politicoeconomic goals. The former has no immediate concern with a national state; the latter makes the creation of a state central to its appeal. These two emphases are perhaps best represented in the Moorish Science Temple movement of Noble Drew Ali and the Universal Negro Improvement Association of Marcus Garvey, both of which flourished about the time of World War I.

The Moorish Science movement was essentially religious; Garvey's UNIA was primarily political. The *raison d'être* of both was to devise some means of escaping the implications of being black in a white-dominated society. Noble Drew sought a psychic escape: by changing their names and the symbols of their culture, his Moors hoped to change their social fortunes. For Garvey, the logical solution was to remove all American Blacks to an independent African state. Drew had a substantial following and Garvey's supporters numbered in the millions. However, neither did much to change the conditions that were ultimately responsible for whatever measure of success they could claim.

*Religious Nationalism: The Moorish Science Temples*

About 1913, a forty-seven-year-old North Carolina black man named Timothy Drew established a "Moorish Science Temple" in Newark, New Jersey.[1] From this seed grew a movement that, at its peak, had established temples in Detroit, Harlem, Chicago, Pittsburgh, Philadelphia, and in numerous cities across the South. Membership may have been as high as twenty or thirty thousand during the lifetime of "the Prophet," as Drew was called.

Drew seems not to have had a formal education, but at some point he apparently had been exposed to Oriental philosophy. He was particularly impressed by the lack of race consciousness in Oriental religious thought and saw in it a possible answer to the Black Man's plight in a color-conscious America. If Blacks could somehow establish an identity with the Oriental peoples, whose religious philosophies either knew nothing of the "curse of Canaan"[2] or else found it irrelevant, they might become less susceptible to the everyday hazards of being "everyday-Negroes" in America.

In pursuing this goal, Drew did not allow himself to be troubled by the inconveniences of history. He simply decreed that, thenceforth, American Blacks were to be known as "Asiatics."

> He became obsessed with the ideal that salvation for the Negro people lay in the discovery by them of their national origin; i.e., they must know whence they came, and refuse longer to be called Negroes, black folk, colored people, or Ethiopians. They must henceforth call themselves Asiatics, to use the generic term, or, more specifically, Moors, or Moorish Americans.[3]

To document this ethnic transformation, he issued "Nationality and Identification Cards" to his followers. Each card bore the Islamic symbol (the star and crescent), an image of clasped hands, and a numeral "7" in a circle. It announced that the bearer honored "all the Divine Prophets, Jesus, Mohammed, Buddha, and Confucius" and pronounced upon him "the blessings of the God of our Father, Allah." The card identified him as "a Moslem under the Divine Laws of the Holy Koran of Mecca, Love, Truth, Peace, Freedom, and Justice" and concluded with the assurance: "I AM A CITIZEN OF THE UNITED STATES." Each card was validated by the subscription, "NOBLE DREW ALI, THE PROPHET."

Drew's movement spread west from New Jersey to Pittsburgh, Detroit, and Chicago, and there were temples in a number of cities across the South. In Chicago the movement rapidly gained momentum and soon became a problem for law enforcement officials. The members of the cult felt an exaggerated sense of security and importance in their new "Asiatic" status, symbolized by the red fezzes which the male members were required to wear at all times. But this sudden metamorphosis was not accepted by the whites, who saw no reason to relinquish their traditional racial prerogatives. The Moors' confidence, however, was not diminished. They were certain that the whites (or "Europeans") were soon to be destroyed and that the "Asiatics" would soon be in control.

A number of disturbances developed. The Moors, made conspicuous by their fezzes, walked the streets, treating white folk with open contempt. In various parts of the Middle West they became anathema to the police.

In Chicago, affairs reached the point where members of the cult would accost white people on the streets, and showing their membership cards or the buttons they wore in their coat lapels, would sing the praises of their prophet, now known as Noble Drew Ali, because he had freed them from the curse of European (white) domination.[4]

The cult members believed that the imminent destruction of the whites was signified by the appearance in the sky of a star within a crescent moon.

As the racial irritations cued by the Moors' aggressive behavior grew worse, Nobel Drew Ali issued a warning to his followers to exercise more restraint. They were cautioned to "stop flashing [their] cards before Europeans" and to avoid making agitating speeches on their jobs. "We did not come to cause confusion," the Prophet observed. "Our work is to uplift the nation."

Despite Drew's sincerity and simple idealism, the Moorish Science movement eventually addressed itself to some new directions not anticipated in its founding philosophy. As is characteristic of mass movements, its growth and expansion began to attract better educated but less dedicated individuals, who saw it as an irresistible opportunity for private gain and exploitation. Anxious to extend the movement and aware of his own limitations, Noble Drew Ali opened the door to these men; but the "new blood" proved to be costly indeed. The less discriminating followers of the Prophet—like their counterparts in other religious sects—were soon duped into buying various charms, relics, magical potions, pictures, and spurious literature concerning their Asiatic heritage. The leaders grew rich off the credulous masses; and when it became apparent that Noble Drew Ali was the chief obstacle to a more complete exploitation, he was shunted aside. Eventually, he was killed.

The responsibility for the death of Noble Drew Ali has never been officially placed. During the struggle for power among the leaders of the cult, one leader was killed. Ali was not in Chicago at the time of the killing, but upon his return he was arrested and charged with murder by police officials, who had become somewhat weary of his movement. He was never brought to trial, for he died mysteriously shortly after being released on bond. The cause of his death is variously attributed to a "third degree" given him while under arrest or to a subsequent beating administered by his rivals for power within the movement.

After the Prophet's death, the cult split into numerous smaller groups. It is no longer a potent force in the black community, though some temples remain active in the industrial cities of the North. Many present-day Moors believe that Noble Drew Ali is reincarnate in their present leaders, and the *Holy Koran* of the Moorish Holy Temple of Science continues to be the sacred book of the various sects. (The *Holy Koran,* not to be confused with the Quran of classical Islam, contains the teachings of the Prophet, Noble Drew Ali, along with various other esoteric materials.) Membership continues to be limited to "Asiatics"—that is, to non-Caucasians—who renounce the traditional category and the implications of being "colored" or "Negro." Each new member attaches the term "el" or "bey" to his name in signification of his Asiatic status. Initiation fees vary, and stipulated dues are paid thereafter.

The cult considers itself Moslem, but it retains many of the familiar markings of Christianity. Jesus, for example, remains a prominent figure in the worship services; and hymns, although revised to appropriate the new teachings, retain the rhythmic chant forms of the familiar black spirituals. Love is taught as the guiding spirit of the universe: "the fallen sons and daughters of the Asiatic Nation of North America need to learn to love instead of hate; and to know of their higher self and lower self."

The Moors believe that "before you can have a God you must have a nationality" and that Noble Drew Ali, who was a prophet ordained of God, gave his people the North African state of Morocco to be their nation. In this connection, they attach great signification to names:

The name means everything; by taking the Asiatic's name from him and calling him Negro, black, colored, or Ethiopian, the European stripped the Moor of his power, his authority, his God, and every other worthwhile possession.[5]

Conversely, each religion has its proper racial adherents, and religious faith should not cross racial lines:

Christianity is for the European (paleface); Moslemism is for the Asiatic (olive-skinned). When each group has its own peculiar religion, there will be peace on earth.

[However], Noble Drew Ali is a kindred personage and spirit to Confucius, Jesus, Buddha, and Zoroaster.[6]

In the Moors' worship services, there is none of the expressive fervor one associates with the stereotype of the typical black church. The services are subdued and quiet. All present are expected to pay careful attention; but there are few responses from the congregation, and even these are hardly audible. Meetings begin and end with undeviating punctuality, and the members are seated separately according to sex. Friday is considered the Sabbath day, but meetings are held on Wednesday and Sunday evenings as well. No baptism or communion is observed. The faithful are required to pray daily at sunrise, noon, and sunset, facing Mecca with hands upraised.

Strict personal morality is a keynote of the movement's teachings. The Moors greet their followers with the salutation "Peace!" or "Islam!" As among the Black Muslims, great emphasis is placed upon the husband's responsibility as protector and provider for his family, while women are enjoined to be good homemakers and to obey their husbands. Divorce is discouraged. Monogamy is the only form of marriage recognized, and the marriage ceremonies are performed by the "Grand Sheik," or Governor, in charge of the local temple. Most secular entertainments are forbidden, as is the use of cosmetics, alcohol, and tobacco. Meat and eggs are taboo. Personal cleanliness is stressed, but men are not expected to shave.

Despite the racial aggressiveness of some of its adherents, the Moorish Science movement did not consider itself "radical." On the contrary, the Moors offered themselves as the nucleus around which a world of truth, peace, freedom, and justice must be built. Despite their hostility to whites, they stressed obedience and loyalty to the flag of the United States, so long as they were to live in America. For the Moors have two homelands. Noble Drew, the Reincarnation of Mohammed, gave them Morocco as the seat of their Nation. But the dark people of the world are also native to the continent of North America, which is temporarily under European dominion. They have no choice but to submit to the harsh rule of the whites until the whites' time to reign comes to an end.

A few Moorish temples remain scattered among the black ghettos today. The congregations believe that they are still led by Noble Drew Ali, with each present Sheik a reincarnation of their revered founder. Many Moors, however, were among the earliest converts to the Black Muslim Movement. They feel quite at home in this new nationalism, which continues them in some aspects of the familiar "Asiatic" religion without requiring them to love the hated "Europeans." In fact, they may now look forward to the predicted destruction of their enemies with increased assurance, for Elijah Muhammad, the Messenger—unlike Noble Drew Ali—is not a man to compromise.

## Political Nationalism: The Garvey Movement

The name of Marcus Garvey is one of the best known in recent black history, yet it is one that some black leadership would like very much to forget. Few Blacks have elicited such consummate scorn from their fellows as did this belligerent little man, caricatured by a contemporary as:

A Jamaican of unmixed stock, squat, stocky, fat and sleek, with protruding jaws, and heavy jowls, small bright pig-like eyes and rather bulldog-like face. Boastful, egotistic, tyrannical, intolerant, cunning, shifty, smooth and suave, avaricious . . . gifted at self-advertisement, without shame in self-laudation . . . without regard for veracity, a lover of pomp and tawdry finery and garish display.[7]

Yet, for all the castigations of his many critics, Garvey enjoyed the admiration of hundreds of thousands of lower-class Blackamericans who followed him with enthusiasm and money, and who received from him a new estimate of their worth and their future. His movement fired the imaginations of a people desperate for a new hope and a new purpose, however unrealistic his programs. Its spirit of racial chauvinism had the sympathy of the overwhelming majority of suffering Blacks, including many of those who opposed its more extreme objectives. For this was the potent spirit of race consciousness and race pride that informed the 'New Negro' " of the 1920s[8] —a period of cultural renaissance and racial militancy among the black intelligentsia as well as among the black masses.

The Garvey movement must inevitably be seen against the background of the post-World War I era, a crucial and difficult time for Blacks in the United States. They had helped to win a war for democracy overseas, only to return to the customary bigotry at home. They had risked death fighting beside the white man in the trenches of France, only to die in America at the white man's hand. In the first year after the war, seventy Blackamericans were lynched, many of them still in uniform. Fourteen Blackamericans were burned publicly by white citizens; eleven of these martyrs were burned alive.[9] During the "Red Summer" of 1919, there were no fewer than twenty-five race riots across the country. A riot in the nation's capital lasted three days; in Chicago, thirty-eight people were killed and 537 injured during thirteen days of mob rule.[10]

Along with the actual physical violence, there was intimidation everywhere. The Ku Klux Klan had been revived; and New York, Illinois, Indiana, Michigan, and several New England states had been added to its traditional roster of Southern states.[11] There was an increasing competition between Blacks and whites for housing and jobs. Despair and militancy were the alternate moods of the black veterans who had fought "to make the world safe for democracy." They were disillusioned about the share of democracy America had reserved for them, but they were determined to bid for their rights—as they had fought for the rights of others.

In the summer of 1914, Marcus Garvey had returned home to Jamaica from a visit to London, his mind pregnant with plans for a new Universal Negro Improvement Association. Ironically, his sense of mission had been triggered by a reading of *Up From Slavery,* the autobiography of Booker T. Washington, who had been despised by many black leaders for his life-pattern of compromise and accommodation.

> I read *Up From Slavery* . . . and then my doom . . . of being a race leader dawned upon me. . . . I asked: "Where is the black man's Government? Where is his King and his kingdom? Where is his President, his country, and his ambassador, his army, his navy, his men of big affairs?" I could not find them, and then I declared, "I will help to make them."[1][2]

And he did. Putting aside Washington's reminiscences of restraint and gratitude for white favors, he originated a movement devoted to extreme black nationalism and self-improvement. As a result, he came to share with Washington the bitter contempt of the black intellectuals.

The manifesto of the UNIA called attention to "the universal disunity existing among the people of the Negro or African race." It challenged "all people of Negro or African parentage" to subscribe to the UNIA program, which read in part:

> To establish a Universal Confraternity among the race; to promote the spirit of race pride and love; to reclaim the fallen of the race . . . to strengthen the imperialism [self-determination] of independent African States . . . to establish Universities, Colleges and Secondary Schools for the further education and culture of the boys and girls of the race to conduct a world-wide commercial and industrial intercourse.[13]

The motto of the Association was: "One God! One Aim! One Destiny!"—a motto which has recently been adopted by the militant Ras Tafarian cult, which also emanates from Jamaica.

In 1916, Marcus Garvey "came screaming out of the British West Indies onto the American Stage."[14] He landed in New York, where at first little attention was paid to his street-corner speeches. Undaunted, he set out to tour thirty-eight states in order to study conditions of black life in America. When he returned to New York a year later, he

had formulated certain opinions which were later to shape the largest
mass movement in the history of the Blackamerican. Important among
these conclusions was the amazing discovery that the "so-called Negro
leaders . . . had no program, but were mere opportunists who were living off their so-called leadership while the poor people were groping in
the dark."[15] He seems to have concluded that too much of the leadership was concentrated in the hands of mulattoes and that these "part-
white Negroes" could not be trusted.[16] He was exceedingly disturbed
that black leadership depended so heavily upon white philanthropy—an
impossible paradox. He was most contemptuous because this dependent
leadership seemed willing "to turn back the clock of progress" at the
whim of the white benefactors.

The New York division of the UNIA soon became the headquarters
of a world-wide organization. By midsummer of 1919, Garvey claimed
to have two million members in thirty branches.[17] His newspaper, *The
Negro World*, was printed in French and Spanish, as well as in English;
at its peak, it claimed a circulation of more than 200,000, "reaching the
mass of Negroes throughout the world." The paper devoted itself mainly to a recapitulation and reinterpretation of the Black Man's contribution to history. It recalled "the stirring heroism of such leaders of
American slave rebellions as Denmark Vesey, Gabriel Prosser, and Nat
Turner. The struggles of Zulu and Hottentot warriors against European
rule, the histories of Moorish and Ethiopian empires, and the intrepid
exploits of Toussaint L'Ouverture . . . were not neglected in the effort
to make Negroes conscious and proud of their racial heritage."[18] Readers were encouraged to speak out on racial matters, and Garvey himself
"delighted in references to the greatness of colored civilizations at a
time when white men were only barbarians and savages."[19]

At the First International Convention of the UNIA, held in New
York in August 1920, no fewer than twenty-five countries were represented. A mammoth parade—led by the African Legion, the Black Cross
Nurses, and other organizations of the UNIA—wound through Harlem
and on to Madison Square Garden, where Garvey set the tone of the
month-long convention with an opening address to 25,000 black people.

We are the descendants of a suffering people; we are the descendants of a people determined to suffer no longer. . . . We shall now

organize the 400,000,000 Negroes of the world into a vast organization to plant the banner of freedom on the great continent of Africa. . . . If Europe is for the Europeans, then Africa shall be for the black peoples of the world. We say it; we mean it. . . .[20]

Later, the UNIA delegates drafted a "Declaration of the Rights of the Negro Peoples of the World," which was adopted on August 13, 1920. The declaration spelled out the Black Man's rights in terms of political and judicial equality, racial self-determination, and an independent Africa under a black government. It alleged that the League of Nations (which had just been organized in Switzerland) "seeks to deprive Negroes of their liberty." The League, it said, is "null and void as far as the Negro is concerned."

The convention also approved a flag for the movement; "red for the blood of the race, nobly shed in the past and dedicated to the future; black to symbolize pride in the color of its skin; and green for the promise of a new and better life in Africa."[21] An order of nobility was created; honorary orders were established; salaries were voted for the leadership; and Garvey was elected Provisional President of the African Republic. Gabriel Johnson, mayor of Monrovia, capital of the free African Republic of Liberia, was named secretary of state in the Provisional Cabinet at a salary of $12,000 a year. So impressed was Johnson that, on his return home, he announced that his office in Garvey's Provisional Government gave him diplomatic precedence over the President of Liberia.

When the convention ended, the Garvey movement had attained world significance. " 'Up, you mighty race,' Garvey thundered, 'you can accomplish what you will,' and the Negro people responded with an enthusiastic determination born of centuries of frustration and despair."[22] They poured a million dollars into the UNIA's Black Star Steamship Line—organized to link the black peoples of the world in commerce and trade, and to transport America's black millions back to their African "home." They gloried in the cooperative possession of grocery stores, laundries, restaurants, and hotels. They took an unconcealed pride in staffing the Universal Black Cross Nurses, the Universal African Motor Corps, the Black Eagle Flying Corps, and other UNIA auxiliaries with black men and women. An unarmed but smartly uniformed Universal African Legion paraded spectacularly through the

streets of Harlem, and the admiring crowds massed along the route
whispered knowingly about the liberation of Africa by force of arms.
Oppressed Blacks everywhere, and especially the despairing millions in
the crowded slums of black America, acclaimed Garvey as the true
leader of great people who had suddenly discovered who they were.

Garvey's political ambitions were never made wholly explicit. The
Ku Klux Klan and the fanatical Anglo-Saxon Clubs of that era assumed
that he intended to lead all the Blacks in America to Africa; for this
reason, they gave him their open support. But Garvey declared, "We do
not want all the Negroes [to settle] in Africa. Some are no good here,
and naturally will be no good there."[23] His real intentions seem to have
been not unlike those of modern Zionism. He wanted to build a state,
somewhere in Africa, to which black people would come from all over
the world, bringing with them a wealth of technical and professional
skills. Within a few years, he hoped, the new state would gain such
prestige and power that it would be recognized as a symbol of accomplishment and protection for Blacks all over the world. For Garvey was
convinced, as is Elijah Muhammad, that the Black Man can hope for
neither peace nor dignity while he lives in and is dependent upon white
society. Like Muhammad, he saw only one solution: the establishment
of a separate nation "so strong as to strike fear" into the hearts of the
oppressor white race.[24]

But, unlike the Zionists, Garvey did not rest his ambitions here. The
eventual liberation of all Africa was never far from his thinking. Presumably his black state, when it became sufficiently powerful, would
begin a revolution that would free all Africa, for he spoke mysteriously
of the hour of "Africa's Redemption": "It is in the wind. It is coming.
One day, like a storm, it will be here." He told a white audience that
"you will find ten years from now, or 100 years from now, Garvey was
not an idle buffoon but was representing the new vision of the Negro. . . ." In what was perhaps a prophetic warning, he declared: "We
say to the white man who now dominates Africa that it is to his interest
to clear out of Africa now, because we are coming . . . 400,000,000
strong." And again, "We shall not ask England or France or Italy or
Belgium, 'Why are you here?' We shall only command them, 'Get out of
here.' "[25]

Garvey's beachhead on the African continent was to be Liberia, the
little country founded on the west coast by American ex-slaves in 1847.

The Liberian government had promised to "afford the association every facility legally possible in effectuating in Liberia its industrial, agricultural, and business projects." Specified settlements were laid out by the Liberian government and set aside for colonization, but Liberia's Acting President Edwin Barclay felt is necessary to warn Garvey that "the British and French have enquired. . . . But it is not always advisable nor politic to openly expose our secret intentions. . . . We don't tell them what we think; we only tell them what we like them to hear—what, in fact, they like to hear."[26]

Garvey's movement was essentially political and social; he did not rest his doctrines and program upon any religious premise. Yet he did not neglect the wellspring of religious fervor—and discontent—in the black community. Then as now, many black people resented the white man's presumption in depicting God and Jesus as Caucasians, in filling the Christian churches and Bibles with pictures of a white God, a white Savior, and an all-white heavenly host. Garvey seized on this resentment and carried it to a logical extreme. Since whatever is white cannot be beneficial to the Black Man, he pointed out, a white God cannot be the God of nonwhite people. This was the God of the white man. The Black Man's God must be black. God made man in His own image.

To promulgate a black religion, Garvey named as Chaplain General of the UNIA a former Episcopal rector, the Reverend George Alexander McGuire. In the Episcopalian fold, Bishop McGuire had long been a nettlesome critic, first agitating in vain for independent status for the black congregations, then organizing an Independent Episcopalian Church. This group followed him into the Garveyite movement and became the nucleus of a new, UNIA-sponsored African Orthodox Church. In his new position, McGuire was ordained a bishop by Archbishop Vilatte of the Syrian Orthodox Church,[27] thus bringing to the African Orthodox Church direct apostolic succession from one of the oldest bodies in Christendom.

Under Garvey's aegis, Bishop McGuire set out to reorder the religious thinking of the vast membership of the UNIA. He established a cathedral and a seminary (named Endich, after an Ethiopian mentioned in the New Testament) for the training of a new order of black priests. The liturgy, based on the Episcopalian ritual, was colorful and impressive. And the new church set high moral demands, seeking "to be true to the principles of Christianity without the shameful hypocrisy of the white churches."[28] But the church was distinguished primarily by its appeal to race consciousness. "Forget the white gods," the bishop demanded. "Erase the white gods from your hearts." By 1924, after four years of his ministry, the Black Madonna and Child had become a standard picture in the homes of the faithful, and the worship of a black Christ became the hallmark of the faith.

In August 1924, at the fourth annual convention of the UNIA, Bishop McGuire issued a public appeal to the black faithful "to name the day when all members of the race would tear down and burn any pictures of the white Madonna and the white Christ found in their homes."[29] The black clergy was loud in protest, and the black press derided the idea of a "black Jesus." But the African Orthodox Church had long since spread its missions through several states and into Canada, Cuba, and Haiti. On both fronts, religious and political, Garvey's black nationalism had become an important source of hope and identity for millions of black people.

From the start, however, Garvey had not been without his troubles. His movement had been kept under constant surveillance by New York State Assistant District Attorney Edwin P. Kilroe, whose interest bordered on harassment. The federal government was hardly sympathetic to Garvey's international ambitions; and abroad, the various colonial governments viewed him with outright alarm. His newspaper—in its English, French, and Spanish editions—had been quickly suppressed throughout the colonial world. In America the newspaper was among several black publications cited by the U.S. Department of Justice in a 1919 report on alleged radicalism and sedition among Blackamericans. The following year the Lusk Committee, investigating sedition in New York State, cited the *Negro World* as one of the most radical elements of the black press. Both the committee and the Department of Justice portrayed Garvey as a dangerous agitator, inimical to the interests of his own people and of the country as a whole; but neither group was able to substantiate its charges.

Meanwhile, the governments of Great Britain and France became increasingly alarmed over the implications of the Garvey movement and spared no effort to keep it out of Africa—even to the extent of bringing indirect pressure to bear on the Republic of Liberia, which had agreed to provide for the settlement of about a hundred thousand Garvey followers in that country. The UNIA had been enthusiastically welcomed there, and the mayor of Monrovia had accepted a post as secretary of state in Garvey's provisional government. Garvey sent several missions to Liberia, one as late as June 1924, to prepare for the settlement of his followers, who were scheduled to begin arriving in October 1924.

In the summer of 1924, the pressure from the British and French (who governed the territories surrounding Liberia) took effect. The Liberian government, under President Charles D. B. King, sent a diplomatic note to the United States announcing that it was "irrevocably opposed both in principle and fact to the incendiary policy of the Universal Negro Improvement Association, headed by Marcus Garvey." The lands promised to Garvey were leased instead to the Firestone Rubber Corporation, and when the new Garvey mission arrived, the members were arrested for immediate deportation. Thereupon, the Liberian president was lionized by the British for his "courage and statesmanship." The British press hailed him for putting "his foot down very firmly on such misguided movements for the people of his own race, as that sponsored . . . by Marcus Garvey and other agitators." The French government made him a Chevalier of the French Legion of Honor.[30]

At home, Garvey was encountering increasing resistance within the black community. The emerging black bourgeoisie and the black intellectuals would have no part of him.[31] Their attempt to mold the public image of Blackamericans as an intelligent, respectable people was undermined by his constant harangues and the spectacle of thousands of his followers parading in flamboyant uniforms through the streets of New York City. At first they simply ignored his movement; but as its notoriety increased, it drew the fire of most of the well-known black leaders, including A. Philip Randolph, Chandler Owen, and W.E.B. Du Bois. Du Bois criticized the UNIA as "bombastic and impractical." He later admitted that competition from Garvey had greatly hampered the development of his own Pan-African Congresses.[32] The NAACP also criticized Garvey's movement, as did the National Urban League.

Nor did Garvey spare his critics. He characterized such leaders as Du Bois, James Weldon Johnson, and Eugene Kinkle Jones as "weak-kneed and cringing . . . sycophant to the white man." He warned that "the 'Uncle Tom' Negroes must give way to the 'New Negro,' who is seeking his place in the sun."[33]

Thus Garvey's troubles closed down upon him. His own lack of business acumen had kept him embroiled in legal wrangles over the Black Star Line and other commercial ventures of the UNIA.[34] Now the apprehensions of the ruling powers on three continents were joined with those of America's conservative black leadership in a demand that the dangerous little Jamaican be cut down to size. The *Messenger* magazine, edited by Chandler Owen and A. Philip Randolph, led the black intellectuals in a direct attack. "Garvey must go!" became the rallying cry of many black leaders who could agree on no other single issue.

Early in 1922, at the urging of the black press, Garvey had been indicted for using the mails to defraud in the promotion of stock in the UNIA's Black Star Steamship Line. But the government's case was weak, and the federal authorities made no move to prosecute. In January 1923, however, the calm was shattered by the murder of James W. H. Eason, an early Garvey admirer who had split with the movement the previous year and was now rumored to have offered himself as a key prosecution witness in the mail-fraud case. There was no evidence linking Garvey or the UNIA to the crime, which remains unsolved, but the hostility of the responsible black leadership was whetted. Less than a week after the murder, a "Committee of Eight"—all prominent Blackamericans, most of them active in the NAACP—sent an open letter to the U.S. Attorney General. The letter condemned Garveyism as a philosophy seeking "to arouse ill-feeling between the races" and urged that he "use his full influence completely to disband and extirpate the vicious movement, and that he vigorously and speedily push the government's case against Marcus Garvey for using the mails to defraud."[35]

Garvey responded with a bitter denunciation of the "good old darkies" who had treacherously sought to curry favor with the white man at the expense of their "fellow Negroes whose only crime has been that of making an effort to improve the condition of the race."[36] But in May the government brought the case to trial and won a conviction. Garvey was fined and sentenced to imprisonment for the maximum term of five years. He remained at liberty for seventeen months while his lawyers vainly appealed the decision, but in February 1925, he was taken to the federal penitentiary at Atlanta, Georgia. In December 1927, his sentence was commuted by President Coolidge; but Garvey had never become an American citizen, and since he had been convicted of a felony, the law required that he be immediately deported. From abroad he labored hard to keep his movement in the United States alive, but it quickly faded, and his death in London in 1940 was scarcely mentioned in the American press.

Garveyism is not dead. William L. Sherrill, once Garvey's representative to the League of Nations, kept open the UNIA headquarters in Detroit and took on the leadership of the movement. The African Orthodox Church also survives, but its membership has dwindled to a few thousand. Various nationalistic cults in America, Africa, and Jamaica still celebrate "Garvey Day" each August 1 with appropriate speeches and ceremony. And Garvey's own stature continues to grow as more and more observers concede that, for all his faults, he had a profound effect on the black communites of the world—in America, the Caribbean, and in Africa herself. The emergent states of contemporary Africa owe much to Marcus Garvey, and the leading African statesmen have been quick to acknowledge it. In America, the recognition of Garvey as an important contributor to the spirit and the impetus of black liberation has been slow to surface. Only after the syndrome of black ethnicity had become firmly established more than forty years after he was broken on the rack of the deep political and personality cleavages in the black ghettos of America, did his true status as a race leader, and as an apostle of black togetherness, begin to emerge. If the notion that "black is beautiful," or that there is power in the recognition of a common experience and a common cause of black people wherever they are, can be said to have a "father," Marcus Garvey must most certainly be the man.

### Preparing the Way for Allah

By the late 1920s, then, Noble Drew Ali was dead and Marcus Garvey deported. Their movements, shorn of their charismatic leadership, were in rapid decline. But there was no change in the experience that gave rise to both movements—the experience of being black among a white majority. This condition was, if anything, more intolerable than ever, for the black masses had been vividly reminded of their lost human dignity and their proud racial heritage. The failure of the Moorish and Garveyite movements left in the black lower class a constrained silence, a vacuum of extremist protest against racial indignities that were soon to be aggravated by the tensions of the Depression. Either America had to come quickly to its senses and live up to its democratic ideals, or a new black nationalist movement would move in to fill that vacuum.

It was just at this time, in the summer of 1930, that Wallace D. Fard appeared in Detroit. Many of those who first came under his spell had been followers of Garvey or Noble Drew. Fard was not alone, of course, in seeking to win over the masses already conditioned to black nationalism, especially those who had flocked to the black, green, and crimson banner of the UNIA. Other black nationalist groups were also active, among them the National Movement for the Establishment of a Forty-Ninth State, the National Union of People of African Descent, the Peace Movement of Ethiopia, and the United African Nationalist Movement. But none of these groups had a leader with Fard's charisma or his ability to seize on the Moorish and Garveyite passions and transform them into a new force, in which religious and political energies were fused. Fard's movement was destined to become the vanguard of black nationalism and, by solving the problem of succession on which earlier movements had foundered, to give that ancient ambition a fresh permanence and power.

# 4  The Faith and the Future

he Black Muslims learned much from Marcus Garvey and
Noble Drew Ali. Like those earlier prophets of black
nationalism, they capitalize on the lower-class Black
Man's despair and reservations about the white man, and
they have developed black consciousness into a confession of faith. The Black Man, they teach, has a manifest destiny, and
the white man is the personification of the evil that separates the Black
Man from his freedom, his moral development, and his God. In such a
confession, the Moors, the Garveyites, and most of the other cults of
black nationalism are able to find satisfactory expression. It matters
little whether the homeland of the dispersed Black Nation is said to be
Asia or Africa. For the black nationalist, the Black Man's Zion is where
the white man is not.

In elaborating their doctrines, the Black Muslims have achieved
what seems to be a paradox: a rigorously high moral standard of personal and group behavior, laced with a very critical view of the white
man's history of black exploitation, and a potentially violent determination that the white man's rule must end. They urge peace among
brothers, but point out that the white man, having scorned brotherhood with nonwhites, can only be a brother to himself. They urge
submission to all authority *except* to the authority of the white man,
which, they assert, is not legitimate but is simply imposed by force and
maintained by intimidation. The Muslims' social morality is, in short,
an in-group morality. They find no mandate, except that of temporary
expediency, for peace and submission between whites and blacks. And
from this point of view, it is the religion of the Negro Christian that
appears as a paradox, if not an outright hypocrisy or madness. For "it is
not possible," said Muhammad's one-time chief spokesman, Malcolm X,

"for you to love a man whose chief purpose in life is to humiliate you and still be what is considered a normal human being."

## I. DOCTRINES AND MYTHOLOGY

Mythologies—and the doctrines they support—are found as the organizing principles of all mass movements, religious and secular. They hold the central position in the most venerable religions and the most specious cults, in social movements as disparate as Fascism and the Townsend Plan, in cultural attitudes ranging from white or black supremacy to the American Creed.

By their very nature, myths are outside the realm of the "true" or the "untrue." They are subject neither to the rules of logic nor to the techniques of scientific investigation. A religious myth, in particular, claims for itself an immunity which is not granted to any other kind of information upon whose authority people commit themselves to action.

Like every other mass movement, the Black Muslims have developed for themselves a unique body of myths and doctrines.[1] Much of this material is elaborative and peripheral. Several major themes, however, are stressed by the Muslims, both in their publications and in their public lectures.

### The Plight of the So-Called Negroes

Like all other black nationalists, the Muslims do not consider themselves "Negroes." They resent and reject the word and its implications: it is no more than "a label the white man placed on us to make his discrimination more convenient." For this reason, they rarely use the word "Negro" without the qualifier "so-called."

The Muslims prefer to be called black men. Malcolm X explained:

If you call yourself "white," why should I not call myself "black"? Because you have taught me that I am a "Negro"! Now then, if you ask a man his nationality and he says he is German, that means he comes from a nation called Germany. If he says his nationality is French, that means he came from a nation called France. The term he uses to identify himself connects him with a nation, a language, a culture and a flag. Now if he says his nationality is "Negro" he has told you nothing—except possibly that he is not good enough to be "American." . . . If Frenchmen are of France and Germans are of Germany, where is "Negroland"? I'll tell you: it's in the mind of the white man! . . . You don't call Minnie Minoso a "Negro," and he's blacker than I am. You call him a Cuban! Nkrumah is an African—a Ghanaian—you don't call him a "Negro." . . . No matter how light or dark a white man is, he's "white." Same way with us. No matter how light or how dark we are, we call ourselves "black" —different shades of black, and we don't feel we have to make apologies about it![2]

America's so-called Negroes, say the Muslims, have been kept in mental slavery by the white man, even while their bodies were free. They have been systematically and diabolically estranged from their heritage and from each other. "They have been educated in ignorance," kept from any knowledge of their origin, history, true names, or religion. Reduced to helplessness under the domination of the whites, they are now so lost that they even seek friendship and acceptance from their mortal enemies, rather than from their own people. They are shackled with the names of the slavemasters; they are duped by the slavemaster's religion; they are divided and have no language, flag, or country of their own. Yet they do not even know enough to be ashamed.

The most unforgivable offense of these so-called Negroes is that they "are guilty of loving the white race and all that that race goes for . . . [for] the white race [is] their arch deceiver." Malcolm X summed up the result of centuries of indoctrination by the white man:

As "Negro Christians" we idolized our Christian Slavemaster, and lived for the day when his plurality of white gods would allow us to mingle and mix up with them. We worshipped the false beauty of the Slavemaster's leprous looking women . . . We regarded them with the utmost respect, courtesy and kindness, bowing, and tipping our hats, showing our teeth. We perfected the art of humility and politeness for their sake . . . but at the same time we treated our own women as if they were mere animals, with no love, respect or protection . . .

We were supposed to be a part of the "Christian Church," yet we lived in a bitter world of dejection . . . being rejected by the white "Christian Church." In large numbers we became victims of drunkenness, drug addiction, reefer smoking . . . in a false and futile attempt to "escape" the reality and horror of the shameful condition that the Slavemaster's Christian religion had placed us in.
· · · · · · · · · · · · · · · · · · · · · · · · · · · · · · · · · · · · · ·

Fear ruled us, but not fear of God. We had fear of the Slavemaster, we had no knowledge of truth and we were apparently afraid to let him see us practicing love and unity towards each other.
· · · · · · · · · · · · · · · · · · · · · · · · · · · · · · · · · · · · · ·

Is it a wonder that the world laughed at us and held us [up] to scorn? We practiced love of others, while hating ourselves . . . patience with others and impatience with our own kind . . . unity with others and disunity with our own kind. We called ourselves "Negro Christians," yet we remained an ignorant, foolish people, despised and REJECTED by the white Christians. We were fools![3]

America's so-called Negroes are the "Lost Nation of Islam in North America." They have now been found, and a Messenger has been sent to prepare them for their day of destiny, for "the judgment of the world has arrived and the gathering together of the people is now going on."[4] The Lost Nation has been as the beggar Lazarus, "the one who was so charmed over the wealth and food of the rich man that he couldn't leave his gate to seek some for himself."[5] But Allah has now found his people, and they must hasten to rise up and be men among men, lest they further disgrace themselves and their God.

The so-called Negroes must be willing to work and to suffer. They must first seek unity among themselves ". . . and then the friendship of others (if there is any friendship in others)." But they must never relent in their striving for a place in the sun:

We must have for our peace and happiness that which other nations have. Allah desires to make the Black Nation the equal or superior of the white race.[6]

If necessary, they must be willing to die for dignity and justice, but they need fear nothing if they will believe in Allah and follow his

Messenger.[7] They must never be aggressors, but "it is a Divine Law for us to defend ourselves if attacked."[8] Indeed, if Jesus had permitted Peter and his other disciples to use the sword on the Jews, Jesus might have been more successful in his work. "For it was the sword that put him to death and the Jews remained unbelievers."[9]

The so-called Negroes are "sacred vessels of the Temple of God"; but "America has poured wine into those sacred vessels," corrupting them, and they will now "have to be chastised into the knowledge of Allah, the God of their Salvation." They have been "absolutely deaf, dumb and blind—brainwashed of all self-respect and knowledge of kind by the white Slavemaster." They are now little more than "free slaves," with no land of their own, no justice in the white man's courts, no vote at the white man's polls, and no voice in the councils whose edicts they must accept. Yet, led by the black clergy, they continue to love their oppressors, while the whites "make fools and Uncle Toms out of our educated professional class of people with a false show of social equality."[10]

"The white man is never going to grant the Negro equal opportunity," says Minister Louis X of New York, "for the white man knows that the Black Man is by nature a leader. Granted equality, he will automatically assume leadership. Since the white man knows this, he grants symbolic status to a few Uncle Toms and keeps the rest of us available for exploitation."

The so-called Negro in America is "sick," the Muslims say. He has been poisoned to death's door by the spurious teachings of the white man. But the white man is sicker: he has been fatally drugged by his own ego. The white man will never recover, for "he is just like a man on dope. If he kicks it, he'll die, and if he doesn't kick it, it'll kill him." The teachings of Elijah Muhammad are "specifically aimed at those suffering from a particular illness we all know about." They are "designed to rectify the ills of the Black Man in the West."

The Muslim leadership particularly condemns the black brother who, having gained a limited acceptance in the white world, dissociates himself from the black masses. Of such a man Malcolm X declared:

No matter how much education he has, everyday things keep reminding him . . . Makes no difference what he is or how great he is. If he is a physicist, he is a *Negro* physicist. If he is a baseball player,

he is a *Negro* baseball player. It's the same if he is in Massachusetts
or Mississippi, he can't escape the stigma the white man has saddled
him with . . . They say that only the people who have been tramped
upon become Muslims. Well, in that case we should be twenty
million strong because there isn't a Negro in America who hasn't
been tramped upon! Some are just too busy licking the boots that
tramped over them to realize what is taking place.[11]

Black moderates—those who undertake to defend whites who have
shown some liberality in their views—come in for a similar upbraiding:

You have a situation where Negroes are too quick to jump up and
shout about what the good white people are doing for them. Well, if
Jesse James robbed a bank and his sons came along later and scattered a few coins before the depositors who lost everything they
had, some people would want to build a monument to the James
boys! . . . So this Negro, he gets elated. He thinks he's making progress when all the time he's catching more hell than any black man
on the face of the earth.[12]

The Black Man's plight was forced upon him by the white man, but
it persists because the Black Man has been willing to remain "in a land
not his own." It can only be solved by separation. So long as Blacks live
among whites, they will be subject to the white man's abuse of power—
economic and political. Separation will provide the only realistic opportunity for mutual respect between the races.

But the Muslims are hardly planning to abandon the country to the
white man. They emphasize that the white man's home is in Europe
and that justice requires a separate "Black Nation here in America,"
built on "some of the land our fathers and mothers paid for in 300
years of slavery . . . right here in America." Marcus Garvey wanted to
found a black nation in Africa. Elijah Muhammad thinks America will
do.

### The Coming of Allah

The so-called Negroes are ignorant and servile, and the behavior
they have copied from the white man is shameful. Yet they remain

sacred to Allah, who has promised to rescue them from their oppressors. Allah's coming had been predicted for six thousand years, ever since the white race began; at his coming, the white race was to reach its end. "America," says Muhammad, "is the place where Allah will make himself felt."

Allah's incarnation was, of course, the stranger in Detroit, who "came from Arabia in 1930" and "used the name of Wallace D. Fard, often signing it W. D. Fard. In the third year (1933) he signed his name 'W. F. Muhammad,' which stands for Wallace Fard Muhammad. He came alone."[13]

Elijah Muhammad, the Messenger, proclaims his own intimacy with Allah—"I know Allah and I am with him"—but he never presumes to Allah's supreme status. Allah alone is the "Author of Islam," and "it is a perfect insult to Allah" to worship anyone other than him. Allah has found his people and will soon punish the white slavemasters for the evil they have done. The period of bondage is ended, and "hell is kindling up."

Allah is not, however, a godhead complete in himself. All black men represent Allah, or at least participate in him, for all black men are divine. A strong Platonic idealism permeates the Black Muslim concept of Allah: Pure Black is equivalent to Absolute Perfection. Again and again the thesis is sounded that *black* is the primogenitor of all that exists. All colors are but shades of black; white is but the absence of color; hence the white man is incomplete and imperfect. All things that are, are made by man; and only Black Man is truly wise and creative.

Allah is a black man, not a spirit or "spook." He is the Supreme Black Man, the Supreme Being among a mighty nation of divine black men. This sharp difference from the Christian concept of God was made clear during a television interview of the Muslim leader in 1959 by Louis Lomax, a black journalist.

*Mr. Lomax:* Now if I have understood your teachings correctly, you teach that all of the members of Islam are God, and that one among you is supreme, and that that one is Allah. Now have I understood you correctly?

*Mr. Elijah Muhammad:* That's right.

*Mr. Lomax:* Now, you have on the other hand said that the devil is the white man—that the white man is a doomed race.

*Mr. Elijah Muhammad:* Yes.

*Mr. Lomax:* Am I correct there, sir?

*Mr. Elijah Muhammad:* Yes.[14]

Elijah must at least be given credit for consistency. At a press conference in Chicago thirteen years later, an interview with a white reporter went like this:

*Reporter:* The press states that you label all white people blue-eyed devils. Is this true?

*Muhammad:* Whether they are actually blue-eyed or not, if they are actually one of the members of that race, they are devils.[15]

It is Allah who exposed the white man: "He gave us information as to the exact birth of the white race and the name of their God who made them, and how, and the end of their time. . . . He taught us the truth of how we were made slaves, and how we are kept in slavery by the slavemaster's children." He taught his people to avoid unclean foods, especially pork; and he instructed them in science and astronomy, the civilizations on other planets, and the knowledge of self. He taught them the history of the two nations—the black and the white— which dominate the earth and "declared the doom of America for her evils to [black men]." That doom is already "past due, and she is number one to be destroyed."[16]

Allah is not unforgiving, and the sins the Lost Nation committed in following and obeying the slavemasters are not held against them *if they return to their own kind.* Allah's greatest teaching is *"Be Yourself."* He demands that "we must give up our slave names . . . give up all evil doings and practices and do only righteousness or we shall be destroyed from the face of the earth." Of those who submit, Allah will make a "new people" who will participate in "unlimited progress."

The coming of Allah signifies the beginning of justice for the Black Man. Allah came to expose the "great enemy of justice and righteousness" before all the world. His very coming is a judgment upon the behavior of those in power. "If justice had prevailed, there would be no judgment," but the slavemaster's yoke grows even more oppressive:

With all of your blood . . . given to help keep America for white

Americans, you return to meet lawlessness and injustice. You are beaten, raped, lynched, burned . . . and denied justice by the government [which is] defended with [your] life's blood. . . . White lynchers and rapers of our people are judged innocent. . . . You continue like sheep among wolves to go on suffering . . . the government makes it clear to you that it is no defense for us against injustice. . . . The only alternative left is to unite as one on the side of Allah. . . . "Fight with those who fight against you," (Holy Quran). "An eye for an eye" (Bible), and fight every injustice against us with every drop of blood that is in us.[17]

Because of the injustices of the Caucasians, "Allah has not come to bring about love and peace between us and the devils, but rather to separate . . . [us] from our open enemies."[18] Allah has further come to bring the "right religion in the right state." He has made it known that Jesus "was only a prophet and not the equal of Moses and Muhammad, and that his [Jesus'] religion was Islam, and not the Christianity of the Pope of Rome."[19]

### The Original Man

The Original Man is, by declaration of Allah himself, "none other than Black Man." Black Man is the first and last: creator of the universe and the primogenitor of all other races—including the white race, for which Black Man used "a special method of birth control." The white man's history is only six thousand years long, but Black Man's is coextensive with the creation of the earth. Original Man includes all nonwhite people, and his primogeniture is undeniable: "everywhere the white race has gone on our planet they have found the Original Man or a sign that he has been there previously."[20]

The so-called Negro in America is a blood-descendant of the Original Man. "Who is better knowing of whom we are than God Himself? He has declared that we are descendants of the Asian Black Nation and of the tribe of Shabazz,"[21] which "came with the earth" when a great explosion divided the earth and the moon "sixty-six trillion years ago." The tribe of Shabazz was first to explore the planet and discover the choicest places in which to live, including the Nile Valley and the area which was to become the Holy City of Mecca in Arabia.

All so-called Negroes are Muslims, whether they know it or not. It is the task of Elijah Muhammad and his followers to teach the so-called Negroes that they are of the tribe of Shabazz and, therefore, "Original." Once they understand this, they will know themselves to be Muslims, heart and soul. Christ himself was a Muslim prophet, and several of his parables refer to the so-called Negroes, especially those of the Lost Sheep, the Prodigal Son, and the Raising of Lazarus. The so-called Negroes are good people and religiously inclined by nature. In fact, "the Black Man by nature is divine."[22]

When the whole world knows who the Original Man is—and only then—wars will cease, for everything depends upon knowing who is the rightful owner of the earth. Lest there be any possible confusion, Muhammad addresses himself specifically to the question:

> The Original Man, Allah has declared, is none other than the Black Man. He is the first and the last, and maker and owner of the universe; from him come all—brown, yellow, red, and white. . . The true knowledge of black and white should be enough to awaken the so-called Negroes . . . [and] put them on their feet and on the road to self-independence.[23]

To know the identity of the Original Man is of crucial importance, for the time of "judgment" is approaching and "Allah is now pointing out to the nations of the earth their rightful places."

### The White Man and Christianity

It would be difficult, probably impossible, to separate the Black Muslim teachings on Christianity from those on race. A fundamental tenet of the sect is that all black men are Muslims by nature and that Christianity is a white man's religion. Thus there is not even a *possibility* of the awakened Black Man accepting Christianity. Nor can the white man accept Islam as taught by Muhammad, for the white man is a devil by nature: "Out of the weak of the Black Nation, the present Caucasian race was created."

The "originality" of the Black Nation and the creation of the white race by Yakub, "a black scientist in rebellion against Allah"—this is the central myth of the Black Muslim Movement. It is the fundamental premise upon which rests the whole theory of black supremacy and white degradation. Muhammad explains in patient detail:

> Who are the white race? I have repeatedly answered that question in this [column] for nearly the past three years. "Why are they white-skinned?" Answer: Allah (God) said this is due to being grafted from the Original Black Nation, as the Black Man has two germs (two people) in him. One is black and the other brown. The brown germ is weaker than the black germ. The brown germ can be grafted into its last stage, and the last stage is white. A scientist by the name of Yakub discovered this knowledge . . . 6,645 years ago, and was successful in doing this job of grafting after 600 years of follow-ing a strict and rigid birth control law.[24]

This experiment in human hybridization was a brilliant scientific accomplishment, but it had one unfortunate side effect. It peopled the world with "blue-eyed devils," who were of comparively low physical and moral stamina—a reflection of their polar distance from the divine black. Hence white athletes are notoriously poor competitors against black athletes, nor should one wonder at the wholesale atrocities com-mitted by the "civilized" whites. Only the white man could herd mil-lions of his fellows into the gas chambers, set off atomic bombs, and run special trains to a lynching at which the women and children are served cokes and ice cream.

In grafting out his creatures' color, Yakub grafted out their very humanity.

> The human beast—the serpent, the dragon, the devil, and Satan—all mean one and the same; the people or race known as the white or Caucasian race, sometimes called the European race.[25]

> Since by nature they were created liars and murderers, they are the enemies of truth and righteousness, and the enemies of those who seek the truth. . .[26]

These devils were given six thousand years to rule. The allotted span of their rule was ended in 1914, and their "years of grace" will last no longer than is necessary for the chosen of Allah to be resurrected from the mental death imposed upon them by the white man. This resurrection is the task of Muhammad himself, Messenger of Allah and Spiritual Leader of the Lost-Found Nation in the West. The period of grace was seventy years; fifty-eight have already elapsed.

During their reign, the devils have "deceived the black nations of the earth, trapped and murdered them by the hundreds of thousands, divided and put black against black, corrupted and committed fornication before your very eyes with your women . . . [and then made] you confess that you love them. . . ."[2 7]

Four hundred years ago, the white Christians stole the Black Muslims away from their homes and brought them to North America, where the whites were already in the process of systematic genocide against the Indian. The whites enslaved the blacks and ensured their bondage by robbing them of their names (identity), language (cultural continuity), and religion (protection of their God). By robbing them of their true names, the whites both shamed them and effectively "hid" them from their own kind. By making the Black Men accept European names, the whites branded them as property. By requiring them to speak English rather than their native Arabic, the whites cut their slaves off from their cultural heritage and the knowledge of self which is essential to dignity and freedom. Such were the secular bonds of servitude.

But the Christian religion was and is the master stratagem for keeping the so-called Negro enslaved. The whites gave him the "poisoned book" and required him to join the "slave religion," which teaches him to love his oppressor and to pray for them who persecute him. It even teaches him that it is God's will that he be the white man's slave! There is, of course, some truth in the Bible, but it is tangled in the white men's contradictions, for "from the first day [they] received the Divine Scripture they started tampering with its truth to make it to suit themselves. . . ."[2 8]

The Bible is the graveyard of my poor people. . . .

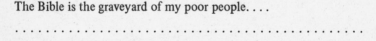

. . . and here I quote another poison addiction of the slavery teaching of the Bible: "Love your enemies, bless them who curse you; pray for those who spitefully use you; him that smiteth thee on one cheek offer the other cheek; him that (robs) taketh away the cloak, forbid not to take (away) thy coat also."... The Slavemasters couldn't have found a better teaching for their protection....[29]

The Bible is also held in some suspicion because "it is dedicated to King James (a white man) rather than to God." Moreover, "it makes God guilty of an act of adultery by charging Him with being the father of Mary's baby; again it charges Noah and Lot with drunkenness and Lot begetting children by his daughter. What a poison book!"[30] On the whole, "Christianity is a religion organized and backed by the devils for the purpose of making slaves of black mankind."[31] It "has caused more bloodshed than any other combination of religions. Its sword is never sheathed."[32]

Islam sent several prophets, including Moses and Jesus, to offer Islam to the white men as a religion of brotherhood. But the white man could not accept it, for the white race is evil by nature and cannot love anyone who is not white. "They are ashamed to even call you a brother or sister in their religion, and their very nature rebels against recognizing you!"[33]

They cannot be trusted. The Caucasians are great deceivers. Their nature is against friendship with black people, although they often fool the black people ... claiming that they are sincere friends....[34]

And: Do not "sweetheart" with white people, your open enemies, for their "sweethearting" with you is not sincere...[35]

The black Christian preacher is the white man's most effective tool for keeping the so-called Negroes pacified and controlled, for he tells convincing lies against nature as well as against God. Throughout nature, God has made provision for every creature to protect itself against its enemies; but the black preacher has taught *his* people to stand still and turn the other cheek. He urges them to fight on foreign battlefields to save the white man from his enemies; but once home again, they must no longer be men. Instead, they must patiently present themselves to be murdered by those they have saved.

Even the Christian God hates his enemies and works to destroy them. This is recorded in the Christian Bible, which all Christians say they accept. "But the black clergy, in trying to ingratiate itself with the whites, will deliver their people up wholesale."[36] Thus, in an unholy and unnatural way, the "Negro clergy class is the white man's right hand over the so-called Negroes,"[37] and the black preacher is the greatest hindrance to their progress and equality.

The so-called Negro clergy, say the Muslims, prostitute themselves to the downtown whites in return for "whatever personal recognition they can get above their followers. North or South it's the same. If a white preacher exchanges pulpits with a so-called Negro minister once a year on Brotherhood Sunday, the black preacher tells his people the millennium is here." And as for their heroics during the "sit-ins" staged by black students in the South, the black preachers' tactic was simply to "put the children out to expose themselves to the brutality of the uncivilized whites, then . . . rush in and 'lead' after the fight is over." In substantiation, the Muslims cite the following article which appeared in a well-known black newspaper:

A shameful display of cowardice and ingratitude was shown last week by certain members of the local clergy. . . . The members took credit for the desegregation of five lunch counters. They neglected to give credit to the students, the persons really responsible. . . . Not one of the ministers sat-in [in] any of the department stores. . . . Brave and persistent activity by the students . . . caused the five lunch counters to be integrated. [But] the ministers, on top secret invitation from the store managers crept downtown to "negotiate." In this, they helped the store ignore the students. Now, after all the hard, dangerous work [had] been done, the ministers have stolen credit for the students' successful work.[38]

The reprehensible behavior of the so-called Negro preachers stems primarily from their desire to be acceptable to the white churches and other religious organizations. Hence the black preacher is far more zealous about adhering to what he has been told are Christian principles than is the white man. The white man does not believe in trying to perfect himself morally, but he wants the Negro to be "past-perfect." As a result, the black preacher is so busy trying to gain the white man's approval by doing what the white man himself has never done, and has no intention of doing, that he has no time to concern himself with the real issues, such as economic justice and the freedom to walk the streets as a man.

## II. MUSLIM MORALITY

In their day-to-day living, the Black Muslims are governed by a stringent code of private and social morality. Since they do not look forward to an afterlife, this morality is not related to any doctrine of salvation. It is, quite simply, the style of living appropriate to a divine black man in his capacity as true ruler of the planet Earth.

Ritual requirements are inextricably mixed with moral injunctions. The Muslim is expected to pray five times a day—at sunrise, noon, midafternoon, sundown, and before retiring—a sixth time if he rises during the night. All prayers are made facing east, toward the Holy City of Mecca. Before each prayer, he must make the proper ablutions: rinsing the mouth, washing the hands, feet, and forearms, and so on. Cleanliness of the body, "inside and outside," is essential.

Certain foods, such as pork and corn bread, are forbidden to the Muslim, for "they are a slow death" to those who eat them. Many other foods common to the diet of Blackamericans, especially in the South, are not to be eaten, since they constitute a "slave diet" and "there are no slaves in Islam." Lamb, chicken, fish, and beef are approved, but all foods must be strictly fresh. The hog is considered filthy—"a poison food, hated of Allah"—and was never intended to be eaten except by the white race.[39]

One Muslim minister explained why the eating of pork is prohibited: "The hog is dirty, brutal, quarrelsome, greedy, ugly, foul, a scavenger which thrives on filth. It is a parasite to all other animals. It will even kill and eat its own young. Do you agree? In short, the hog has all the characteristics of a white man!" Asked to explain the analogy implied in the reference to the hog eating its young, he replied, "Didn't they father a million half-blacks during slavery and sell them off like cattle—for money? Aren't they still bastardizing the race today to keep their wives in servants at subsistence wages? This is eating your own young and picking your teeth with the bones!"

Muhammad himself is vociferous in his dislike of pork and those who eat it:

The hog is absolutely shameless. Most animals have a certain amount of shyness, but not the hog or its eater. . . . The hog eater, it is a fact, will go nude in public if allowed. His temper is easily aroused . . . and he will speak the ugliest, vilest, and most filthy language. . . .[40]

Tobacco is also forbidden, and Muslims are admonished against overeating—a habit to which the so-called Negroes are alleged to be particularly susceptible. An overweight Muslim may be penalized by a fine, which continues until he reduces. In general, one meal a day is considered sufficient, for such restraint eliminates physical and mental sluggishness and leaves more time for industry.

Certain temple activities are considered morally binding and lapses can be swiftly punished. The Muslim is required, for example, to attend two (and occasionally more) temple meetings a week. In extraordinary circumstances he may be excused if he secures permission in advance; but members who fail to attend without such permission are summarily suspended. Male Muslims are also expected to "fish for the dead"—that is, to go into the streets in search of potential members. Unsuccessful "fishermen" are penalized.

Sexual morality is defined in ultrapuritanical terms and is said to be strictly enforced. Any philanderer is answerable to the quasi-judicial militia, the FOI. Courtship or marriage outside the group is discouraged, and unremitting pressure is put on non-Muslim spouses to join the Black Nation. Divorce is frowned upon but allowed. No Muslim woman may be alone in a room with any man except her husband; and provocative or revealing dress and most cosmetics are absolutely forbidden. Any Muslim who participates in an interracial liaison may incur severe punishment, even expulsion, from the Movement. Clear lines are drawn to indicate the behavior and social role appropriate to each sex; and Muslim males are expected to be constantly alert for any show of interest in a Muslim woman on the part of a white man, for whom sex is alleged to be a degrading obsession.

The regeneration of criminals and other fallen persons is a prime concern of the Black Muslims, and they have an enviable record of success. Muhammad claims that his Movement has done more to "clean up the so-called Negroes" than all the churches and social agencies combined. The late Malcolm X scarcely exaggerated when he declared:

It is a known fact, and sociologists agree that when a man becomes a follower of Mr. Muhammad, no matter how bad his morals or habits were [before], he immediately takes upon himself a pronounced change which everyone admits. He [Muhammad] stops them from being dope addicts. He stops them from being alcoholics, [and alcohol] is a curse on the so-called Negroes. He has taken men who were thieves, who broke the law—men who were in prison—and reformed them so that no more do they steal, no more do they commit crimes against the government. I should like to think that this government would thank Mr. Muhammad for doing what it has failed to do toward rehabilitating men who have been classed as hardened criminals. . . . The psychologists and the penologists—all the sociologists—admit that crime is on the increase, in prison and out. Yet when the Black Man who is a hardened criminal hears the teachings of Mr. Muhammad, immediately he makes an about-face. Where the warden couldn't straighten him out through solitary confinement, as soon as he becomes a Muslim, he begins to become a model prisoner right in that institution, far more so than whites or so-called Negroes who confess Christianity.[41]

Eric Hoffer, however, in his perceptive study of mass movements, comments on this phenomenon from a rather different point of view:

It sometimes seems that mass movements are custom-made to fit the needs of the criminal—not only for the catharsis of his soul but also for the exercise of his inclinations and talents. . . . There is a tender spot for the criminal and an ardent wooing of him in all mass movements. . . . It is perhaps true that the criminal who embraces a holy cause is more ready to risk his life and go to extremes in its defense than people who are awed by the sanctity of life and property.[42]

Crime, he suggests, is a kind of escape-valve in which "the underground pressure of malcontents and misfits often leaks out." The mass movement draws this scattered energy to itself and harnesses it for its own purposes. Whether this portends an increased hazard for society as a result of the Black Muslims' assiduous rehabilitation, time alone will tell.

But the rank-and-file Muslim is expected to evince general character traits that can only benefit the society as a whole. Men are expected to live soberly and with dignity, to work hard, to devote themselves to their families' welfare, and to deal honestly with all men. They are expected to obey all constituted authority—even the usurped and corrupt authority of the white man, until the Black Nation returns to power. Women are especially enjoined not to imitate "the silly and often immoral habits of the white woman," which can only wreck their marriages and their children. While equal in every way to their husbands, they are taught to obey them. Modesty, thrift, and service are recommended as their chief concerns.

Above all, self-reliance and a sense of mutual responsibility are the hallmarks of Muslim morality. Muhammad urges his people:

Put your brains to thinking for self; your feet to walking in the direction of self; your hands to working for self and your children. . . . Stop begging for what others have and help yourself to some of this good earth. . . . We must go for ourselves. . . . This calls for the unity of us all to accomplish it![43]

### III. THE GOALS OF THE MOVEMENT

The ends toward which the Muslim organization is directed are the most nebulous points of its entire body of doctrine. This is the area in which the Muslim is almost certain to become vague, mystical, eschatalogical, and evasive under questioning. He may give a misleading impression that the Movement has no well-defined objective or that it lacks the ability to accomplish its goal. But the facts are quite to the contrary. The Muslim knows where he is going, or at least thinks he does, and what appears to be haziness or naivete is only shrewd diplomacy.

Some uncritical observers have tended to dismiss the Movement as "confused and inconsistent" or else as having "improbable" or "fantastic" goals. Muhammad is more often written off as an "illiterate crackpot" or a "self-seeking charlatan" than taken seriously as a "race leader." His followers are frequently categorized by their better-educated critics as "ignorant Southern-type Negroes who don't know any better," and their Movement is dismissed as "just another Harlem-type cult." There are probably elements of truth in all this, but they are not the whole truth, and they do not answer any of the really important questions. To ignore the Movement on such grounds would be absurd.

The Black Muslims exist. They are a viable, visible, present reality. The Black Muslim Movement has a vitality unmatched by any other organized movement with a large black membership. The pertinent question is *why* this is so. An examination of the goals of the Movement—as they have been stated or implied in its literature and public lectures, and as they may be inferred from careful observation and analysis—may offer some insight regarding the Muslims' ability to attract and hold an important segment of the black masses.

### The United Front of Black Men

Elijah Muhammad's program demands that "every Black Man in America be reunited with his own." This means, of course, that every black Christian is the target of the Movement. At the present time the Movement is predominantly lower class, and the Muslims are aware that the middle and upper classes will be harder to reach, for these classes, say the Muslims, are the "satisfied black men who think they have the least to gain." Yet Muhammad declares: "We are trying to reach *all* black men, those in the colleges and those in the jails. We need leaders at every level to challenge the lies of the white man. We need scholars to search out the truth independently of what the white man has written."[44]

The Muslim goal of five million members by 1965 proved unrealistic. That phenomenal growth was expected to result from an intensive recruitment drive, and from the increasing disillusion of the black middle and upper classes. "By then even the Uncle Toms will know that no matter *who* they put in the White House, the so-called Negroes are right where they were before." It is probable that the sixties saw an actual decrease in registered Muslim membership, but when consideration is allowed for the extraordinary competition from other movements of this period (e.g., King, SNCC, CORE, the Panthers, etc.), as well as for the new black militance (so far still contained in the churches, but threatening to form new religious movements), to say nothing of the moderation of some of our most abrasive racial policies, the Muslims' lack of spectacular growth takes on perspective.

The Muslim ideal is "a United Front of Black Men," who will "take the offensive and carry the fight for justice and freedom to the enemy." Through such a United Front, "the American Negroes will discover themselves, elevate their distinguished men and women . . . give outlets to their talented youth, and assume the contours of a nation."[45] Because he pursues a United Front, Muhammad's attacks against black leadership have been mainly retaliatory, and the necessity for such a public display of disunity is distressing to him. Special attention is given to removing the differences which divide Muslim and black leadership. In an address delivered in Detroit in January 1960, Raymond Sharrieff, Supreme Captain of the FOI, announced:

> Nineteen sixty marks the beginning of a new era, an era in which our Leader, the Honorable Mr. Elijah Muhammad, plans to unite every stratum of the American Black Man. . . . Even if not a member of our Temple. . . . Religious, economic and political differences are luxuries we American Black Men cannot afford. We must, in the Sixties, sit together and counsel.[46]

Ten years later the Muslims were in fact widely accepted in the black liberation movement. Black unity—the "Black Man's one hope for freedom"—is held by the Muslims to be the white man's most haunting fear. And the white man can bring intensely divisive pressures to bear, because the American Blacks, "a nation within a nation," are an "occupied people." The whites not only control communications, arms, jobs, housing, education, etc., but from the Muslim point of view, they still control the thinking of the loyalty of vital segments of the so-called Negro leadership as thoroughly and effectively as they did during World War II.[47] Operating through professional Uncle Toms, they have thrown up barriers to black unity; and the divided black people have no way to protect their rights or make themselves heard.

From the white perspective, any talk about black unity is considered seditious. "Stool pigeons are planted everywhere to spy on their own people." "The same Negroes whose fathers were sold at auction in the town square sell themselves and their people at the white man's dinner table," one Muslim minister declared with disgust. But these traitors are known, and they will be dealt with in due time. *Muhammad Speaks* scoffs at the effectiveness of infiltrators and publishes the names of those who have been exposed:

Plots and scenarious [*sic*] of all descriptions . . . have been aimed at the Nation of Islam for more than 40 years—infiltrators . . . who "registered" as Muslim in the Chicago and Washington Mosque respectively, and later wrote so-called "expose" articles, and others— have failed to stop the spread of Islam or disunite the Muslims.

The axiomatic recruitment policies of spy outfits—that of selecting prison inmates, homosexuals or others who can be bribed to work as informants, "fifth columnists" or saboteurs—has been of no avail against the teachings of Messenger Muhammad and the unity of the Muslims.[48]

The white man can hire them one against the other for just a few dollars . . . or even a smile. The Negroes must put a stop to the white man's stool pigeons among them . . . if they are ever to become a nation recognized by the nations of the earth.[49]

We have found a few who are being paid to keep the enemy well informed of all we say. One day they will be out.[50]

Muhammad warns the black community that "the government makes every Negro who opens his mouth in favor of their own kind a promoter of sedition, and labels their teaching as being subversive or un-American." Even " 'divine truth' is un-American if it is on the side of the poor Negroes." But the black community should not be panicked into avoiding Muhammad's teachings as seditious, for this accusation is only a white trick to isolate the Muslims and frighten the black masses. "The government is not after me, they are after you to keep you from following me."[51]

Are Muhammad's teachings in fact seditious? No one can say, for his goals—and the ultimate methods he would use to reach them—are never stated explicitly. "You are about to become the Head," he tells his followers, "and this should be good news. . . . 25,000,000 people should not be satisfied with anything short of a country for themselves. If you cannot think like a Muslim, it is because you are a coward. . . . The time has come for me to do something for my beautiful nation."[52] His goal sounds *possibly* like secession, and his methods are *apparently* not for cowards, but his only actual commitment is a cryptic promise to "do something." What that something is, or will be, remains in the secret fastness of Muslim esoterica.

Muhammad walks the precipice between sedition and religious license with consummate skill. He speaks knowingly of an impending "Battle of Armageddon" and has promised that Blacks "will soon gain control of New York City—and that 'white rule' in the United States will be overthrown."[53] Later this is explained to mean that the white nations would destroy each other and that the Black Nation would inherit the spoils. When asked what hope there was for whites, the Messenger said:

Now, I must tell you the truth. There will be no such thing as elimination of all white people from the earth, at the present time or at the break out of the Holy War. No, because there are some white people today who have faith in Allah and Islam though they are white, and their faith is given credit. They are not born or created Muslims, but they have faith in what the Muslims are and trying to live. It is only through Islam that white people can be saved. But you see there would be a Holy War (they call it a Holy War which means right is against wrong and wrong against right).

*Quest*: You do not mean white fighting Blacks or that sort of thing?

*Muhammad*: I do not say I should say "no," because the right is the Black and the wrong is the white, and naturally the Muslim world is bound to clash with the unrighteous world.[54]

A return to the Mosaic *lex talionis* is encouraged, for example, as the only possible guarantor of meaningful survival; and Muslims are urged to "fight like 'hell' with those who fight like 'hell' against you, and the world of mankind will respect us as equals."[55]

In a black leadership conference held in New York City, Malcolm X reminded his confrères that they must surely "recognize that anyone who can assemble so many well-disciplined young Negroes together as swiftly as we, should never be underestimated as a force to be recognized and reckoned with here in Harlem's community affairs and conferences."[56] The point could not have been lost on the assembled leaders, who could hardly imagine the necessity of swiftly assembling many well-disciplined young men for a *conference*.

Such, then, is the Muslim vision of a United Front of Black Men—a phalanx of American Blacks no longer torn by dissension but standing shoulder to shoulder, ready for battle. The leader and the enemy are known, but everything else is shrouded in mystery: the methods of combat, the terms of surrender, and the new way of life to be established after the victory.

### Racial Separation

The Black Muslims demand absolute separation of the black and the white races. They are willing to approach this goal by stages—the economic and political links, for example, need not be severed immediately—but all personal relationships between the races must be broken *now*. Economic severance, the next major step, is already under way, and political severance will follow in good time. But only with complete racial separation will the perfect harmony of the universe be restored.

Those so-called Negroes who seek integration with the American white man are, say the Muslims, unrealistic and stupid. The white man is not suddenly going to share with his erstwhile slaves the advantages and privileges because of their subordinate position. America became the richest and most powerful nation in the world because she harnessed, for more than three hundred years, the free labor of millions of human beings. But she hasn't the slightest intention to share her wealth and privileges with "those who worked so long for nothing, and even now receive but a pittance." The so-called Negroes are still "free slaves." Millions of them are not allowed to vote, and few are permitted to hold office. None can wholly escape the implications of color. Ralph Bunche, the most distinguished Blackamerican on the world scene, refused a sub-Cabinet post in the federal government because he could not live and move in the nation's capital with the freedom accorded to the most illiterate white thug. Even the recognized enemies of the country, so long as they are white, come to America and immediately enjoy the privileges routinely denied to black citizens—hundreds of thousands of whom have fought and died for their nation.

Again, the Muslims maintain that only the so-called Negro leaders want to integrate. The black masses have no love for the white man and no desire to be in his company. "But for the pseudo-Negro leaders, to be accepted by whites and to be in their company is worth more than heaven itself." These leaders are forever "begging and licking the white man's boots for [him] to smile and pat [them] on the back."

Finally, the whole scheme of integration is only a stratagem through which the white man hopes to save himself from an inevitable fate. He has sowed the wind, and now he must reap the whirlwind. The ascendancy of the white West is ended. The wheel must turn. When the white man was the undisputed ruler of the earth, who spoke of integration? Now he has seen his empires crumble, his slaves shake off their bonds, his enemies multiply all over the world—"so he is willing to throw his faithful dog the driest bone he has, hoping that dog will once more forget the past and rush out to save his master." But the Blacks will still be the loser, for the white man will only "integrate them" where it serves his own advantage, and this will always be at the bottom.

Muhammad urges the Black Man to stand aloof. Why integrate with a dying world?

Today's world is floating in corruption; its complete disintegration is both imminent and inescapable. Any man who integrates with the world must share in its disintegration and destruction. If the Black Man would but listen, he need not be a part of this certain doom.[57]

The Muslims reject the ultimate integration—racial intermarriage—as sternly as any Southern white, and for much the same reasons.

Usually, when the white man says "integrate," he has reservations. He doesn't want to see a black man marry his woman. We all agree on that. Muslims who follow Mr. Muhammad are absolutely against intermarriage. When you say "integration," if you mean that everyone should have equal opportunities economically, that everyone should have the right to socialize with whom they please, that everyone should have the right to all the cultural advantages and things of that sort, well and good. But if [to] integrate means that a Black Man should run out and marry a white woman, or that a white man should run out and get my woman, then I'm against it. *We're absolutely against intermarriage!*[58]

The Muslims are convinced of their superior racial heritage and believe that a further admixture of white blood will only weaken the Black Nation physically and morally, as well as increase the loss of face the so-called Negro has already suffered by permitting the white man to bastardize the race. The white race will soon perish, and then even a trace of white blood will automatically consign its possessor to an inferior status.

Muhammad conceives his mission to include the repurification of the "Lost-Found-Nation-in-the-West"—ideologically, morally, and, above all, biologically. Only when this has been done can the black people of America assume their rightful place of dignity and leadership among the triumphant black nations of the world. The United Front of Black Men, therefore, will countenance no interracial dallying. The intelligent Black Man must look beyond today's personal whimsies to the building of the Black Nation of tomorrow.

### Economic Separation

The call for a Black Front has important economic overtones, for the Muslims' economic policies are a fundamental aspect of the total Movement. Their basic premise is that the white man's economic dominance gives him the power of life and death over the blacks. "You can't whip a man when he's helping you," says Muhammad; and his oft-quoted aphorism is economically, if not socially or politically, cogent.

Economic security was stressed from the first days of the Movement. As early as 1937 it was observed that:

> The prophet taught them that they are descendants of nobles. . . .
> To show their escape from slavery and their restoration to their
> original high status, they feel obliged to live in good houses and
> wear good clothes . . . and are ashamed that they have not been able
> to purchase better commodities or rent finer homes.[59]

As we have seen, the pendulum has swung back toward the center. The Muslims still prize industriousness and a sense of responsibility, but they shy away from conspicuous consumption. They do not live in the residential sections generally preferred by the black business and professional classes, and they do not sport the flashy automobiles usually associated with black revivalistic cults. On the contrary, they strongly affirm their identify with the working class. There is a strong emphasis on the equality of the ministers and the "brothers," and all tend to live pretty much alike in terms of housing and visible goods, but there is some recent evidence that this ideal of brotherly equality is being modified in its application to the life styles of some of those closest to the center of the power.

Thrift is encouraged; and while credit purchasing is not forbidden, Muslims are reminded that "debt is slavery." These counsels have had a clearly salutary effect. Indeed, the more faithful a Muslim is to the teachings of his leaders, the better his economic condition is likely to be.

> The ascetic manner of life of the Moslems [Muslims] also has contributed to their economic improvement. No money whatever is spent by them on liquor, tobacco, or pork. Their one meal of the day consists almost entirely of vegetables and fruits. Consequently their expenditure on food is significantly smaller than is that of other Negroes. . . . [60]

Money must not be wasted, and no Muslim is expected to live beyond his means.

> Stop wasting your money! Your money was not given to you, so why should you give it away for what you can do without? . . . We could save millions of dollars [for] education . . . land, machines . . . cattle . . . homes and factories . . . Feed your own stomachs and hire your own scientists from among yourselves. . . .
>
> How can we begin? Stop spending money for tobacco, dope, cigarettes, whiskey, fine clothes, fine automobiles, expensive rugs and carpets, idleness, sport and gambling. Stop . . . living on credit loans . . . seeking the highest priced merchandise. . . . If you must have a car, buy the low-priced car. . . . We must make a better future for ourselves and our children . . . . [61]

Such rigorous self-discipline is not only a virtue in itself but also a step toward the establishment of the Black Nation. Until the economic independence of the Black Nation can be assured, however, some Muslims will find it necessary to work for the white man. There is no shame in that, for all work is honest and even the meanest job can be done with dignity.

The Muslims are urged to be competent and honest in all their dealings, giving a full day's work for the wages received. Muslims are expected to "respect authority, on the job and wherever else it is legitimately exercised." Each working day is to be considered a learning experience against the time when the Black Nation will operate its own factories, farms, and other enterprises. But this policy pays immediate dividends as well:

> The members of the cult claim they have secured work more easily than have other Negroes. To some extent their claim seems to be justified.... Through the Nation of Islam they have gained a new status and a new confidence in themselves. When they meet Caucasians, they rejoice in the knowledge that they themselves are superiors meeting members of an inferior race. Employment managers tend to accept more readily persons whose appearance gives evidence of clean living and self-reliance, than those who show the marks of debauchery, defeat and despair.[62]

As an ideal, the Muslims advocate a complete economic withdrawal from the white community. Their transitional goals seem to hinge on the establishment of black businesses and industries which will reduce interracial contact to a minimum, provide jobs and capital for black workers and entrepreneurs, and offer the sense of group security proper to an "independent" people. To accomplish this end, Muhammad has drawn up an "Economic Blueprint" which is published occasionally in some elements of the black press and which is the basic text for Muslim lectures on the economic plight of the so-called Negro. The Blueprint opens with a description of the Black Man in white, Christian America as a Lazarus under the table of the rich, "begging for crumbs" and "entangled in want in the midst of plenty." Lazarus is asleep—"but I go," says Muhammad, "that I may wake him."

The key to the Black Man's economic security consists of five simple propositions:

1. Know thyself and be yourself. Islam makes a true Brother to

[every other] Brother. . . . Acknowledge and recognize that you
are a member of the Creator's [i.e., the Black] Nation, and act
accordingly. . . . Recognize the necessity for unity. . . . This requires action and deeds, not words and lip service.
2. Pool your resources, physically as well as financially.
3. Stop wanton criticism of everything that is black-owned and
   black-operated.
4. Keep in mind—*Jealousy Destroys From Within.*
5. Observe the operations of the white man. He is successful. He
   makes no excuses for his failures. He works hard—in a collective
   manner. You do the same.[63]

Muslims are urged to pool their resources and techniques in merchandising, manufacturing, building, maintenance—any field in which unity
and harmony will contribute to efficiency and effectiveness. Those who
lack skills or education are urged to ask help from their brothers with
more training or experience.

Above all, Muslims are encouraged to "buy black" whenever possible. "The white man spends his money with his own kind, which is
natural. You too, must do this. Help to make jobs for your own kind.
Take a lesson from the Chinese and Japanese . . . and go all out to
support your own kind." Business and professional men must not ex-
ploit their black customers or clients; but the black consumer must not
hesitate to spend the few extra pennies the black businessman may have
to charge in order to meet the competition of the advantaged whites.

The Muslims themselves maintain numerous small businesses and
other enterprises. In Chicago they operate department stores, groceries,
bakeries, restaurants, and various kinds of service establishments. They
own large farms in Michigan, Alabama, and Georgia; and in practically
every city with a temple, they have restaurants, barber shops, clothing
stores, and occasionally other businesses. All are run with efficiency
and aplomb. A low-rent housing complex is under way in Chicago, and
a hospital is planned. Large-scale building projects are also slated for
Phoenix and some other cities with sizeable contingents of Muslims.
The Nation already boasts an ultramodern, multipurpose building in
Chicago housing a department store, doctors' offices, and a showplace
dental suite—all Muslim enterprises. The building cost almost a half
million dollars, "paid for by the 100 per cent Black Nation of Islam."

Early in 1972 the Muslims reputedly paid four million dollars for the St. Constantine Greek Orthodox church on the Chicago South Side. The church is to be used as an administration building for a four-year college planned by the Muslims.

True Muslims are reminded that if *one* has a bowl of soup, all have soup. "Everywhere, the Negro is exploited by the white man; now, the Black Man must learn to protect his own, using the white man's techniques." By way of demonstration, Muhammad once bought a large modern apartment building in Chicago, evicted the white tenants, moved in house-hungry Blacks from the South Side ghetto and lowered the rents.

Muhammad believes that much of the Blackamerican's "sickness" is economic. In February 1960, as a gesture toward strengthening this "Lost Nation," he gave free exhibition space to black businesses at his Annual Convention, held at the giant Coliseum in Chicago. The three-day convention attracted some fifteen thousand delegates and visitors, and the exhibition was designed to "provide the opportunity for Negro businessmen to promote their businesses in line with Mr. Muhammad's program of Economic Security for the American Negro." There were Asian and African exhibits as well, but the emphasis was on the Black-american potential for economic independence. The exhibition also represented an open bid by Muslims for an increasing share of leadership among Blacks—a display of the Muslim potential for inducing the kind of race-consciousness to which black business must ordinarily look for survival.

A decade later, the Black Muslims were the most potent organized economic force in the black community. What they had tried to demonstrate symbolically at the Chicago convention of 1960, they had gone out and done for themselves—and by themselves. In an interview with Elijah Muhammad, Jr., the Muslim Farm Inspector, in November of 1971, he offered the following statistics:

... we now have herds totaling in the thousands; where we only had a few chickens, we now have 20,000 on one farm alone; where we only had a few sheep, we now come to our own slaughter house periodically with hundreds of sheep.

At this point in our growth we own approximately 10,000 acres of farming land and every acre goes towards feeding people, whether it's green beans for market or grain—feed for raising cattle which comes to the market.

We presently deal with truckloads of produce coming and going from places as far away as California, Texas, Georgia and Alabama, and as near (to the Home office in Chicago) as Michigan, Wisconsin, Indiana, etc.

We cater not only to our Muslim-owned businesses, the Messenger created GOOD FOODS, CORP. which serves chain stores and individually-owned markets large and small, giving them all the best in produce, meats, eggs, poultry and fish.

We market truckloads of beef every week with one truck holding 35,000 pounds. We produce and sell 12,000 dozen of eggs a week and we need more. One dairy alone gives us 2200 gallons of milk per week and we need to increase that. Our apple orchard gave us 25,000 3 lb. bags of apples and this was not sufficient to meet the demand. We handled 30 truckloads of watermelons, each containing approximately 40,000 lbs. We warehouse hundreds of 100 lb.-bags of navy beans, which depart each week from the warehouse to be consumed by people in many ways, from Muslim soup to the famous bean pie.

We slaughter and sell over 200 lambs a day. We sell thousands of pounds of fish a week in our local fish markets. We transport these food items in our own trucks, and on our own plane to markets around the country. If we are not in your area now, we soon will be.[64]

Robert C. Vowels, Dean of the School of Business Administration at Atlanta University, suggests that "in terms of getting Blacks to do something for themselves and feel a sense of accomplishment in doing it, Elijah Muhammad has to be seriously considered in leadership terms." Dr. Vowels believes that "most of the black economic development programs are . . . poorly conceived, undercapitalized, and horribly managed. . . . The single most influential system of thought now making the rounds is the Nation."[65]

### Some Good Earth

It would be hazardous to assume that the Black Muslim Movement is all religion and economics. That these are fundamental aspects of the Movement is not open to serious doubt. But what does Muhammad envisage beyond a well-fed black nation under the sign of the Star and Crescent?

When Marcus Garvey began to speak too plainly about the political aspirations of the Universal Negro Improvement Association, his movement was labeled "seditious." Elijah Muhammad, who is not only a student of Garvey but was himself arrested and charged with sedition very early in his Muslim career, has learned the hazards of plain talk in the area of politics. It is doubtful whether any except the top leadership know exactly what the Movement's political aspirations are, or why. The characteristic mood of the Muslim laity is simply a blind faith—a complete confidence in Elijah Muhammad, who "has a plan for all of us" and is considered well-nigh infallible. The Muslim brotherhood has a sense of manifest destiny, an awareness of some kind of impending social cataclysm in which they will figure prominently. They are not certain what this cataclysm will be or when it will take place, but they are unshakably convinced that Messenger Muhammad knows. And they are prepared to lay down their lives at a signal from their leader, if dying will forward the goal he has in mind.

Doubtless the Federal Bureau of Investigation could relax its constant vigilance if Muhammad were more explicit about this goal. It is alleged that no fewer than fifteen FBI agents are regularly assigned to cover his New York temple alone, and Muhammad complains that the FBI could readily catch "all the lynchers and school-bombers in the South" with a fraction of the agents assigned to cover his personal movements. Responsible black leadership and the concerned white community would similarly be obliged if Muhammad's political goals were known. But the Muslims have shown little inclination to announce their ultimate intentions. They revel in the guessing game in which they are "it." The stock reply to unacceptable questions is "Those who say don't know, and those who know don't say."

At best, Muslim statements about their political goals are couched in mystical and eschatological innuendo or else in cryptic allusions to "a separate nation for ourselves, right here in America" or to "some good earth, right here in America, where we can go off to ourselves." Muhammad announced to some ten thousand listeners in Washington, D.C.:

You can't blame the government for not giving you anything when you are not asking for anything. . . . It is certainly evident by now

that you were never intended to be a full citizen. . . . Your role was
that of a slave and today, even . . . that intent underlies your role in
the body politic.
. . . . . . . . . . . . . . . . . . . . . . . . . . . . . . . . . . . . . . . . . . . . . . . . . . . . .

Our oppressors are determined to keep our eyes in the sky while
they control the land under our feet, . . . smite our cheeks and rob
our pockets.
. . . . . . . . . . . . . . . . . . . . . . . . . . . . . . . . . . . . . . . . . . . . . . . . . . . . .

To integrate with Evil is to be destroyed with evil. What we want—
indeed, justice for us is to be set apart. We want, and must insist
upon an area in this land that we can call our own, somewhere
[where] we can hold our heads [up] with pride and dignity without the continued harassments and indignities of our oppressors.
. . . . . . . . . . . . . . . . . . . . . . . . . . . . . . . . . . . . . . . . . . . . . . . . . . . . .

. . . .let us carry in our hearts the doctrine of separation from our
oppressors; let us demand a home we can call our own, support for
ourselves until we are able to become self-sufficient.[66]

Usually the quantity of land mentioned is "two or three states,"
but the figure has sometimes been raised. In an address at the Muslim
Convention of 1960, Muhammad suggested:

The best thing the white man can do is give us justice and stop
giving us hell. I'm asking for justice. If they won't give us justice,
then let us separate ourselves from them and live in four or five
states in America, or leave the country altogether.[67]

Malcolm X once thought that "nine or ten states would be enough."
The Muslims have never indicated what states would be acceptable to
them or just how they propose to acquire them, but the Southwest has
featured prominently in speculation.

The Muslims often mention the alternative of leaving the country.
In his column in the *Los Angeles Herald-Dispatch,* for example, Muhammad said: "All we are asking for is a separate state or territory. . . .
It doesn't have to be in America."[68] But this alternative is never emphasized, and Muhammad repeatedly calls attention to the Black Nation's inherent right to land in America. This claim is grounded on two
propositions: (1) the white man stole the country from the Indians,

who are nonwhite peoples and brothers to the so-called Negroes, and (2) the so-called Negroes worked for three hundred years as absolute slaves and an additional one hundred years as "free slaves," thereby earning a share in the country. Yet what share have they received?

> We are kicked around . . . until they say: "Move out n———r," even though they killed our people, the Indians, in order to possess the country for themselves.[69]

> We have not been given anything but hell in return for 400 years of hard labor, sweat and blood, without justice. We are not wanted in their society and are hunted like rabbits all over the country. . . .
> After 100 years of so-called freedom . . . the slavemasters have not offered you [a home] even in the worst part of this country, though our labor and our poor fathers' labor before us helped make America what it is.[70]

The late Malcolm X, speaking to a group of white listeners, made the first modern demand for reparations. It was a dramatic demand— not only for territory but also for a subsidy from the United States government. Millions of black men, he reminded his audience, "worked 300 years without a pay day. We feel that we've got something due us, and I don't mean this phony integration stuff." The United States, he declared, must "compensate us for the labor stolen from us." And he explained how:

> The United States can subsidize Israel to start a state—Israel hasn't fought for this country. The United States can subsidize India and Latin America—and *they* tell the Americans to "go home!" We even subsidize Poland and Yugoslavia *and those are Communist countries!*
> Why can't the Black Man in America have a piece of land with technical help and money to get his own nation established? What's so fantastic about that? We fought, died and helped to build this country, and since we can't be citizens here, then help us to build a nation of our own. We don't have to go to Africa. We can do it right here.[71]

There are indications that Muhammad does not really consider the physical separation of the races in this country a viable issue. He has offered no concrete proposal for effecting such a separation or for a partition of the country. The Muslims' real-estate holdings are scattered across the country, from Boston to Los Angeles, and they are preparing to spend additional millions in the cities they now share with the blue-eyed devils. The implications are that the devils are to be tolerated for the indefinite future.

These facts, however, are capable of another interpretation. The Muslims are convinced that "the white race . . . will never agree to divide America with us, though our blood is spilled on this soil and on foreign soil for the freedom of white Americans and their European friends."[72] But the white man's rule is at an end, and a "Superior Power" will now "create a 'New World,' a New People, a New Order, and a New Government."[73] What measures will this New Government take? If the Muslims will not leave America, and if the white man will not share the land with them, one drastic alternative remains:

The wicked must be punished for their wickedness poured out upon us. . . . This country is large enough to separate the two (black and white), and they both [could] live here, but that would not be successful. The best solution is for everyone to go to his own country. . . . The native home of the white race is in Europe.[74]

# 5 Reaching for the Masses

nlike Athena, the Black Muslim Movement did not spring full-blown into maturity. It evolved over a generation and only gradually became a well-known symbol of protest—at least in the black ghettos of America's principal industrial cities. How shall we account for its growth and its attractiveness to the black masses as a social movement, quite apart from its identity as a religion?

Organizations such as the NAACP and the National Urban League, for all their virtues, have not caught the imagination of the black masses. Their memberships tend to comprise middle- and upper-class Blacks and whites, in each case the *least* disprivileged of their race. It is true that the mass man stands to benefit most from their services, for he is most deprived of the values they attempt to make available. But the mass man's needs tend to be visceral and immediate, and highly personal. Neither legal precedent nor symbolic breakthroughs have much meaning for him. He is likely to see the NAACP and the Urban League as *class* movements. He enjoys a vicarious participation in their accomplishments, but they are not "his" in the way that his lodge or his church is his, and his sense of identification with them is tentative and nebulous.

The Black Muslims, by contrast, are undeniably a mass movement. They are reaching for the support of the entire black lower class—and, ultimately, of all Blackamericans. This ambition is of crucial importance, for it controls every public statement and activity of the Muslims, every gesture by which their myths and doctrines are expressed in action.

## I. THE NATURE OF A MASS MOVEMENT

### The Importance of Mass Membership

A mass movement usually begins with the degeneration of some familiar corporate structure—a church, in the sense of a religious denomination, or a major social or political unity—which has formerly maintained the social equilibrium. So long as this established structure is strong and vigorous in its social concern, mass movements do not develop. There is no need of them. But as these corporate ties dissolve— as the masses are dislocated from their "hereditary milieu"—many individuals become highly receptive to the new corporate unity implicit in a mass movement.[1]

Such people are the strength of a mass movement. Neither money nor prestige nor heritage approaches in importance the physical fact of a *participating* membership. The effectiveness of what a mass leader has to say depends upon how many people believe him and trust him for deliverance. Those who do believe him will be in the movement, and they are the most impressive arguments for the potential converts.

The principal rewards of a mass movement are always in the future, and the future takes on security in terms of the number of persons who are willing to identify themselves with it. The few are induced to follow the many, not because the collective mind of the many is presumed to be wiser, but because there is a certain loneliness in social isolation that is somewhat relieved by identification with a cause. Fifty million Frenchmen may very well be wrong, but they make reassuring company. Moreover, for the oppressed, the remotest hope is more acceptable than the present reality, and the strength of hope is intensified geometrically as those who share the hope increase in number.

A mass movement, therefore, does not begin with logic or a program, or even a defined goal. It begins with people who participate in a common hope for a better tomorrow. The task of the leader of a mass movement is to make that hope inclusive and vivid for all who find their present circumstances painful or unacceptable.

### The True Believer[2]

It is a popular misconception that mass movements are formed by the most destitute elements of the society. This is almost never true.

The destitute do not revolt. The mass movement may become a symbol of hope which draws the destitute to membership, but the movement draws its initial followers from the ranks of the merely discontented, those who have not yet lost all hope for better things. They see in the leader and his doctrine a chance to fulfill the desires and longings they have not quite relinquished, even in the face of the most discouraging adversity. In short, it is not present suffering but future expectation that impels the dissatisfied and the deprived to unite in protest.

The hard-core members of a mass movement, the "true believers," may vary greatly among themselves, but they have certain unmistakable traits in common. Their most pronounced characteristic is a desire for a personal rebirth—an escape to a new identity, in which they will be freed of their present restrictions and oppressions. A mass movement promises them a new "face." The old, unappreciated self is abandonded; in its place is a new self, neatly designed to inspire pride, confidence, and hope.

Except for the opportunist and the adventurer, the mass movement offers no appeal to the individual interested in personal advancement on his own merit. Those who have learned to accept themselves or who have gained approval and acceptance in the society at large are not moved to exchange their individuality for a corporate identity. They do not wish to be lost in the mass. Only those who have lost all hope of gaining acceptance for themselves as they are—but who still hunger for acceptance—will seek to compel that acceptance by participation in a corporate identity. The true believer, despised or ignored as John Smith, will be respected as, say, a Black Muslim; and he will count the submergence of his individual personality a trivial price to pay.

The true believer is ordinarily a misfit in the society he rejects. He may be a *temporary* misfit who has not yet found his niche—perhaps a returned veteran, an unemployed college graduate, a juvenile, or a recent immigrant. Such people tend to exhibit a nervous restlessness and dissatisfaction. They envy the apparently unhampered progress of other men, and they are haunted by a fear that their best years will be wasted before they can realize their personal goals. These temporary misfits are receptive to the promises of the mass movement, but they are not totally committed to its doctrines, for they have not completely repudiated themselves. Any significant change in their personal fortunes will reconcile them to the larger society.

The *permanent* misfit's allegiance is without reservation, for he can

find salvation only in escape from his repudiated self. Such a man may
be an artist, composer, preacher, scientist, or writer who has failed
decisively to achieve a meaningful success. He may be an ex-criminal or
a guilt-ridden individual striving to lose his past vileness by participating
in a holy crusade. Perhaps the most tragic of the permanent misfits is
the corporate minority, bent on assimilation but blocked by visibility—
that "irreparable defect in body" which precludes acceptance. In such a
minority:

> . . . . the individual stands alone, pitted against prejudice and dis-
> crimination. He is also burdened with the sense of guilt, however
> vague, of a renegade. . . Within a minority bent on assimilation, the
> least and most successful (economically and culturally) are likely to
> be more frustrated than those in between. The man who fails sees
> himself as an outsider; and, in the case of a member of a minority
> group who wants to blend with the majority, failure intensifies the
> feeling of not belonging. . . . Thus it is to be expected that the least
> and most successful of a minority bent on assimilation should be the
> most responsive to the appeal of a proselytizing mass move-
> ment. . . . The least and most successful among the Negroes are the
> most race conscious.[3]

The true believer has no purpose and no goal except in relation to
the movement with which he has identified himself. His acceptance and
assimilation into the group is so complete that his personal identity *is*
the corporate image. His confidence is the confidence born of the
strength and unity of the movement, which can perform miracles of
accomplishment beyond the reach of any individual. Most important,
he is no longer alone. He is now accepted and wanted, rather than
rejected and despised. And as long as the movement lives, the true
believer cannot really die, for his life is in the corporate identity. To be
expelled from it, or to have it destroyed by an external force, would be
a death almost as real as physical death itself.

### Leadership in the Mass Movement

The leader of a mass movement, like his true believers, is a product
of the circumstances which make the movement possible. Ordinarily he
is neither elected nor appointed, though he may have already held a

post at some level within the movement. More often than not, the leader is simply "acclaimed" or "recognized," with formal investiture coming later if at all.

It has been said that the successful leader is a man who determines where his followers want to go and leads them there. Such a description applies *a fortiori* to the leader of a mass movement. Whatever his morals or his motives, he must have an almost uncanny sensitivity—an ability to empathize with and reflect the unspoken (and often unrecognized) yearnings of the people he undertakes to lead. He must, in his own behavior, reassure them by displaying a complete absence of fear and a constant concern for their welfare. He must demonstrate an unshakable conviction in the ultimate success of his cause, in which he alone is aware of some unique and essential truth.

The leader's most important asset is his ability to surround himself with a small coterie of worshipers who draw their inspiration from him, are categorically willing to accept his will as their own, and are themselves capable leaders and organizers. No other single factor will more clearly determine his failure or success. But the leader can never rely wholly on his lieutenants; he must be indomitable himself. He must have "a joy in defiance . . . faith in his destiny and luck; a capacity for passionate hatred; contempt for the present . . . [and] a disregard of consistency and fairness."[4] He must also be able to estimate and manipulate the human craving for the sense of security inherent in a communion of cause and kind. Assemblages, parades, rituals, ceremonies, uniforms—all the badges of belonging—are part of his repertoire of leadership and control.

Originality is *not* important: the leader of a mass movement appropriates from every source whatever ideas or techniques he finds useful and presents them as originating with his own people. Nor must he be a thinker in his own right. Many times in history, the leaders of mass movements have been brilliant men, but their appeal was not rooted in the quality of their ideas. "What counts is the arrogant gesture, the complete disregard of the opinion of others, the singlehanded defiance of the world."[5]

The mass movement tends to be associated with the person of the leader as though it were his creation. In reality, the leader does not create the movement; he capitalizes upon conditons which are the product of social interactions too diverse and too momentous to be the work of one man. In a very real sense, mass movements are set up and waiting to happen before the leader arrives on the scene.

> There is a period of waiting in the wings—often a very long period—
> for all the great leaders whose entrance on the scene seems to us a
> most crucial point in the course of a mass movement. Accidents and
> the activities of other men have to set the stage for them before
> they can enter and start their performance. "The commanding man
> in a momentous day seems only to be the last accident in a series."[6]

But a coalescence of the peculiarly volatile elements of social change
does not automatically produce a mass movement. The right man must
be there. The elements must come together in the presence of the
unique personality which can successfully catalyze or ignite them.

### The Instruments of Unification

The characteristic feature of a mass movement is its unique capacity
for united action without consideration for the individual sacrifices of
its members. The personal self is lost in the corporate whole and is
expendable in the interests of the whole. Personal privacy, personal
judgment, and often personal possessions, freedom, and life itself are
laid upon the corporate altar. The mass movement exists as an instrument for united action and self-sacrifice, not for the advancement of
individuals. Whenever there is a relaxation of collectivity, or when individual self-interest appears, the distinguishing character and the effectiveness of the movement are lost.

Absolute self-sacrifice is the lifeblood of the movement; contempt
for death is the sure sign of faith. The true believer places all his trust in
the destiny of the movement, its doctrines, and its leader. He forsakes
all values not sanctioned by the movement and not among its stated
objectives. He lives not for the present but for the future; and not for
his own future, but for the glorious triumph of his cause. He has renounced all self-interest, and even his most pragmatic affairs—earning a
living, raising a family—assume the character of a holy crusade.

> What seems to count more than possession of instruments of power
> is faith in the future . . . extravagant hope, even when not backed
> by actual power, is likely to generate a most reckless daring. For the

hopeful can draw strength from the most ridiculous sources of power—a slogan, a word, a button. No faith is potent unless it . . . has a millenial component.[7]

A mass movement, then, is unified first by faith, carried to the extreme of self-sacrifice. It is unified also by its doctrines, for the mass movement claims to possess the absolute truth—an esoteric knowledge of the past, a pellucid understanding of the present, a perfect awareness of the future. This "truth" is a formidable source of the movement's power, and the true believer "knows" the "truth" through faith. He knows it with his heart rather than with his mind.

The doctrines of a mass movement derive their power not from their meaning but from their certitude. The leader's utterances may be replete with the grossest nonsense, and rational critics may search them in vain for some clue to his power. But they miss the point. Reason and truth are not important; the masses are roused to action by what they *accept* as true. A proposition that can be tested can be proved false. A prophecy or a revelation cannot. A doctrine that is understood loses its power to compel its hearers: he who accepts a mystery can only obey, but he who understands it draws the power into himself. The true believer, however, wants only to accept. Understanding is personal, and he has renounced self, so he feels no need to understand. He has no doubts; he truly believes.

Self-mastery is another potent instrument of unification for the mass movement. On the one hand, as the members overcome in themselves the decadent habits and corrupt appetites of the rejected society, their own last shreds of identification with that society are symbolically overcome. On the other hand, certain moral commitments claimed by the general society but imperfectly observed by it take on an exaggerated importance within the movement. As the members successfully (indeed, fanatically) honor these commitments, they assert their moral superiority over all those from whom they have set themselves apart. The true believer is thus, in one sense, inevitably ambivalent: he seeks the approval of the general society by accomplishing what it has failed to accomplish, yet he scorns that society as worthless and its opinions as insignificant.

The mass movement also establishes its own exclusive code of behavior and institutes its own taboos. In the Black Muslim Movement, for example, every Muslim is committed to defend and protect every other "brother," even, if necessary, at the forfeiture of his life. Timidity or any hint of reluctance in this regard is absolutely taboo, and the rare lapses are punished summarily by ostracism or rejection by the group. Moreover, there can be no deviation from the party line as defined by the Messenger and enunciated by his ministers. Independent interpretations are absolutely taboo. The ministers speak with the voice of Muhammad; the laity speak with the voice of the ministers; and on subjects on which the Messenger has not spoken, no one else in the Movement will venture to speak. When Malcolm X violated this very fundamental rule of protocol, he was suspended from his office of Minister and shunned by all those who previously called him "brother." It is a truism illustrated in all such movements that the true believer must relentlessly master his own errant impulses and mold himself to the movement's unique image. But in doing so, he lowers still further the stubborn barriers of personal will that stand between his old, rejected self and his new corporate identity.

Finally, the mass movement is drawn together and held together by hatred, "the most accessible and comprehensive of all unifying agents." Eric Hoffer describes the effect of hatred upon the true believer:

> It pulls and whirls the individual away from his own self, makes him oblivious of his weal and future, frees him of jealousies and self-seeking. He becomes an anonymous particle quivering with a craving to fuse and coalesce with his like into one flaming mass. . . . Common hatred unites the most heterogeneous elements.[8]

Hatred requires an object, a devil.

> Mass movements can rise and spread without belief in a God, but never without belief in a devil. Usually the strength of a mass movement is proportionate to the vividness and tangibility of its devil.[9]

The genius of the leader of a mass movement is displayed in his timing and his choice of who the devil is to be. The devil must be an individual or group which is a socially legitimate hate-object, but he must also be omnipresent. Every difficulty must be ascribed to his evil nature, and every accomplishment must be vaunted as a triumph over him.

Hatred of the devil is the driving force of a mass movement. It is, without doubt, the most immediate instrument of unification. And, to complete the circle, it is the final product of every mass movement.

... we have never, since the world began, heard of a merciful nation. Nor ... of a merciful church or a merciful revolutionary party. The hatred and cruelty which have their source in selfishness are ineffectual things compared with the venom and ruthlessness born of selflessness ... we usually blame this shameful perversion on a cynical, power-hungry leadership. Actually it is the unification set in motion by these enthusiasms, rather than the manipulations of a scheming leadership, that transmutes noble impulses into a reality of hatred and violence. The deindividualization which is a prerequisite for thorough integration and selfless dedication is also, to a considerable extent, a process of dehumanization.[10]

## II. THE BLACK MUSLIMS AS A MASS MOVEMENT

### Reaching for the Masses

Under Fard, the Muslims never had more than eight thousand members, although the conditions for rapid growth were almost ideal. Muhammad claims "a few hundred thousand,"[11] and while no objective source is in position to verify that allegation, the evidence does seem to suggest that over the long span of Muhammad's leadership the number of Blacks who have been attracted to the movement has been substantial. The difference may well lie in the fact that Fard was the leader of a cult. Muhammad made that cult a movement.

Muhammad's strategy has been to put the cult on parade—on the streets, in the press, in the temples, *wherever there are people.* And he has done this with impressive success. For local action, he has had an able corps of ministers in the field; but there were not many at first, and their fight was uphill. The press gave him his first major assist, for it made him "controversial": as a columnist in one of the most important black papers in the country, he became a conversation piece for hundreds of thousands of Blacks across America. Thousands of letters were sent to Muhammad and to the *Pittsburgh Courier,* denouncing and defending both the Messenger and the newspaper which provided space for his message.

People went to the temples to see the man whose columns they read. For the most part they were simply curious, but Muhammad and his ministers are masters at capturing the curious. In the temples Muhammad preached a somewhat different message—not completely different, but different in emphasis. His writings in the newspapers were generally filled with vague and cryptic biblical interpretations. But in the privacy of the temples, the white man was unmasked; his mistreatment of the so-called Negro was rehearsed in bizarre detail and with militant outrage.

Moreover, Muhammad appealed to the newcomers not as individuals but as a crowd. All persons entering a temple were (and still are) searched for weapons as a precaution against the assassination of a minister. This requirement intrigued the curious and excited their sense of personal importance. Even to be thought capable of assassinating an important leader was gratifying to some who, in the structure of things, had no real identity whatsoever. At the same time, they were awed and flattered at being admitted, while all white men were rigidly excluded. The initiative had passed to the Muslims: it was now the newcomers who were tentatively accepted, but on trial.

Inside the temples, they were fascinated by the black-suited young males with the red ties and the military bearing. They were impressed by Muhammad's bold denunciation of the white man, and they were enlightened by hearing for the first time the "truth" about themselves, the Black Nation of Islam. For the most receptive among them, the potential true believers, a new vision dawned. They joined—a few at first and then more and more—and the character of the association began to change. The cult had quietly died. The Movement had begun.

The black press helped to supply the initial impetus that brought Muhammad and the Muslims to the attention of his potential followers. The white press has made him famous, and notoriety sharply enhanced his attraction for the masses. In the summer of 1959, Mike Wallace presented a television documentary featuring the Muslim leader,[12] and articles soon followed in *Time, U.S. News and World Report, Reader's Digest,* and other elements of the national press. Muhammad's total following was then less than thirty thousand. A month after he had been "discovered" by the mass media, his following had doubled, and it continued to climb for most of a decade. Ironically, many of these magazines and newspapers sought to "expose" Muhammad as "a purveyor of cold black hatred," [13] or otherwise as a social anomaly with no real future. They underestimated his appeal to an important segment of the dissatisfied black masses, who, being born with a cause, needed only a leader. A New England journalist correctly assesses Muhammad's timeliness as a leader for the disprivileged:

> Muhammad cannot be laughed at as Father Divine has been. Muhammad's movement, with its promises of swiftly approaching social and economic superiority for the Negro race, has captured the imagination of a segment of the suppressed and inarticulate Negro masses as few things have since Marcus Garvey. . . .[14]

Muhammad's first and most crucial task is to keep the Movement a *movement* rather than permit it to become an institution. This does not mean that the Muslims must forsake structure and direction; on the contrary, they have one of the most effective organizational structures to be seen outside the military. But to lure the masses, they must seem to be going somewhere, not settling down. They must reflect and mobilize the masses' own dissatisfaction and urgency, building these into the corporate identity. A successful mass movement is always arriving, but never quite arrives.

Muhammad is not unaware of the frustrations and the free-floating hostilities which are the corollaries of America's caste system, and he will continue to use these as capital in his program to bring every "lost black brother" under the Star and Crescent of Islam. This is, to be sure, an ambitious undertaking; but it is well to remember that only Billy Graham has attracted and converted more people in recent years than has Elijah Muhammad, Messenger of Allah, and Dr. Graham enjoys the advantages of social approval, a magnificent TV presence, and a product most Americans are committed to buying anyway. Elijah has none of these, but, unlike Billy Graham's converts, the Blacks who make "decisions for Allah" do not return to the anonymity from which they so briefly emerged. They take on a new identity that is *really* different, and they find a new and satisfying visibility in the corporate image of the Muslim brotherhood.

### Lures for the True Believer

To clinch the conversion of those true believers who approach the Movement in simple curiosity, Muhammad offers the lure of personal rebirth. The true believer who becomes a Muslim casts off at last his old self and takes on a new identity. He changes his name, his religion, his homeland, his "natural" language, his moral and cultural values, his very purpose in living. He is no longer a Negro, so long despised by the white man that he has come almost to despise himself. Now he is a black man—divine, ruler of the universe, different only in degree from Allah Himself. He is no longer discontent and baffled, harried by social obloquy and a gnawing sense of personal inadequacy. Now he is a Muslim, bearing in himself the power of the Black Nation and its glorious destiny. His new life is not an easy one: it demands unquestioning faith, unrelenting self-mastery, unremitting loyalty, and a singularity of purpose. He may have to sacrifice his family and friends, his trade or profession, if they do not serve his new-found cause. But he is not alone, and he now knows *why* his life matters. He has seen the truth, and the truth has set him free.

When he has seen the light and has decided to join the Movement, the potential convert is put through certain rites of passage before he is admitted. First he is given a copy of the following letter, which he himself must copy by hand:

*Address*
*City and State*
*Date*

*Mr. W. F. Muhammad*
*4847 So. Woodlawn Avenue*
*Chicago, Illinois 60015*

*Dear Savior Allah, Our Deliverer:*

*I have been attending the teachings of Islam by one of your Ministers, two or three times. I believe in It, and I bear witness that there is no God but Thee, and that Muhammad is Thy Servant and Apostle. I desire to reclaim my Own. Please give me my Original Name. My slave name is as follows:*

*Name*
*Address*
*City and State*

The applicant's letter is sent to Chicago, where it is scrutinized. If it contains any errors, it is returned and must be recopied correctly. If the letter is perfect, the applicant receives a questionnaire concerning his marital status and dependents. When this and other forms have been completed and approved, the convert enters his new life as a member of the Black Nation of Islam.

To commemorate his rebirth, the convert drops his last name and is known simply by his first bame and the letter X. To facilitate identification among Muslims having the same first name and belonging to the same temple, numbers are prefixed to the X. Thus the first man named John to join the temple is named John X; the second becomes John 2X; and so on. Some temples have gone as high as X to the "17th power"! At a later date, Muhammad may grant the convert a new—that is, an "original"—surname, such as Majied, or Hassan.

The symbol X has a double meaning: implying "ex," it signifies that the Muslim is no longer what he was; and as "X," it signifies an unknown quality or quantity. It at once repudiates the white man's name and announces the rebirth of Black Man, endowed with a set of qualities the white man does not have and does not know. "In short," Malcolm X explained, " 'X' is for mystery. The mystery confronting the Negro as to who he was before the white man made him a slave and put a European label on him. That mystery is now resolved. But 'X' is also for the mystery confronting the white man as to what the Negro has become." That mystery will be resolved only when the teachings of Elijah Muhammad have been received by enough of the "Lost Nation" to counter "three hundred years of systematic brainwashing by the white man." When the Lost Nation of Islam in the West has learned its true identity, has gained a realistic appreciation of its past accomplishments, and has seen the "truth about the white man," then the white man will see the black man in a new light—"and he will have no reason to rejoice."

Most Muslims also retain their "slave" surnames for use in such pragmatic affairs as signing checks. On these occasions, however, the surname is always preceded by an X to indicate that the Muslim repudiates it. On other occasions, Muslims may use the tribal name "Shabazz." For example, when Malcolm X toured Egypt and several other Moslem countries in Africa and Asia for the first time, he traveled as Malik Shabazz "so that my brothers in the East would recognize me as one of them." If he had used his "European" name (Malcolm Little), he explained, he would have been rejected as an imposter or ridiculed for retaining that symbol of the white man's ownership.

This change of name is, of course, only the most outward token of rebirth. Perhaps the deepest change promised—and delivered—is the release of energies that had been dammed or buried in the old personality. This release may account in part for the regeneration of criminals, alcoholics, and marcotic addicts which is a hallmark of the Movement. At the other extreme, it is often apparent in a change from gentle bewilderment to dogmatic and barely leashed hostility. "When I was in the Pacific," said a Muslim veteran of World War II, "I prayed to God every day that He would not let me die in the jungle, fighting some Japanese who had never done anything to me. I was a Christian then. Now I pray to Allah to let me live to help my people find out who their real enemies are, right here in America."

### Recruitment

In pursuit of his goal to make Black Muslims out of black Christians, Muhammad has an ambitious program of recruitment. His ministers go into jails and penitentiaries, pool halls and bars, barbershops and drugstores to talk about Islam. They invade the college campuses, the settlement houses, and the YMCAs. Young Muslim brothers hawk their newspapers along with insistent invitations to attend lectures at the Muslim temples. They speak from street corners and in parks, and they distribute literature wherever large crowds of Blacks may be gathered. Invariably, the proselytizers are young, personable, urbane, and well-dressed men of confidence and conviction.

It is a Muslim boast that the black intellectual will be hardest to reach ("he has been brainwahsed more thoroughly than any of the rest of us"), but he will ultimately have no choice other than to accept Islam. He can never be more than marginally acceptable to the white man, so "he will have nobody to lead and no one to honor him when the common people have all become Muslims." Muhammad himself has a sort of calculated patience with black intelligentsia. He regards them as doubly damned: "They have stayed in the white man's schools too long, learning nothing of themselves," and they are fervid in their "hopes that the white man is going to change and treat them like men instead of boys." The late Malcolm X was more philosophical: "The

American Black Man has worked hard to accomplish something and to be somebody. The whole system was against him, but some made it to a point where the white man will show some isolated individuals a little respect; not much, but more than he shows the rest of us. That man isn't going to join us until the white man is more respectful of us than of him."[15]

In their proselytizing, the Muslims carefully select their approach and their language—and often their speaker—to match the particular audience in mind. For example, Muhammad's long center-fold column in *Muhammad Speaks,* the official Muslim newspaper, is very deftly aimed at the *lumpen proletariat*, the common man. In one of the best edited newspapers published by Blacks, Muhammad's column is filled with biblical eschatology, numerology, and "mystery," all to the embarrassment and shame of the educated classes. However, the pitch here is being made not to the educated classes but to the masses, who are successfully attracted by such techniques. Inside the brotherhood these exotic elements are deemphasized, and more practical concerns are introduced.

When the Muslim is called upon to confront a highly critical audience, the whole panoply of the occult is usually discarded, except when it is needed to protect the speaker or the Movement against too close examination. In the privacy of his home, Mr. Muhammad is not only "rational," but gracious and friendly as well. He does not greet his guests with *"As-salaam-alaikum"* unless they happen to be Muslims. There are no guards anywhere about the house, and none of the physical trappings of the Movement is in evidence. Conversation is at a level consistent with his appraisal of the visitor. To be sure, Muhammad has a professional hostility against the white man, but this hostility does not dominate his private conversation. The Messenger's concern is more likely to center around the Black Man's economic plight. On the other hand, he may become totally incomprehensible about any matter he does not wish to discuss, usually calling upon "Allah" in answer to any questions which might put him at a disadvantage or give away any statistics or other secrets about his movement.

As it is with his erstwhile master, so it was with Malcolm X, who was characterized in the early days of his ministry as "whip-smart"[16] and able to think on his feet under adverse conditions. Despite his conversational adroitness, or perhaps because of it, Malcolm would take refuge behind any convenient obfuscation rather than allow himself to be trapped into saying more than he thought expedient. If he did not invoke Allah, he would refer the insistent prober to Mr. Muhammad—who would not hesitate to invoke Allah if the situation demanded it.

The Muslims boast of a considerable amount of professional talent. Dr. Leo McCallum of Chicago is a first-rate dentist who has kept abreast of the latest technical and therapeutical progress in his field. Dr. Lonnie Cross, who heads the Washington Mosque, was once chairman of the mathematics department at a leading university. Minister Louis Farrakhan of the Harlem Mosque is an accomplished musician. The rather handsome and personable minister plays the violin and is accomplished on several other instruments. As a calypso singer, he was commanding top pay in the better night clubs before he renounced Christianity and became a Muslim. Since then he has performed only under the aegis of Islam. He has written and directed two stage productions, *Orgena* and *The Trial*, both propaganda pieces designed to show the cupidity of the white man and the depths to which the Blacks have fallen in trying to be like him. In *The Trial*, as we have seen, the white man finally pays for his crimes against humanity, and the Black Nation is restored to its former moral and cultural excellence. Minister Farrakhan has also written and recorded several popular Muslim songs, the best known of which are *White Man's Heaven Is Black Man's Hell!* and *Look At My Chains!*

Dramatic productions, songs, and other such entertainment are effective recruiting devices. "People who can put on a play like that—and who wrote it themselves are not just 'everyday' folks," is a common consensus in the black ghetto. But Muhammad does not make entertainment ability the chief attraction of his Movement. Indeed, he is careful to emphasize "that the so-called Negro has already done too much singing and dancing," when he should have been giving his attention to more serious matters like factories and supermarkets. Apart from the public meetings and publications, a good deal of recruiting is done in jails and prisons, among men and women whose resentment against society increases with each day of imprisonment. Here their smoldering hatred against the white man builds up to the point of explosion. But Muhammad's ministers are trained to prevent any such release; they are adept at channeling aggression and hostility into a kind of leakproof reservoir for future use. No act of violence or retaliation against the white man is permitted. Instead, Muslims who join the sect while in prison invariably improve in behavior and outlook. Every Muslim *must* respect constituted authority—no matter what the authority may be. This is one of the cardinal rules of membership in the sect.

The black prisoner is reminded that he is in an institution administered by whites, guarded by whites, built by whites. Even the chaplains are white, "to continue to force upon you the poisonous doctrine that you are blessed by being persecuted." The judge who tried him, the jury who heard his case, the officers who arrested him—all were white. Can he, then, be justly imprisoned?

> If in fact you *did* steal, from whom did you steal? Only the white man has anything, and if you stole from him, you got but a fraction of what he owes you. Did you kill? If you killed a white man, they murder us at will. They decorate their trees with the bodies of our people. Or they kill us by "law," but they cannot enforce the same "law" to protect us or let us vote.[17]

If prisoners have committed crimes against other black men, they are told they committed these unnatural acts out of frustration and the inability to see who the real devil is. "You may have killed your black brother with your hand, but in your heart you have tried to kill your true tormentor."

When the prisoner is discharged, he is not often wanted by the Christian churches, but a ready-made fellowship awaits him at the Muslim temple. The new brother is welcomed and immediately made to feel a part of the group. A job is found for him, usually in one of the Muslim enterprises, and in a short time he is indistinguishable from any other Muslim. The routine of work, coupled with the obligations of the temple, leave him little time for regression or for any contacts with the criminal element.

Occasionally, a man or woman will join the Muslims "to keep out of trouble" or to find help in trying to overcome addiction to dope or alcohol. One woman in Milwaukee said that she joined "because I was tired of hating myself every time I looked in the mirror."

Muhammad's reclamation program promises a kind of moral and social perfectionism, which is available to all who adopt Islam. In his public addresses, he chides the black community for its juvenile delinquency, which is "caused by parental immorality" and "rips apart the seams of the Christian society." In Islam, echoed Malcolm X, "we don't have any delinquency, either juvenile or adult, and if Mr. Muhammad is given a chance he will clean up the slums and the ghettos—something all the leaders and the social workers and the policemen put together have not been able to do."

The Muslims visualize the reclamation of thousands of Blacks who, through ignorance, despair, and defeat, have found themselves in the gutter or in jail. They have had some impressive successes in rehabilitating certain categories of social outcasts, including narcotic addicts and alcoholics. Muhammad operates on the premise that "knowledge of self" and of the "truth about the white man"—when tied in with a constructive program, such as building the Black Nation—is sufficient to reclaim the most incorrigible. "By nature," the Muslims are taught, "you are divine." Their social tragedies are caused by the white devil's "tricknology," but truth and hard work will soon make them free.

### Visit to a Mosque

The real recruitment is done in the temples, or mosques, for there the import of Muhammad's message may be heard at best advantage. The mosque is typically located in the area of densest concentration in the black ghetto. In this way, the bars, pool halls, and chicken shacks—all crowded with potential converts—are readily accessible to the proselytizing Muslim brothers. Conversely, the mosque is in a neighborhood familiar and convenient to most of those to whom its basic appeal is directed. On Wednesday nights the clean-shaven, dark-suited Muslims may be seen posted near the liquor stores or canvassing the bars and cafes, "fishing for the dead"—that is, inviting the most lost of the Lost Nation to repair to the nearby temple to learn the truth about themselves and their future.

On Sunday mornings the crusading brothers may station themselves outside the Christian churches—High-Church or apostolic, cathedral or store-front, it doesn't matter to the self-confident Muslims, for the message they have is ultimately intended for the entire Black Nation. They march silently up and down in front of the churches, passing out handbills inviting the Christians to come to the Muslim temple that afternoon "to hear the truth." The Muslims are invariably polite and friendly, quietly dressed, and soft-spoken. But most impressive of all is their self-assurance, their utter confidence in their "program for the Black Man which does not require you to love those who do not love you."

The temple itself may be a vacant store or a lodge hall, if the Muslims have but newly organized or if the Movement has not yet caught on in that area. Where the size of the congregation warrants, the Muslims have typically bought abandoned Jewish temples or Christian churches as the whites have fled from the changing neighborhood. Occasionally the nascent Muslim organizations meet in black churches or even in funeral chapels.

Arriving at the temple, the new visitor may discover that it has a number rather than a name. A large sign across the front of the building or a signboard on the lawn may proclaim it to be, say, MUHAMMAD'S MOSQUE OF ISLAM NO. 5. However, because law enforcement and other agencies have shown increasing interest in the Movement in recent times, the wily Muslim leader has now stopped numbering his temples in order to keep the strength of the Movement secret.

The lawn bulletin, as in Christian churches, announces the speaker for the day. Whenever a program of unusual importance is held at a local temple, it is supported by busloads of Muslims from all nearby cities and from national headquarters in Chicago. At a rally held by the Atlanta Temple, Muslim caravans came from as far away as Boston and Los Angeles. This kind of mobility promotes a rather widespread cohesiveness within the brotherhood; most of the ministers eventually become known to all other ministers and to congregations scattered across the country.

The black visitor is welcomed at the entrance to the temple by a committee of the dark-suited brethren. The white visitor is politely but firmly turned away, with an explanation that this is a meeting for the victims of the white man and not for the white man himself. It may be further explained that what will be said in the temple may sound offensive to white people and that white visitors who become offended may find themselves in danger; consequently it will be better for all concerned if only black people attend.

Blacks are readily admitted and are shown into the temple with elaborate courtesy and ceremony. In an anteroom just off the sanctuary, a Muslim sister waits to record the visitors' names and addresses, which are then added to the temple's mailing list. Following this registration, the visitor is asked to submit to "a little ceremony we always go through." The "little ceremony" is, in fact, an elaborate and systematic search for concealed weapons. All pocket knives, nail files, and any other instruments capable of inflicting serious injury are taken from the visitor and checked in a plastic bag, along with lip rouge, chewing gum, cigarettes, and all other "articles of defilement." The visitor is asked to open his wallet and remove his money. Both the wallet and the money are then examined, but the owner is permitted to retain these.

Two Muslims are assigned to go over each new arrival, and they do it with a thoroughness that would delight the heart of a police sergeant. Pockets must be turned inside out; coat lapels, collars, and trouser cuffs are all given attention. The trouser legs must be raised to show that nothing is concealed in the socks. While the visitor's arms are held aloft, a Muslim brother places his outspread hands on either side of the neck and in one continuous sweep carefully trails them down the sides of the body to the ankles. The armpits and the inside of a man's legs are given close attention. Women are given similar treatment in a room set aside for that purpose.

The Muslims are remarkably adept in the searching procedure. The whole thing takes only about a minute and is done with as little inconvenience and embarrassment to the bewildered newcomer as possible. On special occasions, such as when the Messenger is speaking, a double line of perhaps fifty to sixty Muslim brothers is assigned to this detail, thus enabling several thousand people to be "cleared" and seated within an hour or two preceding the meeting. At the big meetings the paramilitary FOI is in charge, and the Muslims as well as non-Muslims are searched.

Once the visitor has been cleared, he is escorted into the sanctuary by one of the Muslims. The entrance to this room is typically guarded on the inside by two members of the FOI, who stand, one on each side of the doorway, facing the front of the room. If there is a double entrance (as in most churches), guards are posted at each. The entrances near the chancel at the front of the room are similarly guarded. There may also be two guards flanking the speaker, one on each side; or there may be a guard opposite the front row of seats on each side of the room. The escort will lead the visitor to the front of the room, making certain that all seats on the front row are filled first, and so on with the succeeding rows. Men are seated to the right, women to the left. There is no mixed seating whatsoever.

Before the minister enters to deliver the main lecture for the day, one of the brothers may instruct the audience in a Muslim prayer or in the understanding of certain Arabic phrases. The prayer posture may be taught—palms upward, face to the East—and its meaning explained.

There is a flurry of excitement when the minister enters. He walks rapidly to the lectern and bows slightly, with his palms up and slightly extended. Then he smiles at his congregation and greets them in Arabic. *"As-salaam alaikum!"* ("Peace be unto you!") The greeting is returned in unison: *"Wa-alaikum salaam!"* ("And unto you be peace!") This exchange is usually made three times, after which the minister launches immediately into his address, which is the heart of the service and usually lasts two or three hours. Unlike the traditional Christian sermon, it is not confined to a single topic each week. Instead, the minister attempts every week to present the entire gamut of Muhammad's teachings. He speaks almost without pause and is interrupted only by the changing of the guard—a ceremony in which, at intervals, the guards at the rear of the hall march forward, exchange phrases in Arabic with the guards down front, and then exchange stations with them.

Throughout the lecture, the audience is attentive and earnest. It is eager and seems enraptured by its exclusive possession of the truth; yet it is always restrained. There are no "happy" people in the congregation, and the foot-thumping, head-wagging-amen stereotype of the store-front churchgoer is conspicuously absent. There is no singing and no "shouting." Emotional displays are limited to frequent ejaculations of "That's right!" or "Right on!" when the minister scores a point upon which there is wide agreement. Often, the minister asks a rhetorical question for emotional effect. He may wonder, for example, "Now what do you think would happen if you tried to do some of the things the Constitution says you have a right to do?" At this there is an uneasy rumble of snickering, interspersed with the cynical response: "Now *that's* a good question, Brother Minister! That's a *good* question!"

While the minister lectures, money receptacles are in continuous circulation, and the challenge to "support your own" is insistently urged by young ushers moving among the audience. The receptacles are not inconspicuous: they are plastic wastebaskets or large brown paper bags. Such collections are a relatively recent innovation. The Muslim brothers formerly took no public offerings and announced proudly: "Islam takes care of its own." Now they explain that, since Muhammad has become well-known and his aims and integrity are established, the public can be permitted to contribute toward his work, especially the proposed building of an Islamic Center and a hospital in Chicago.

The minister nearly always begins his lecture by writing several Arabic phrases on a blackboard, explaining that Arabic is the original language of the Black Man and that he must begin to relearn the langauge of which the white man has deprived him. The first phrase is the Muslim greeting: *As-salaam alaikum.* The proper response is then written and explained: *Wa-alaikum salaam.* "It is proper," the minister explains, "to begin the study of Islam and the worship of Allah in the presence of peace. Islam is the religion of peace, and Muslims should be at peace with each other and, insofar as is possible, with all others."

Peace having been disposed of, the minister launches into a long discussion of the primacy of the Black Man and his remarkable accomplishments. To this end, he cites pertinent passages from the Islamic Quran, the Old Testament, and other literature, as well as the writings of Muhammad himself. The hearers are reminded that their earlier knowledge of themselves and their past has been derived from the spurious teachings of the white man, who has prostituted truth and defiled history to serve his own ends. Black men must no longer accept the white man's teachings at face value. They must search out the facts and make intelligent judgments for themselves. The ministers will help them, for the Messenger knows the truth about the white man and he has taught his ministers well.

Often the minister reads passages from well-known historical, sociological, or anthropological works and finds in them documentary references to the Black Man's true history in the world. Black men in Asia and Africa were enjoying advanced civilizations when the white man was eating his meat raw in the caves of Europe. Yet the whites, through their control of informational media (including the black preachers), have succeeded in making the so-called Negroes accept themselves as inferior.

Black men sat on the thrones of Egypt and Ethiopia, fought beside the Romans in conquering the savages of Britain, discovered America long before Columbus, and then piloted the ship on which Columbus sailed. Black men ruled Spain and Southern Europe, reigned as popes in the Eternal City of Rome, and built great civilizations on the west coast of Africa. They produced many Moslem scholars of whom the white Christians profess to be ignorant, though the white civilization has stolen much knowledge from them. But the whites have taught the so-called Negro nothing of all this, and he has a mental block against searching out the information for himself. The so-called Negro doesn't want to know about his own history; he wants to know about the white man's history. He has been taught that his own history will only deposit him in the jungle, whereas the white man's history begins with Socrates dying nobly to illustrate a moral principle.

Occasionally the minister chides the audience for its skepticism: "I know you don't believe me because I happen to be black. Well, you can look it up in a book I'm going to tell you about that was written by a *white* man." He then reads off references, which his hearers are challenged to check for themselves. A single documented statement, however, may become the basis of a wide range of generalized *non sequiturs.* The fact that a North Carolina slaveholder owned an Arabic-speaking Moslem slave of unusual mathematical ability may be offered as evidence that *all* slaves brought to America were Moslem, Arabic-speaking, and learned.

Similarly, historical facts may be indiscriminately mingled with myths and countermyths. The information that Aesop was black and that the great University of Sankore in Timbuktu sent its professors to learn in the universities of Cairo, Granada, and Morocco at a time when Europe was just emerging from the Dark Ages—allegations easily documented from standard sources[18]—may be interspersed among claims that "all history is written in advance by twenty-four Black Scientists" under a twenty-fifth black man who serves as "Judge," or that the tribe of Shabazz (to which all black men belong) represents "Original Man" who "came with the earth sixty-six trillion years ago."

The minister next turns his attention to the evil and divisive influences of the white man and to the white man's equally repulsive religion. The white man has come but lately to the table of civilization. "When the black princes of Asia and Africa were wearing silks and plotting the stars, the white man was crawling around on his all-fours in the caves of Europe. The reason why the white man keeps dogs in the house today, and sleeps with them and rides them about in cars is that he slept with the dogs in the caves of Europe and he has never broken the habit."[19]

The audience is urged to give the Christian religion back to the white man, for it is a religion of slavery and death. Blacks must also give the white man back the names he has labeled them with, for these are badges of slavery. "If a Chinaman tells you his name is 'Whitfield,' you know there's something wrong somewhere. Well, there's also something wrong about a black man named 'Jones'."[20] Wherever the white man's name is attached to the so-called Negro, it is a symbol of possession. "Every time you sign your name you tell the world you're still the white man's chattel. If your body happens to be partly free, you're still his chattel in mind."

At this point, the minister may point to a painting which, in most temples, hangs on the wall behind the lectern. On the right half of the canvas are shown the symbols of Islam—the star and crescent—and the legend "Freedom-Justice-Equality." On the left are depicted the American flag, the Christian cross, and a black man hanging by his neck from a tree. These three, the minister explains, are the symbols of Christianity and what it has offered the Black Man. But now the Black Man has a choice: Islam, or continued abuse in subservience to the white Christians.

The men are reminded that they have been helpless even when their homes have been invaded. Resistance, even to protect their families, has meant death. Further, their economic conditions are so contrived that they must send their womenfolk out to work in the homes and offices of Christian white men. This is no accident: the white man controls the economy, and he knows the Black Man is at his mercy. He deliberately castrates the Black Man by paying his wife higher wages, so that the male is no longer head of his family. The wife then comes to despise her husband and to admire the white man, who is economically independent. And the white man not only employs the Black Man's women but proceeds forthwith to send them home to their black husbands with blue-eyed babies. "These same robbers," says Muhammad, "disgrace and corrupt them with all kinds of diseases besides spotting up [their] children like the animal family."[21]

> We stand by with folded arms, cowards to the core, and allow the human brute . . . to take our women . . . the most priceless gift of a nation. . . . We cannot produce a pure, chaste nation with a "free-for-all" woman. If we [cannot] protect her from the human beast's advances, we should kill ourselves and our women.[22]

Christianity is dealt with summarily. It is considered a religion of ignominy and disgrace for the Black Man, but of great convenience and practicality for the white man. For the white man neither believes its teachings nor makes any attempt to practice them. The white man wants the so-called Negro to accept Christianity and live according to its teachings; but he then laughs at the so-called Negro for being a fool.

"Love thy neighbor"; I have yet to meet one white man that loved his neighbor. . . . "Thou shalt not kill"; I have yet to meet such a Christian. . . . Where is a good Christian among this race?[23]

. . . you fear and love [the white Christians] though you are even disgraced, beaten and killed by them, from your ministers of their slavery religion . . . down to the lowly, ignorant man in the mud. You have made yourselves the most foolish people on earth by loving and following after the ways of Slavemasters, whom Allah has revealed to me to be none other than real devils, and that their so-called Christianity is not His religion, nor the religion of Jesus or any other prophet of Allah (God).[24]

The audience is encouraged to disavow a religion which worships "a dead Jesus and his dead disciples," for such behavior distracts them from the business of trying to live in *this* world. "The white man has 'given you Jesus' while he has robbed you blind." Heaven is right here, and we must try to share in it now, rather than after death. Jesus has not "gone anywhere."

No one after death has ever gone any place but where they were carried. There is no heaven or hell other than on earth for you and me, and Jesus was no exception. His body is still . . . in Palestine and will remain there.[25]

With this transition, the minister next gives his attention to the Messenger's economic program. The hearers are chided for thriftlessness, conspicuous consumption, and living beyond their means. Such self-indulgence will not build the Black Nation. The white man still owns the so-called Negro, because the white man owns the factories, the land, the houses, and everything else needed for survival. When he decides to kill a black man, he does not shoot him—except for amusement. "All he needs to do is to deny the Negro a job, and he will soon be just as dead." The Black, in an attempt to protect himself against economic reprisal, adopts a posture of servility. "The so-called Negro's principles are always in pawn to the slavemaster. The white man can make him bark and roll over any day in the week!" He is no more than a "free slave," for he dares not assert his manhood, no matter what indignities are heaped upon him or what atrocities are directed his way.

"Mr. Muhammad has an economic program," the minister continues, "which, if followed, will soon free the Black Man and make him equal to the other nations of the world." But the Black Man must be prepared to work:

> Many of us, the so-called Negroes, today are so lazy that we are willing to suffer anything rather than go to work. It is true that God has come to sit us in heaven, but not a heaven wherein we won't have to work.[26]

Integration comes under heavy attack. It is anathema to the Movement, and the minister is trained to denounce it with especial vehemence. He may read from Muhammad's *The Supreme Wisdom,* in which the Messenger condemns integration as a kind of social opiate.

> The Slavemaster's children are doing everything in their power to prevent the so-called Negroes from accepting their own God and salvation, by putting on a great show of false love and friendship.
>
> This is being done through "integration," as it is called; that is, so-called Negroes and whites mixing together such as in schools, churches, and even intermarriage. . . . The poor slaves really think they are entering a condition of heaven with their former slaveholders, but it will prove to be their doom.
>
> Today . . . we are living in a time of great separation between the blacks and white. . . . The so-called Negroes must now return to their own; nothing else will solve the problem.[27]

The integration controversy is presented as a private quarrel between Northern and Southern whites:

> The Northern whites don't really care about the Negroes, but they

don't like it because the crackers in the South disgrace the country and embarrass the nation. They can't keep out of the Black Man's bed, and they have to keep lynching Negroes and try to keep it covered up. Now today, this makes for bad international relations. But the Southern cracker isn't going to clean himself up and stay on his side of town just to please the Yankees or to put the country in a better light. He can't. He was born a dog, and he'll be a dog. But he'll get up on Sunday morning and look pious in his pew![28]

The minister denounces integration as a stratagem of the white man to insure his survival in a world he has managed badly. The white man's time is up, and he knows it. He has no friends anywhere. He now hopes that by integrating with the rising Black Man, he can avoid paying for the long list of crimes he has perpetrated against humanity. So he has undertaken to "sweetheart" with the only people who are stupid enough to listen, the dupes he has trained to love him. But the Muslims are not taken in by all this. Minister Bernard Cushmeer writes:

Messenger Muhammad has put it in the clearest language when he says that the Black Man must be free and must have justice. Justice involves his being separated from the white man. He can never enjoy justice living under the rule of a people who by nature cannot govern with justice. Moreover, the Messenger has made known that the God has something in mind for the future of the Black Man. In no way does that future include Black and white together.[29]

If the so-called American Negro were not so much in love with his deceivers, he would be preparing to be master now, rather than continuing to be satisfied as a free slave. For the white man's doom is sure.

The minister then speaks again of Islam, the religion of "peace, justice and equality." It is the *only* religion, he asserts, in which the Black Man in America—or anywhere else in the world—can find communion in brotherhood. Islam is hateful to the white man because it "equalizes" him, and "the white man would rather be dead than to be equal." But there are as many professing believers in Islam alone as there are white men in the entire world, and all nonwhite men everywhere are *by nature* Muslims, whether they profess it or not. The white race is thus hopelessly outnumbered by the Muslim brotherhood, which stretches across the world.

The Holy Quran of Islam is the "book which makes a distinction between the God of the righteous and the God of evil." This is the book which the slavemaster has willfully kept from the Blacks in America, for it contains all knowledge: "the Guidance of Light and Truth and of Wisdom and Judgment."

This book the *Holy Quran Sharrieff,* pulls the cover off the covered and shows the nation for the first time that which deceived 90 per cent of the people of the earth without knowledge of the deceiver.[30]

At present the Holy Quran must be taught by the leaders, but all Muslims should learn Arabic (which is taught at some temples) so that they may read it for themselves in the original. Meanwhile, only those translations approved by Muhammad should be used.[31]

Near the end of the meeting and at the conclusion of the minister's lecture, the congregation is asked whether it agrees with what has been said. Any who do not agree are asked to state the points of disagreement, so that the minister may try to provide the clarification necessary to unity. If the minister cannot provide a satisfactory answer, he promises to relay the question to the Messenger himself for resolution. No questions or problems are deemed beyond the capacities of the Messenger, for it is because of his wisdom and insight that he has been chosen leader of the Black Nation.

When all questions raised from the floor by those not yet returned to Islam have been spoken to, the minister invites those who believe what they have heard and who have the courage of their convictions to come forward and declare for Islam. There are rarely more than fifteen or twenty in any one meeting; but in a three-hour lecture before 8,500 persons in Los Angeles' Olympic Auditorium, "Mr. Elijah Muhammad . . . persuaded more than 143 Christians to renounce Christianity and embrace Islam."[32]

Those who elect to join are warmly welcomed by the Muslim brotherhood and are assigned to classes of instruction. Those who are impressed, but are not yet willing to separate themselves from the Christian tradition, are urged to continue attending the public meetings, in the expectation that they will eventually overcome this hesitation. The merely curious and those suspected of being "stooges for the FBI" are not encouraged to return.

## Schools and the Center

A powerful and long-range recruiting device of the Movement is its parochial schools, with their massive emphasis on education about the Black Man—his resplendent past, his divine nature, his triumphant future. Many lower-class Blacks find this approach, for all its exaggerations, a welcome change from the white-oriented teaching in nearly all public schools, which has so long cast black children adrift in a sea of nonidentiy and nonbelonging. Today, to have their children learn something of themselves and their heritage is strong among black people of all classes. The parents who send their children to the Muslim schools are impressed with the concrete evidence of the Muslims' determination to free themselves from all white influence and to prepare their youth for roles as reclaimers of the Black Man's heritage. Finally, the schools have important status value as private schools for the low-income families, who could never hope to afford the luxury of ordinary private schools.

The Muslims had fourteen parochial schools (called Universities) in operation in early 1972.[33] This is a far cry from the initial school Muhammad opened in Detroit in the early thirties. The schools are staffed by Muslim and non-Muslim teachers, and most of them are accredited by the local accrediting agencies. The school year is fifty weeks long. The future leaders of black Islam cannot afford to take three months off for frivolity. There is no vacation from the realities of life and the tricknology of the white man. Sports and the usual extracurricular activities are not a part of the Muslim program except insofar as they contribute directly to the serious search for knowledge. Elijah Muhammad, whose own formal education did not exceed the fourth grade, has very definite ideas about what education can accomplish:

The so-called American Negro needs self-education . . . in order to get the respect and recognition of others. . . . He needs even more than an equal education. He needs a superior education to that which is ruling the nations of the earth today.

Muhammad is echoed by Minister Farrakhan, who explains:

We are 400 years behind, 100 years up from slavery. We have a lot of catching up to do, and though we are to enjoy life, we have no time for a lot of play and a lot of sport.

The Muslim curriculum consists of science, reading, mathematics, history, arts, and language. Language (Arabic) and math are taught to children from the age of three. All classes at the more developed schools are taught in Arabic and English:

> English is a bastard language. This is the truth. English is a bastard language, for it is a language that is made up of other languages. It is a dependent language, so we see here why it is necessary for us to have a new language.[34]

Much is made of the fact that Muhammad's young son, Akbar, a graduate of the University of Islam in Chicago, acted as interpreter for his father's party during a tour of Islamic countries in Africa and Asia.

The Detroit school dates back to the early years of the Movement, when it was a constant thorn in the side of the Detroit police and school officials. In 1934, Muhammad was found guilty of contributing to the delinquency of a minor and given six months' probation when he refused to withdraw his children from the University of Islam and enroll them in the city's public schools. At about the same time, when the city attempted to interfere with the operation of the school, the Muslims began "a severe riot" in which the Muslims "tried to storm the police headquarters. Fearful of race riots, the judges of the recorder's office released with suspended sentences almost all of the rioters."[35] But the trouble continued:

> Several . . . cult members were in and out of court on . . . charges, most resulting from their insistence on sending their children to cult schools. "Universities of Islam" were operated in various places around Detroit for more than a decade as the Board of Education sought to close them. . . . The school system finally decided to "join" the Muslims instead of fighting them. . . . Cult leaders, working through their attorney . . . got together with the State Department of Public Instruction representatives to work out an approved private school for the cult. The court cases were dropped on the assumption the school had been approved. . . .[36].

The school was closed again in August 1959, after "a State Police sergeant, an agent of the State Department of Public Instruction, two Buildings and Safety Engineering Department inspectors, a Health Department investigator, and a Detroit Fire Department inspector poked through the musty, crumbling former theatre building. . . ."[37] A few weeks later, the school was again in operation.

By contrast, the school attached to Mosque No. 7 in contemporary Harlem has an enrollment of seven hundred with a waiting list of two hundred Muslim and non-Muslim applicants. The teachers all have bachelors' degrees in the areas of their subject matter, and many of them have earned advanced degrees. Standard textbooks are used, but their subject matter is taught selectively and supplemented by parochial materials. Another six hundred children attend Muhammad's University No. 2 in Chicago. Again, the waiting list for admission is long. Non-Muslim children attending the Muslim schools usually convert to Islam (along with their parents) within a year after enrollment.

### Intibah, Hah!

School is a very serious matter for Muslim boys and girls. The Muslim teachers have few of the problems of discipline common to other schools. They assert with the confidence of certainty: "There is no juvenile delinquency among our children." Discipline begins early:

> "Intibah, hah!" a young woman called to a class of first-level boys, most of whom, until that moment, were sitting quietly in their seats, wearing suits, white shirts and either bow or string ties.
>
> At the sound of the Arabic command, the students rose swiftly to attention.
>
> A second command in Arabic, and the boys, aged 4 to 6, turned left face, then right face, all the while chanting multiplication tables.
>
> At the end of the exercise, the teacher gave the command to sit, and jubilantly concluded the exercise with the words: "Give Praise to Muhammad!"[38]

The children are separated by sex. In some schools boys attend in the morning, girls in the afternoon. There are no play or rest periods. No time off for lunch. The boys wear jackets (except in summer) and ties. The girls dress in ankle-length, flowing white gowns with matching head-wraps. "You make a child shyless," says Elijah Muhammad, "when you allow them to wear dresses above their knees or place young girls in the same classroom with young boys." "There is a natural attraction between male and female," explains Farrakhan. "When they are close together, that attraction begins to work, and they're not so attracted to the wisdom they are here to learn. . . . We won't have sweethearting going on while education is supposed to be going on." Minister Yusef Shah, Dean of Boys at the Chicago school, writes:

> One can readily see that the system of education proposed and instituted by Messenger Muhammad . . . is the successful formula in effectively educating the black children. . . . Coeducation does not exist in the Muhammad Universities of Islam. Coeducation is the Western way of educating youth. Separate education is the Islamic way of educating youth. Separate education . . . destroys such social atrocities as immorality, social diseases, promiscuity and other social filth and indecencies. . . . It is a fact that coeducation does not and will not foster a moral education.[39]

The Muslim students are inculcated with the notion that their education is the best available: Sister Beverly Maraud, National Director of Education for the Nation, assures her graduates that:

> You are, with the help of Allah, being given an education that is superior to any other education received anywhere in any school in any of the cities and towns in which you live. . . . As a Muslim student you are blessed. We thank Allah for young people such as you who have disassociated yourself from the corrupt ways of the generation and civilization in which you live. . . . An Islamic education is the key to your future.[40]

The Muslims place a high premium upon special education for wives and mothers, and their Muslim Girls' Training and General Civilization Class is an effective means of drawing black women into the Movement. The MGT, as it is generally known, concentrates primarily on the art of homemaking. It meets on week nights at the local temples, and the women are "taught how to sew, cook, keep house, rear their children, care for their husbands, and how to behave at home and abroad." High moral behavior is an absolute requirement, for "a Muslim can rise no higher than his women." Minister Yusek Shah explains:

> Mr. Muhammad teaches us that the man is the God, the Maker and
> the Owner and the Father of Civilization. He is the provider, where-
> as the woman is the Mother of Civilization; she is the man's heaven.
> . . . We can agree that the nature of the man and the woman are
> different. Since their natures are different, it is necessary to teach
> and train them separately.[41]

Perhaps the most ambitious undertaking Muhammad has announced
is the building of an Islamic Center in Chicago. The center is to include
"a mosque in which to pray . . . an educational institution in which to
enlighten our youth, a library in which to deepen their knowledge and
understanding, a hospital in which to cure the sick and strengthen the
healthy."[42] The initial cost of the center is put at $20 million, and
funds are solicited from all who attend the various meetings of the
Muslims, on the promise that the facilities of the center will not be
restricted to Muslims.

The Muslims acquired a five-acre tract on Chicago's far South Side
for which they paid a reputed $150,000. When residents in the area
became convinced that the Muslims really intend to build the center,
they sought to have the tract condemned for a public park. Muhammed
lashed out at the program in terms reminiscent of Garvey:

> The short-sighted so-called Negroes seem to rather have a play-
> ground to sit, eat and sleep on [and] to be criticized by the civil-
> ized people of earth as the laziest and most foolish people of all.
> . . . I warn you my people who are trying to oppose me and my
> followers—to the joy of our enemies, (the devils) by our Allah, all
> of your efforts shall fail . . . if we are forced by the city to give it up
> or sell, by the help of our God, Allah—we will most certainly retal-
> iate; this we are assured of.[43]

### Mr. Muhammad Speaks

The Black Muslims have spared no effort to contact the black
masses through every available medium of mass communication. Wherever Muhammad speaks, his audiences are numbered in the thousands.
Baltimore, Pittsburgh, New York, Boston, Philadelphia, Los Angeles,
Chicago, Atlanta, Washington, and other cities across the country have

turned out impressive crowds to hear the Messenger, but since the mid-sixties, Muhammad has kept close to his Chicago mansion and his public appearances have been few. Films, tapes, and other sophisticated media are used increasingly to reach his public. His interviews with the press are rare.

For several years, Muhammad's column in the *Pittsburgh Courier* attracted wide attention among Blacks and stirred a lively debate between those who supported his views and those who were indignant that he was granted space in the paper. During his tenure as a *Courier* columnist, no other single writer drew as many letters to the editor; and the newspaper, which had been steadily losing readers, suddenly found its circulation increasing. This was partially due to the fact that the Muslims took to the street corners and the housing projects to hawk the papers—each brother being assigned a quota. In 1959, however, the controlling interest in the paper was bought by S. B. Fuller, a Chicago manufacturer, and Muhammad's column was dropped.

Subsequently the column began to appear in the weekly *Los Angeles Herald-Dispatch,* which became in effect the official Muslim organ. Following its alliance with the Muslims, the *Dispatch* began to publish a regional edition in Chicago, and local offices were opened in other cities where there are large numbers of Muslims. The paper was published by Sanford Alexander of Los Angeles. Raymond Sharrieff, son-in-law of Muhammad and Supreme Captain of the FOI, was in charge of its Chicago offices. The paper was sold at all Muslim enterprises across the country, and individual Muslims were given quotas to sell in the black ghettos. Circulation soon reached forty thousand a week.

Malcolm X called the *Dispatch* "the most outspoken newspaper in America . . . 100 per cent pro-black." The paper denounced "the so-called Negro leaders," ridiculed the commitment to nonviolence and passive resistance, and gave unequivocal support to the Black Muslims.

. . . Mr. Muhammad's program . . . and the racial policy of the *Herald-Dispatch* is one and the same. . . . Mr. Muhammad maintains and the *Herald-Dispatch* concurs, that the salvation for the so-called American Negro is unity of purpose . . . one goal, spiritually, economically, and politically, such as embracing Islam, . . . building business enterprises among the black race, supporting the Negro businessman, learning self-respect. And above all else, [we must] stop begging our oppressor for the crumbs from his table. Prepare for the day when his beastlike action against the non-white population . . . will be stopped with force.[44]

The feature news of each issue of the *Dispatch* was mainly concerned with Muslim affairs, and the addresses of Muhammad, Malcolm X, and others prominent in the Movement were invariably given extensive coverage. Guest columns by various Muslim ministers were featured regularly, as were stories about the activities of local temples. Muhammad's "Economic Blueprint" was featured in most issues. The back page was often devoted entirely to a graphic projection of the proposed Islamic Center and a listing of the Muslim temples and their addresses. Considerable space was devoted to advertising from Muslim temples, enterprises, and individuals.

News of interest to the general black community was also published in the *Dispatch*, but relatively little space was given to social events—an important feature in most black newspapers. Some straight news pertaining to Christian churches was carried, as was news about such organizations as the NAACP. Foreign news was usually limited to items concerning the Afro-Asian community:

In February 1960, the *Dispatch* presented Elijah Muhammad an award on the occasion of its eighth anniversary celebration. In anticipation of the event, the *Dispatch* said editorially:

Mr. Muhammad has succeeded in organizing approximately one half million so-called Negroes. . . . He is uplifting fallen humanity. He is not concerned with other races, he teaches the so-called Negro to be pro-black. This is not teaching hate . . . because of his teachings, his program of positive action, the *Herald-Dispatch* will give him the highest Achievement Award ever given to an individual by this publication. . . . [45]

Both Christianity and Judaism came under frequent attack from the *Dispatch*. An editorial entitled "The Evils of Christianity" declared:

The Christian, the white man with a gun and a Bible in one hand and a bottle of gin in the other . . . enslaved [the Black Man] . . .

[and is guilty of] economic oppression, lynchings, bombing of [Negro] churches, segregation, disenfranchisement. . . . Christianity in Germany used fiendish gas ovens to "scientifically" rid the world of millions of Jews; the U.S. under Christianity performed the most heinous crime ever committed on the planet Earth—the dropping of the atomic bombs on the Japanese. . . .[46]

The "Christian Belgians" are charged with slaughtering the Congolese; the "Christian French," with bombing the Algerians and Tunisians, "supported by the Christian United States and Britain." In a particularly bitter editorial, the *Dispatch* challenged its readers as follows:

We ask Negroes: where was Ralph Bunche, the stooge of the Western Powers when the Belgians murdered 10,000 Africans on January 4, 5, and 6, 1959? We ask the Negroes where was the United Nations when the South Africans were shooting down Africans like flies? . . . Where was Ralph Bunche when the British, using rockets were killing the Africans in Kenya? . . . Russia saved Egypt in 1956. . . . Russia ordered Israel out of the Sinai Desert . . . it was Russia again who ordered the Belgians out of the Congo. We are thankful for Russia.[47]

This praise of Russia seemed a startling departure from the Muslim line. Muhammad holds no brief for *any* white nation, including the Soviet Union. Hence, it must be concluded that the *Dispatch* either forgot momentarily its new associations or the gesture toward Russia was no more than a ploy to discomfit white America.

Judaism, "from which Christianity spread"—the *Dispatch* does not mention Islam's similar origin—is condemned for "her brutal treatment of the Palestine Arabs who had befriended the Jews in an hour of need." The Jews are referred to as "educated and highly cultured," and it is emphasized that their "crimes were conducted with the aid and sanction of the Christian countries." All black people are called upon to "renounce Christianity in all its facets, [for] Christianity . . . is not for the Black Man."[48]

Eventually, the *Dispatch* faded into oblivion when the Black Muslims founded their own newspaper, *Muhammad Speaks.*

The Muslims have at times offered various special publications designed to attract the attention of the black masses to Muhammad's work and teachings. Among the most important has been a volume called *The Supreme Wisdom: Solution to the So-Called Negroes' Problem,* an early hornbook of the Movement. In its fifty-six pages, Muhammad addresses himself to such diverse topics as "The Bible and its Teachings," "Christianity," "What Our Enemy Is Doing," "No 'Integration,' " "Kinky Hair," "The Hog and Its Eaters," "Heaven on Earth" and "Other Notable Aspects of Islam." An early edition lists ten formal require-ments of practice, or "Principles of Belief," including the following: "Keep up prayer; speak the truth regardless of circumstances; keep clean internally and externally at all times; set at liberty the captured believer; fear no one but Allah, and kill no one whom Allah has not ordered you to kill." *The Supreme Wisdom* has been through several editions, but on the whole it is poorly written and poorly organized. Not many outside the fold have seen it.

In 1959 and 1960, the Muslims launched a number of publications in keeping with their new resolve to add a million converts to Muham-mad's following. One such publication was *The Messenger,* a magazine edited by Malcolm X and devoted to a pictorial presentation of "typical Muslim activities." Several pages were devoted to the Muslim schools and show the eager young faces of the Muslim children in their classes. Other sections show Muslim women (busy with the tasks of homemak-ing), the Muslims' various commercial enterprises, and a display of newspapers headlining news about Muslims. There is a feature story on "a typical Muslim family"—that of Supreme Captain Raymond Shar-rieff. Subsequent issues were planned but were never published.

One issue of *The Islamic News,* a tabloid-sized paper, appeared in July 1959. Its eight pages were mainly devoted to an "Exclusive Ver-batim Transcript of [Muhammad's] Historic Washington Speech." The issue is obviously the work of a professional journalist, and the speech as presented is probably not a "verbatim transcript." This address is particularly important, however, because in it Muhammad is obviously tweaking the nose of the government, which, on his previous visit to Washington during the lean years of the Movement, had humiliated him and put him in jail.

Another tabloid-sized Muslim paper, *Muhammad Speaks,* began as "a militant monthly dedicated to Justice for the Black Man." This paper was launched in May 1960 and went on sale at fifteen cents. Now published weekly and costing a quarter, it is devoted to the general news of Muslim interest, including features of special interest to women, and to the problems and interests of the black community. This is probably the best publication the Muslims have developed to date. First published at 113 Lenox Avenue, in "The Heart of Harlem," *MS*, as it is called, has a current circulation of over 600,000, making it by far the most widely read paper in the black community. Its news coverage of the "Third World" is extensive, and its editorial policy is an important instrument of Black Muslim ideology. *MS* photography is generally excellent, and its political cartoons are apt, imaginative, and powerful. It is now published in Chicago at a modern printing plant owned by the Muslims.

In July 1960, a pocket-sized magazine called *Salaam* appeared. It was essentially a picture magazine, and its first issue featured Muhammad's trip to Mecca, the University of Islam in Detroit, and the 1960 Muslim Convention in Chicago. *Salaam* was published in Philadelphia by L. Masco Young. It is now defunct.

Yet another pocket-sized Muslim magazine was *Muhammad Speaks to the Blackman.* It was a shallow publication, playing upon racial feeling in such a way as to be nauseous even to some pro-Muslims. Dan Burley, a well-known Chicago newspaperman, was listed as editor. *Salaam* expired after a few issues. Other Muslim publications continue to appear sporadically as the need for them is indicated.

In addition to these publications and such attention as they receive in the non-Muslim black press, the Muslims lose no opportunity to offer themselves to public attention through television and radio. Malcolm X became famous as the chief spokesman interpreting the Movement through these media. Malcolm's polemical adroitness, displayed during numerous radio and television debates, led an admirer to name him "the Harlem Asp." Also known as "the Big X," Malcolm tilted with newsmen, politicians, black leaders, and any others who cared to subject themselves to his barbed wit and slashing satire. After Malcolm's assassination, one of his former proteges, Minister (Louis) Farrakhan of Boston, succeeded him as minister of the Harlem Mosque, and became Muhammad's National Representative as well. Soft-spoken, patient, and gentle to the point of self-effacement, Farrakhan's low-keyed, scholarly approach is in stark contrast to the eager polemics of Malcolm X.

The Muslims have an extensive series of weekly radio lectures. In

1972 a listing of "Muhammad's Nationwide Radio Schedule" in *Muhammad Speaks* covered seventy-eight stations, each reaching cities within a hundred-mile-or-more radius of a major metropolitan area. The list keeps growing, but the Muslim leadership is looking beyond this "limited expedient." The next major enterprise the Movement hopes to undertake in its constant reaching for the masses is its own radio station—"The Voice of Islam," broadcasting from "the wilderness of North America."

In a book entitled *Message to the Blackman* (first published in 1965), Muhammad spelled out the essential doctrines of Black Islam as taught him by Fard, with his own elaborations. *Message to the Blackman* is required reading by the faithful, and it has found its way into the homes and libraries of non-Muslims. Since proper diet is a key aspect of Muslim commitment, *Message* was logically followed by a volume entitled *How to Eat to Live,* also by Muhammad. Together, these two books refine and extend the doctrines laid down in *The Supreme Wisdom.* Some of the Messenger's lectures are available on long-playing records.

Like most religious movements, the Nation of Islam has developed its own apologists. While Malcolm X was internationally known as the most effective polemicist the movement has produced, Malcolm seldom committed his convictions to paper. The same is true of Minister Farrakhan who succeeded Malcolm as public spokesman for the Nation. In a book called *This Is The One* ( *We Need Not Look For Another*), Bernard Cushmeer has marshaled an impressive array of arguments to support the basic tenets of Black Islam as taught by Elijah Muhammad. The sociologists, journalists, theologians, and others who have exprssed themselves on the movement are one by one examined for error and generally found wanting for truth as the Muslims see it. Cushmeer, Minister of the Phoenix (Arizona) Mosque, thus becomes the Black Muslim counterpart of a developing school of Christian black theologians writing about the black religious experience in America from the inside.

# 6 Tensions:
# With the Outside World

he Black Muslims are psychologically indrawn: they feel responsible only to each other and derive most of their satisfaction from their own mutual approval. Yet they are also aware of the world around them—and confidently aware that the world is aware of them.

To a great extent, the Muslims define their Movement by contrast to their most important audiences: Christian Blacks, Jews, the orthodox Moslems in America, and the hated whites. They assert their own strength and purity by castigating the weakness and depravity they claim to see among these others. The Nation (i.e., The "Nation of Islam"), is its own best evidence of success. The Black Muslims have *done* (for Blackamericans) what others are still talking about doing. They have demonstrated to their own satisfaction that black unity is possible . . . and potent. "The white devils and their Negro stooges know this and spare no effort, long or short range, to divide us." The Muslims are consciously not at all like the world from which they have drawn themselves apart.

But more is involved in the traffic between the Movement and its surrounding world than a mere exercise in self-glorification. The Muslim statements are often complex, foreshadowing ultimate goals and hopes even while they make explicit the dogma of the moment. And in the response of the black, Jewish, Moslem, and white communities to the Black Muslim challenge, it is possible to read some hints, at least, of the onrushing future as the Black Muslims envision it.

## I. THE BLACK COMMUNITY

### Individual Black Leadership

The sudden prominence of the Black Muslim Movement and its rapidly increasing appeal to the black masses have become a source of major concern for the less radical black leadership. Some of this concern may be attributed to professional jealousy, for each Muslim was once potentially a member and a supporter of some other black organization. But beneath this surface jealousy lie far more serious apprehensions—a recognition of the Muslims as a dangerous threat to the areas of harmony that have been won through years of painstaking interracial negotiation and experimentation.

Black leadership in America—politicians, intellectuals, and businessmen—has been uniformly dedicated to the principle of cooperation with the white man in any attempt to relieve the Blackamerican's condition without exacerbating it by unnecessarily increasing the level of white fear and white hostility. Muhammad's harangues on "the truth about the white man" are therefore considered dangerous and destructive, regardless of their truth or falsity. One leader who has spent a lifetime in patient negotiation with the white community declared that Muhammad's allegations are "intemperate enough to be insulting and true enough to be embarrassing."

The strategy of black leadership has characteristically been to avoid embarrassing the white man, even at the cost of some delay in attaining a desired end. This has not been just a matter of strategy. The Blackamerican has clung tenaciously to his belief in the American Creed and the Christian ideal, and he has wanted to believe in the white man's essential integrity. Indeed, he has often been much more willing to see the mote in his own eye than to argue about the beam in the eye of the white man. John Steinbeck sensed this when he wrote:

I am constantly amazed at the qualities we expect in Negroes. No race has ever offered another such high regard. We expect Negroes to be wiser than we are, more tolerant than we are, braver, more dignified than we, more self-controlled and self-disciplined. . . . We expect them to obey rules of conduct we flout, to be more courteous, more gallant, more proud, more steadfast. In a word, while maintaining that Negroes are inferior to us, by our unquestioning faith in them we prove our conviction that they are superior in many fields, even fields we are presumed to be trained and conditioned in and they are not.[1]

Not until recently has responsible black leadership seriously considered whether the Black Man might solve his problems without help. Traditional black leadership sees Blacks as an integral part of the American society, and their problems as America's problem—the problem of all the people, created by all the people—and it is considered in the interest of all the people to participate in its solution. Besides, in the complex set of relationships that constitutes a modern society, it is considered unrealistic to think of any one group solving an intergroup problem alone—except by annihilating the offending group or by a complete physical separation from them. Few black leaders have envisaged either extreme.

The Black Muslims do not repudiate either possibility. On the contrary, they already are demanding physical separation; and while they are cautious in discussing the *means* by which the white man may be annihilated, they proclaim openly that his time is up. Listen to Minister Malcolm X as he addresses a white audience at Boston University:

A child stays within the mother until the time of birth. When the time of birth arrives, the child must be separated or it will destroy the mother and itself. The mother can't carry the child after its time—the child wants to be free. It cries for a world of its own. If the mother will not give it up naturally, the doctors must forcibly take it from her, which sometimes causes her death. If she can set it free naturally, easily, so much the better; if not, it must be taken. Twenty million so-called Negroes in America number a nation within a nation, crying for freedom. We must be free. We must be born. We must be separated or cause the destruction of both.[2]

This notion—that separation is the only final solution to the race problem in this country and throughout the world—is still appalling to most Blacks, but has fascinated and converted a substantial minority as the Muslims have increased their respectability and vastly extended their range of effective contacts in the black community. Ten years ago the following portrayal of the mood of the black community was essentially accurate:

In the long struggle over racial discrimination in the United States, the American Negro has almost always behaved with fortitude and restraint.

He has pressed the battle for his rights through orderly and legal means. He has borne insult and injury without resorting to violence. He has faced the hate-mongers without adopting hatred as his creed.

His passive resistance campaign against discrimination on busses in Montgomery, Alabama, showed a moral strength and self-discipline that has few parallels in our history.[3]

Today, such a portrayal would have to be evaluated and modified.

When black leadership attempted to ignore Muhammad and his Muslims, Malcolm X complained:

Mr. Muhammad has done more to make the Black Man in America think than all the Negro teachers and leaders together.... If he were not responsible for doing this, he would not be the object of so much comment and so much concern. For a long time, they tried to cover him up—to put him under the rug. They figured he would just evaporate or go away. No matter what he did, nothing was said about it in the white press or any other press. It looked like it was an agreed method to just not say anything about him.[4]

But the Movement could not be realistically ignored. Muhammad was drawing thousands wherever he spoke, and it was inevitable that black leadership would have to take official recognition of him, because the *black people* were already listening.

The politicians were among the first to yield. In Harlem, at a two-day "Unity Feast" held in July 1958, Muhammad was greeted by Manhattan Borough President Hulan Jack, who referred to him as "our distinguished visitor from Chicago" and welcomed him on behalf of Manhattan's two million residents. City Councilman Earl Brown told the eight thousand Muslims and other nationalists present: "I have been inspired by being with you.... As I gaze upon you I recognize fully our power as a people." Judge Carson DeWitt Baker and State Senator

James Watson were also present. U.S. Congressman Adam Clayton Powell wired his regrets at being unable to attend and offered his sentiments for the success of the meeting. The celebration was also attended by the late J. A. Rogers, historian and columnist for the *Pittsburgh Courier;* Colonel Walters of the Universal Negro Improvement Association—Marcus Garvey's old organization; Noel Austin, Director of the Manhattan Elks Civil Liberties League; and other notables of political, labor, and fraternal organizations.[5]

Muslim relations with black politicians have always been more consistently cordial than their relations with any other group of black leaders, even though Muslims have yet to demonstrate their voting strength. In August 1960, for example, Martin Luther King, Jackie Robinson, Adam Clayton Powell, Thurgood Marshall, Hulan Jack, Roy Wilkins, and other black leaders were invited to attend a Harlem rally and "debate key issues" before the public. Seven thousand came to hear them, but only Hulan Jack, the Harlem politician, put in an appearance. Mr. Jack expressed great appreciation and admiration for Elijah Muhammad as "a spiritual leader whose purpose is to bring about better understanding and cooperation." Malcolm X, who hosted the meeting, called upon all black leaders to set aside "petty differences" and to "reason together and keep open minds." Some leaders had failed to appear, he explained, because they were afraid "of irking their white bosses [or] embarrassing their white liberal friends."

Minister Bernard Cushmeer of Phoenix concludes that:

The Black Man's rejective behavior of Messenger Muhammad . . . is rooted in the unnatural condition the white man put him in. . . . The Black man is waking up. As he better understands the Messenger's words and works, his understanding rises and he accepts his own. . . . These black people will wish they were practicing Muslims.[6]

An earlier Leadership Conference, held in Harlem in January 1960, was attended by an impressive array of New York politicians—this time including Adam Powell. Malcolm X commended these leaders for "at last catching up with the progressive thinking of the enlightened Negro masses." He also warned them that, while the Muslims have thus far

refrained from active political participation, they should not be discounted when political decisions are made that affect the black community.

The late United Nations Under Secretary Ralph Bunche came under
direct fire from the Black Muslims. They excoriated him as "the George
Washington of Israel," presumably because they suspected him of favor-
ing Israel in his negotiation of the Israeli-Arab dispute. This negotiation
was elsewhere hailed as a diplomatic achievement; it brought Dr.
Bunche a Nobel Prize in spite of the denunciation of the Black Nation
of Islam.[7]

Black intellectuals systematically ignored Muhammad at first. Like
most Blacks outside the lower class, they did not feel impelled to
attend his meetings and their knowledge of the Muslims came, for the
most part, through occasional conversations with persons who had
read about the Movement. In a nationwide sampling of intellectual
opinion, a surprising percentage of "informed" black intellectuals was
found to know practically nothing about the Movement,[8] even though
it had been constantly reported in the black press for several years,
featured in almost all of the national news magazines, and covered
repeatedly in the white press. Even in the cities where Muslim activities
regularly outdrew Christian and fraternal affairs and received national
coverage, the intellectuals remained oblivious of the Muslims' existence.

Some of this "ignorance" was, of course, a kind of psychological
insulation. It represented a refusal to acknowledge the existence of *any*
phenomenon that might be interpreted—by the white community, at
least—as casting doubt on the social and intellectual acceptability of
black people. At first the intellectuals considered it indicative of their
status to "know nothing of these people." They "rarely read the Negro
press," they explained, and none of their friends were aware of any
Muslim activity. After a spate of articles on the Black Muslims in *Time,
the New York Times, the Christian Science Monitor, Reader's Digest,*
and other middle-class media, the intellectuals at last admitted having
"heard something about the Movement" but tended to dismiss it as
"just another Harlem-type cult of ignorant Negroes." An article by Nat
Hentoff in *The Reporter* magazine, in August 1960, brought polite
inquiries from the black elite. It is anomolous that some Blacks first
learned of the Muslims from white people when the Muslim mosques
were invariably in their own back yards. Today, while many black intel-

lectuals talk knowingly about Malcolm X, they still don't buy Elijah Muhammad, and the Muslim Movement is still something they wish would go away.

The Muslims are ambivalent toward the intellectuals, who, they say, "have been in the white man's schools longer and have been more thoroughly brainwashed." Those few who join the sect are acclaimed as the true race leaders, who have sacrificed status to service, and great pride is taken in their "professional" or "college" training. But intellectuals are more acceptable than other Blacks to the white community, and nearly all of them spurn Muslim-type protest organizations. Such intellectuals are scored for permitting the white man to "make fools and Uncle Toms out of our educated and professional class of people with a false show of social equality."[9] The Muslims also charge the intellectuals with "giving their education back to the teachers" rather than teaching in the black schools and colleges, where they are more sorely needed.

The Muslims do not expect to make many converts among the black intellectuals, for these are held to be the "satisfied Black Men" who are least concerned with the problems confronting the majority of black people. To the intellectuals, on the other hand, the Black Muslim Movement looms as a threat—not to themselves, but to their hopes and aspirations for black people in general who commit themselves to a self-defeating goal of black separatism.

Black businessmen, like black politicians, are very much aware of the Muslims—and especially of their economic potential. They do not like Muhammad's religious and racial extremism, but they welcome his continued stress upon economic self-sufficiency and upon racial solidarity in protecting and strengthening black financial interests. Those who do business with the Muslims report them to be reliable and businesslike. The Muslims do not buy beyond their means, but they tend to buy merchandise of good quality, usually for cash.

Black businesses are usually well represented at the Muslim Bazaar and Convention. Banks, insurance companies, retail stores, small manufacturers, and service enterprises accepted Muhammad's invitation to display their wares and advertise their services as an important contribution to their advertising and merchandising efforts. However, the Muslims were not always so well appreciated. Said an executive of a black insurance company which spurned an invitation to be represented at the Muslim's annual convention in the Chicago Coliseum in 1960:

> In my opinion the "Muslim" movement or cult has not had, and will not have in the future, any appreciable appeal to American Negroes in either the Low- Middle- or Upper-social Class. . . . It is my further opinion that this movement is rendering a definite disservice to the effort being made in the realm of human relations to make democracy in its fullest sense a reality in this country, and should be resisted to the utmost by the intelligent leadership of our group, as well as the authorities vested with the responsibility of guaranteeing the security of our country against such dangerous and radical movements.

Whether he spoke for a significant number of black businessmen is doubtful from the vantage point of twelve years later, when the Muslims seem to be enjoying the general acclaim of the world of black business.

### The Black Press

The important elements of the black press have not supported Muhammad, nor have they in any way endorsed the Muslim teachings. They have, however, given impetus to the Movement by providing the medium through which it became known to the black community. In this, the press has had little choice: it exists to keep the public informed, and the Muslims were and are news.

The Muslim leadership is fully aware of the importance of the press to its interests. In the *Messenger* magazine, a Muslim publication, Editor Malcolm X devoted two full pages to an article expressing his support of the black press:

> The daily [white] press can make even the "Negro" public eat your flesh with its powerful . . . propaganda. . . . The Negro press may have its shortcomings, but when the die is cast and your "downtown" friends ready you for the dogs, there must be a NEGRO PRESS to present your case to the "Negro" public. The Negro press is our only medium for voicing the true plight of our oppressed people to the world.[10]

He gave specific endorsement to four black newspapers: the *Pittsburgh Courier,* the *Los Angeles Herald-Dispatch,* the *New Jersey Herald News*, and the *New York Amsterdam News.* Readers were encouraged to examine each of the black papers and "then support the one you find to be the most fearless, uncompromising, and outspoken in behalf of our downtrodden people."

The *Pittsburgh Courier* is one of the biggest and best known black newspapers in the country. It has a nationwide coverage, implemented through several regional editions (such as the *New York Courier*), and it was the first paper to give any significant coverage to the Black Muslim Movement. For about three years, from 1956 until the summer of 1959, it served in some ways as a spokesman for the Movement. It carried Muhammad's column, as well as news about Muslim activities, and in 1957 it presented Muhammad with the "Courier Achievement Award."

The *Courier*'s editors and columnists also came frequently to the Muslims' defense. For example, George S. Schuyler, New York editor of the *Courier* and one of the most widely read black journalists, wrote in his column, "Views and Reviews":

The recent uproar over Mr. Muhammad's movement . . . seems to me to be quite superficial. . . . There is no point in inveighing against Mr. Muhammad's followers as anti-white when the whole climate surrounding them is anti-black. . . . Mr. Muhammad may be a rogue and a charlatan, but when anybody can get tens of thousands of Negroes to practice economic solidarity, respect their women, alter their atrocious diet, give up liquor, stop crime, juvenile delinquency and adultery, he is doing more for the Negro's welfare than any current Negro leader I know.[11]

In October 1959, the *Courier* took *Time* magazine to task for "flippancy" in its treatment of the facts in an exposé of Muhammad. The *Courier* said editorially:

*Time* magazine . . . is relentless in its frenetic search for *le bon mot.* It seems frequently more interested in the good word than in the good reputation. If it can get its writers to turn a good, or bad, phrase, so long as it "clicks," *Time's* editors do not seem to be concerned. They have the same penchant for "facts" unadorned or unexplained.[1 2]

The *Courier* was complaining about *Time's* unamplified reference to Elijah Muhammad's arrest on a charge of contributing to the delinquency of a minor in 1934, and to *Time's* assertion that the Muslim leader was jailed for draft-dodging in 1941. The *Courier* editorial pointed out that the charge of "contributing to the delinquency of a minor" was brought against Muhammad for refusing to withdraw his children from the sect's parochial school and send them to public schools. With reference to Muhammad's alleged draft-dodging, the *Courier* pointed out that Muhammad was forty-five years old in 1941 and, therefore, ineligible for the draft. It did not offer the further clarification that Muhammad was jailed for exhorting his *followers* not to register for the draft.

In 1959, when ownership of the *Courier* passed to more conservative hands, Muhammad's column was discontinued, and coverage of Muslim affairs was sharply curtailed. The Messenger's column soon began to appear in another black paper, the *Los Agneles Herald-Dispatch,* which quickly became the de facto official organ of the Black Muslim Movement.

The *New York Amsterdam News* is the only other newspaper of significant circulation giving important coverage to the Muslims. The *News* displays little if any overt bias toward the Movement or against it. It gives considerable attention to Muslim affairs, particularly in New York City, where there is a large Muslim contingent; but its policy is clearly one of impartial reporting. The *News* treats the Muslims as an important and potentially powerful group in the Harlem community, but not as unusual or bizarre. (Harlem abounds in exotic cults, sects, and nationalistic organizations, and the *News* displays a certain sophistication regarding all such movements.)

Characteristically, the *News* invited an African Moslem, Isa S. Wali, to write a series of articles interpreting orthodox Islam for its readers. Against this background, it invited its readers to judge for themselves whether the Black Muslims are a bona fide Islamic sect. The paper observed:

Due to the rapid growth of the followers of Elijah Muhammad in Harlem, one of the most frequently asked questions in Harlem today is "What is Islam?"

Mr. Muhammad's followers call themselves Moslems and their religion Islam. There are those who dispute their claims and charge that they are not true Moslems and that their religion is not true Islam.

Without attempting to take any sides in the controversy, the *Amsterdam News* herewith publishes this interpretation of Islam as it was interpreted by a Moslem of Africa at the second annual conference of the American Society of African Culture.

The hope is that our readers, having been told just what Islam is, will be able themselves to determine who is not practicing it.[13]

One of the few papers which has ever been harshly critical of the Muslims is *The New Crusader,* a tabloid published in Chicago. In the autumn of 1959, when Balm L. Leavell, Jr., was editor, the *Crusader* published a series of articles "exposing" Muhammad. The paper has a limited circulation, however, even in Chicago, where it must compete with the long-established *Chicago Daily Defender.* Outside Chicago, the *Crusader* is virtually unknown.

The *Crusader* devoted several issues to its exposé[14] and claimed that, on one occasion, the Muslims bought ten thousand copies of the paper in bundles as they hit the newsstands and burned them in the streets "to curtail circulation of any unfavorable stories about their leader." The keystone of the exposé was an article quoting Talib Ahmad Dawud, a rival Moslem leader, who denied that Muhammad was a bona fide Moslem or that he would be permitted to make the pilgrimage to Mecca—a prediction that turned out to be mistaken.

It is worth noting that even this paper did not criticize Muhammad's racial attitudes, preferring to question his religion instead. Indeed, the *Crusader*'s racial views appear to parallel closely those of Muhammad and the *Herald-Dispatch.* In an editorial which appeared in the same issue with an installment of the "exposé," the *Crusader* said:

... Negroes have labored so long under the illusion that there is a WHITE SUPREMACY, that ... IT'S TIME we got some IDEA ABOUT BLACK ALSO BEING SUPREME! ... History bears out the contention that the NEGRO IS OF SUPERIOR BACK-

GROUND. . . . No, we don't go along with Rev. King on hollering down BLACK SUPREMACY . . . our leaders, INCLUDING DR. KING, persist in teaching that old time religion in which THE WHITE MAN IS ALWAYS SUPREME. . . . Most Negroes today are hungry for AGGRESSIVE LEADERSHIP. . . . They WANT AC-TION NOW, VIOLENT ACTION if the situation calls for it. That's why ELIJAH MUHAMMAD is TROUBLING THE WHITE FOLKS TODAY. . . . WE NEED BLACK SUPREMACY to get Negroes OFF THEIR KNEES in churches that preach a WHITE HEAVEN, a WHITE GOD, and a WHITE UNIVERSE.[15]

At one time it was obvious to anyone who read the *Crusader* that it was anti-Muslim, even though its principal circulation is among the classes from which the Muslim membership is drawn. The coincidence was striking. But times change, and the *Crusader* abandoned its anti-Muslim crusade. By a not-quite-so-striking coincidence, the *Crusader*'s new editor happened also to be the editor of one of Muhammad's then current pocket-sized magazines, *Muhammad Speaks to the Blackman*.

### Institutional Black Leadership

The National Association for the Advancement of Colored People is the organization upon which most Blackamericans have looked for a solution to the problem of racial subordination. In earlier generations they had relied respectively upon the church, the major political parties, and the moral consciousness of the "better class" white people. Failed each time they trusted, they now tend to rely principally upon themselves, expressing their moral and civil convictions through the NAACP.

The NAACP, in turn, has placed its chief confidence in the adequacy of the law, the competence of its own lawyers, the sense of moral responsibility in our judiciary, and the integrity of those sworn to enforce the courts' decisions. The NAACP's legal arm has won some encouraging legal decisions, which—when they have been enforced—have made the lot of the Blackamerican citizen increasingly less onerous.

But to the Blacks farthest down and hurting most, the way of the NAACP is too slow, too expensive, and too uncertain. The fact that the NAACP may have accomplished more concrete results than has religion, politics, or the appeal to moral responsibility seems inconsequential to the now generation of today. The black youth of today cannot understand why they must spend time and money again and again to have the courts secure for them privileges that all other Americans—and many resident aliens—take for granted. This is especially true of those who may lack the sophistication necessary to rationalize their status, but no longer accept it as necessary or inevitable.

The Black Muslims are just such a group. They do not trust the NAACP, partly because they do not understand either the organization or the complex of politicosocial relations that make it necessary. Yet even those Muslims who claim to understand the NAACP vigorously reject it. They reject it because white people, and "Negroes who want the white man's acceptance," are identified with it. The Muslims claim that *any* black group the white man is identified with inhibits or qualifies the black member's sense of freedom and his ability to see clearly his own interests.

At first, the leadership of the Black Muslims was not antagonistic toward the NAACP. It had courted the notion that, as soon as Blacks understood the Movement, they would all embrace it—leaders and laymen alike. The total orientation of the Black Muslim is away from the white man; and this is not merely a creedal expression but an attitude that informs his whole way of life. It is inconceivable to the Muslim that, after "learning the truth"—as taught by Muhammad—any sensible Black would prefer to retain his white associations. The Muslim leadership fully expected—and still does expect, though more patiently —that black leadership will eventually join freely in a "United Front of Black Men." Moreover, the Movement abhors all intraracial strife and will seduluously avoid it, except when it feels compelled to maintain face.

In an interview in April 1959, Muhammad praised the NAACP as doing a good job "within its limitations." The "limitations" were, of course, its interracial board and its partial dependence upon white philanthropy. Muhammad's preference is *not* to destroy interracial contacts willy-nilly wherever they exist, particularly those of a practical nature. What he wants is a "Black Council" *above* such contacts, a council that will coordinate a grand strategy looking forward to eventual independence from all contact with the white man. Presumably, as Messenger to the Lost-Found-Nation, Muhammad himself would head such a council. This idea is, needless to say, rather less than acceptable to the NAACP.

At first, the NAACP, like most other black or interracial organizations, paid no official attention to the Muslims. The NAACP itself was under fire from conservatives for "pushing too fast," and it may well have been relieved by the sudden arrival of a group which is bent on pushing very much faster, and a good deal further. During a television interview in July 1959, Roy Wilkins, Executive Secretary of the NAACP, was asked what he thought of the Muslims. He replied only that "for years the NAACP has been opposed to white extremists preaching hatred of Negro people, and we are equally opposed to Negro extremists preaching against white people simply for the sake of whiteness." The following month, however, after some excitement in the white press about "the Muslim menace," Blacks and whites alike demanded an official statement from the NAACP. A strong indictment seemed indicated, and Mr. Wilkins complied:

> The NAACP opposes and regards as dangerous any group, white or black, political or religious, that preaches hatred among men. Hatred destroys men—the haters and the hated.
>
> The so-called Moslems who teach black supremacy and hatred of all white people have gained a following only because America has been so slow in granting equal opportunities and has permitted the abuse and persecution of Negro citizens. At this very moment the Congress is shadowboxing with a milk-and-water civil rights bill. All this furnishes ammunition for the use of opportunistic leaders.
>
> The clearest rejection of the "hate-white" doctrine of these so-called Moslems is to be found in the new states of Africa where leaders recognize the need for cooperation with white nations and with their economies.
>
> Prime Minister Nkrumah of Ghana cannot build the Volta Dam with hot-air hatred from American Negro cultists.[16]

The most comprehensive statement on the Muslims issued by an NAACP official was made by Derrick Bell, Executive Secretary of the Pittsburgh Branch, in a radio address over station KDKA. Mr. Bell addressed himself principally to certain "sincere individuals" who had advised that the NAACP "must denounce the Muslims in no uncertain terms" and suggested "full-page ads in the local newspapers" for the purpose. Many concerned persons had offered money to finance such an advertisement. Others called for a condemnation of the *Pittsburgh Courier* for publishing Muhammad's column. In answer, Mr. Bell said in part:

> I question the wisdom of either of these proposals . . . not because either the NAACP or I agree with the . . . Muslims. On the contrary we could not disagree more. We are convinced that . . . racial superiority is just as wrong when preached by black men as by white men. Those who have . . . watched the NAACP's struggle for freedom . . . will not likely confuse the NAACP with the Muslims merely because there are Negroes in both groups. . . . [Further] to urge the *Courier* to discontinue a column which thousands of its readers find of interest [is not the remedy]. The Muslims would simply find another medium to disseminate the same material.[17]

Thurgood Marshall, at that time chief legal counsel for the NAACP, was less diplomatic and considerably more direct. In an address at Princeton University, Marshall denounced the Muslims as "run by a bunch of thugs organized from prisons and jails, and financed, I am sure, by Nasser or some Arab group." He called the Muslims "vicious" and a real threat to the FBI, the NAACP, and all state law-enforcement agencies.[18]

The Muslims fought back. Malcolm X referred to Marshall as a "twentieth-century Uncle Tom" and declared that Muhammad was "too busy to worry about the envious yapping of every jealous dog that is paid to bark at him." The *Los Angeles Herald-Dispatch* devoted its editorial columns to a discussion of "The Ugly American"—that is, "the American Negro who has made a career of being a good Uncle Tom." Yet the *Dispatch* offered Marshall an excuse by blaming "Zionism" for the statement he had made at Princeton:

> Marshall is a competent attorney who has consciously or unconsciously accepted Zionism as his philosophy. While speaking at Princeton University to a group of white Americans, he denounced the followers of the Islamic faith as "a bunch of thugs financed by Nasser or some Arab group." This is Zionist ideology at its ugli-

est. . . . The Zionists are the most subtle, successful, and insidious
[hate group] . . . and have injected their poison into the ugly American, the Uncle Tom.[19]

The Jews, said the *Dispatch*, have infiltrated the NAACP, whose primary function is to promote the interests of the Jews in the guise of
helping black people.

In the early thirty's, a large percentage of European Jews were
engaged in trade, living in the rear of stores, markets and generally
making their living from the Negro in the Negro community. Thus
they had an excellent opportunity to study the habits and weak-
nesses of the Negro. The depression of the 30's, through the activities of the Communist Party, allowed the Jews to further intrench
themselves into the community, to infect his thinking to the extent
that by 1940 the Negro was almost entirely dependent upon the
Jews and had accepted the thinking and ideology of the Jewish
people. In the late 30's and by the early 50's the Jews had finally
gained control of the NAACP.[20]

The NAACP has permitted itself to be sidetracked by the Jews into a
struggle for integration, but, the Muslims alleged, integration is a stratagem of the Jews "to divert the Negro from basic economic problems
by keeping him chasing butterflies," while the Jew works feverishly to
establish himself economically at the Black Man's expense. Each time
the Black Man tries to establish his own leadership, he is blocked by the
Jews, who fear a great economic loss if the Black Man takes over his
own destiny.

Our main task then . . . is to rid ourselves of this phony Jewish
leadership, to work and cooperate with all groups but as equals and
not to permit ourselves to be dominated by any of them.[21]

As if to prove their willingness to forget past differences with the
NAACP, the Muslims made a public gesture of togetherness. Wallace D.
Muhammad, a son of Elijah and minister of the Philadelphia Temple,
helped to launch an NAACP fund drive on behalf of Mrs. Daisy Bates,
NAACP regional executive, and her husband, who had lost their news-

paper and their personal fortune because of their activities in the integration crisis. Young Muhammad contributed fifty dollars with the assurance that:

> We Muslims have always admired Mrs. Daisy Bates for her strong courage in the face of great odds in the Little Rock, Arkansas situation. And since our organization, under the leadership of Mr. Elijah Muhammad is striving for the same goal as the NAACP in their fight for our people's rights in this country, we feel that Mrs. Bates is more than deserving of this small contribution. . . .[22]

This overture was a significant reversal of the behavior charged to Muslims in New York some time earlier. At a reception given in Harlem for President and Mrs. Séku Touré of the Republic of Guinea, L. Joseph Overton, president of the New York branch NAACP, was so roundly booed that he was unable to perform his scheduled function as master of ceremonies. Overton himself was quite popular with Harlem's black nationalists; his NAACP was not. The Muslims had not sponsored the reception, but they were present in force, and they were accused by their critics of starting the demonstration against the NAACP, which then became "spontaneous."

Malcolm X categorically denied this accusation. He warned that "the Negro masses are unsympathetic to any Negro leader handpicked by the white man," but he denounced this act of discourtesy as "a terrible thing." James Lawson, president of the United African Nationalist Movement, who had directed the reception, supported Malcolm's position. He insisted that the booing had not been organized. Rather, he said, it was "spontaneous and unanimous," for "the name 'NAACP' is tantamount to waving a red flag in front of a bull." The common people, Lawson said, remember the NAACP as "the enemy of Marcus Garvey and Booker T. Washington, and they did not want the mention of that group on any program honoring the African Chief of State."

Whatever the Muslims' share of responsibility for the demonstration, Mr. Overton—whom the Harlem Muslims call "one of the few NAACP leaders who knows anything at all about what the common people are thinking"—seems to have remained unperturbed. The *New York Times* later reported:

Despite his unpleasant experience at the reception for President

Touré, Mr. Overton was moved in a recent interview to praise the Temple of Islam [i.e., the Black Muslims]. Since his work for the NAACP is in Harlem, this may be an indication of the movement's strength.

"I daresay there is no group with higher moral standards," Mr. Overton commented. "Many vices have been dominated; mutual love has been cultivated."

Mr. Overton expressed confidence that his type of "grassroots leadership" would lead to a measure of understanding with Malcolm X and his followers.[23]

In return, Malcolm X admitted that "Overton is out there in the street with the rest of us. He's got some idea of what the Black Man wants— what he's thinking. It's not so with the others. Every time I've seen Roy Wilkins he's been at the Waldorf, or in the vicinity of the Waldorf. I have never seen him with black people unless they were looking for white people!"

In short, those NAACP leaders who live closest to the experiences of the Muslim class seem to have a more sympathetic understanding of the Movement. They do not condone the Muslims' extremist policies, nor do they share the Muslims' extreme antipathy for and distrust of the white man. But they can appreciate the individual Muslim's sense of futility—his awareness that he is hemmed in by powerful forces which are brutally indifferent to his sense of dignity and personal worth.

The Muslims look upon the National Urban League, like the NAACP, as "controlled by white men, for its existence is dependent upon white philanthropy." Like the NAACP, it is no more than a way station: "It is not the answer."

Because of the nature of its program, the Urban League has not been brought into direct conflict with the Movement. Some league officials, however, have expressed concern about the negative publicity they feel the Muslims have brought upon the entire black community. Former Executive Secretary Lester B. Granger conceded that the Muslims had momentarily caught the public attention, but he felt that they are only a temporary symptom of the crisis in race relations. "These racist, hate movements," he explained, "appear at intervals of crisis, spend themselves and fade into oblivion, while the truly significant improvements in the Negro's status are being made through patient cooperation of Negroes and whites, working together in the common interest."

The Urban League issued no official statement regarding the Muslims. Asked about this apparent lack of official concern, Mr. Granger explained:

> It is true that there has been expressed a great deal of interest in this variant among Negro protest expressions. However, my own feeling is that the discussion has been out of all proportion to the significance of the movement whether one gauges that significance in the relationship to the number it involves or the historical record of similar movements that have regularly occurred over a period of more than 40 years.
>
> In short, I do not believe that any good purpose is served by having an organization such as mine make an official expression of opinion in view of the many truly significant developments with which we are concerned.[24]

Not all of the Urban League's executives in the local offices across the country share Mr. Granger's detached aloofness. In Ohio, for example, Andrew G. Freeman, executive director of the Columbus Urban League, felt constrained to sound a public note of warning:

> The basic faiths with which we are familiar meet the needs of all men. Our philosophy of government is based on the belief in the brotherhood of man under God. Any teaching contrary to this principle is extremely dangerous and should be viewed with concern.[25]

Edwin C. Berry, director of the Chicago Urban League, was more emphatic, perhaps because his work brings him into more personal contact with the average ghetto Black. In an informal statement that has been widely quoted in the national press. Berry said: "A guy like this Muslim leader makes more sense than I do to the man on the street who's getting his teeth kicked out. I have a sinking feeling that Elijah Muhammad is very significant."[26]

Whitney Young, who succeeded Granger as executive director of the League, agreed with Berry. Trained as a social worker, Young's experiences in the nether world of the black ghetto equipped him to understand the Black Muslims without compromising his commitment to a quite different approach to the same constellation of problems: poverty, alienation, racism, and nonidentity. In 1968, the Los Angeles Urban League gave Elijah Muhammad a "Ghetto Award," citing "the unyielding and unrelenting efforts of the Nation of Islam to unite the black community."

The Black Muslims are emphatically opposed to passive resistance as expressed by the followers of Martin Luther King, Jr. They opposed King because he emphasized the Christian principle of loving the oppressor rather than retaliating against him. This is precisely the "slave philosophy" the Muslims have sought to escape in their repudiation of Christianity. Hence, King represents to the Muslims a capitulation to the cunning Christian strategy of the white man. "How long do you think we'd last," asked a Muslim leader, "if the white man thought we'd all bow our heads and present our necks to the axe? About long enough for him to get the axe!"

The Muslims scored King for having turned many potential freedom-fighting Negroes into "contented, docile slaves,"[27] and they repeatedly questioned his "fitness to lead American Negroes." His decision to leave Montgomery to become associate minister at his father's church in Atlanta brought a bitter denunciation from the *Los Angeles Herald-Dispatch:*

In February, the same Reverend Martin Luther King, the Darling of the South, Honey Boy of the North, is now moving his headquarters from the increasingly hostile atmosphere of Alabama to the more lucrative haven of Atlanta. Is this a retreat from the bloody racial struggle soon to erupt in Alabama? Has his philosophy developed from "turn the other cheek" to "turn and run away"?

If all of us are going to die and go to heaven as the Negro Christian ministers have been preaching, why must Reverend King flee the "portals of death" in Alabama, conveniently seeking safer reffuge among the wealthier Negroes of Atlanta? . . .

Reverend Martin Luther King could clear his conscience simply by taking a firm stand on the side of TRUTH. Tell the Negroes in America the TRUTH—that they will never get anything up in the sky after they die, nor will they ever get anything here on earth either until they are ready and willing to shed blood or die fighting for it.[28]

Dr. King did not reply to this attack; but in an earlier address before the National Bar Association, meeting in Milwaukee, he had cited the Muslims as "one of the hate groups arising in our midst which would preach a doctrine of black supremacy," a new kind of bigotry as bad as the old one of white supremacy.

The Muslims ridicule the charge that teaching the Black Man to defend his person and his dignity has anything to do with black supremacy. The Black Man is by nature peaceful and respectful, they say, but it is also the nature of a man to fight to protect himself. The so-called Negro, however, has been so psychologically paralyzed by the black preachers and their religion that he is no longer a man.

No one can react to persecution like this but the Negro, and he does it under the counseling of the Negro preacher. . . . Were it not for the Negro pastor, our people would be just like the Hungarians, we'd be fighters. . . . The Negro is a fighting man all right. He fought in Korea; he fought in Germany; he fought in the jungles of Iwo Jima. But that same Negro will come back here, and the white man will hang his mother on a tree, and he will take the Bible and say, "Forgive them Lord, for they know not what they do." This Negro preacher makes them that way. . . . Where there is a slave like that, why you have a slave-making religion.[29]

Nothing short of an eye for an eye will have a lasting impression upon the white man, for he "has never stolen an acre of land or chained a single black to be his slave without force." Hence Malcolm urged the Black Man to "be peaceful and loving. Agree with everyone, but if anyone comes to take advantage of you, do the same thing the white man does; *lay down your life!* and the Black Man will be respected all over the planet Earth."[30]

Passivity, say the Muslims, robs the Black Man of his only weapon. This is especially true in America, where the whites are morally indifferent and the Blacks are a numerical minority. One Muslim brother explained: "When the Ghanaians got ready for the British to go, they told the British to 'get out!' and the British got out. The same was true of the Belgians—and when they were a little slow, why the Congolese helped them to go. But the Ghanaians and the Congolese were at home and in the majority. When the South Africans get ready for the white man to go, why they can just all sit down, and the white man has to go or starve. It's not so here. When the white man here gets tired of your 'sitting down' or 'sitting in,' you *know* what he's going to do."

Martin Luther King was challenged by Malcolm X to "come to Harlem and prove that 'peaceful suffering' is the solution to the atrocities suffered daily by Negroes throughout America."[31] Dr. King did not respond. The Muslims then announced that they would hold a rally in Atlanta to demonstrate that Southern Blacks were "tired of suffering, peacefully or otherwise."

Elijah Muhammad chided Dr. King for accepting the Nobel prize and for denouncing any notion of black supremacy when he preached at St. Paul's Cathedral in London:

Reverend Martin Luther King, Jr., the 1964 Nobel Peace Prize winner, would have honored himself and his people if he had refused the medal. He won neither peace nor justice for his people. . . . Reverend King sharply warned in St. Paul's Cathedral that "A doctrine of black supremacy was as great a danger as one of white supremacy." . . . Of his own people he said, "We must not seek to rise from a position of disadvantage to one of advantage substituting injustice of one type for that of another."

I have never heard of any such talk coming from a leader's mouth in all of my life. If a man is NOT going to rise from a position of disadvantage why is he preaching for the passage of the Civil Rights Bill for his people? No wonder he had the privilege of going into a cathedral where no so-called Negro had ever stood in the pulpit. He is ignorant, preaching for brotherhood of white people and destruction of his own people, because brotherhood with the white people means the destruction of the black people. . . .

He said, "God is not interested in the freedom of white, black or yellow man, but in the freedom of the whole human race." Here, again the Reverend shows that he has not studied the scripture . . . This kind of talk coming from a theological college graduate is almost unbelievable. How many American so-called Negroes would like to follow a man who speaks like one who cares nothing about them?

Reverend King has made it clear that he never wants the black man to rule, because he knows it will be "just as dangerous as white supremacy." This shows that all black people should disregard any-thing that a man like that says. He disagreed that his people should ever rise from the level of a subjected people of slavery. I would like to ask the Reverend under whom he would like to live, since he condemns the ability of both for the supreme character of ruling the nations of the earth, as the white man has done and enjoyed for the last 4,000 years.

He wants to be a brother to the white man and wants the black man to be like the white man. This is continued enslavement. I am just wondering how many followers he has after his last statements.

I heard the Rev. King say on television that he wanted white people to be his brothers and not his brothers-in-law. He loves our enemies. Any black person who believes in himself should not go near or even listen to this type of teaching. It is really awful to hear a man say such things when he has been beaten and thrown into jail seeking the right to exercise the rights of a member of his own black nation.

So, in view of such statements, Rev. King is of no good among black people.[32]

The sit-ins were denounced, not for passivity, but for aggressively "going into these stores where we are neither wanted nor invited." Instead of pointlessly jeopardizing their lives, Blacks are urged to "ignore the whites and develop [their] own business as [the whites] have." Separatism, the Muslims point out, hits the white man where it hurts. The whites have begun a nationwide campaign against Muhammad as a "hate teacher" because he excludes whites from his temples "on the same basis that Negroes are excluded from white churches." This is proof that if black people want the white man's respect, they need only turn the white man's policy against him.

The sit-ins were described as being led by CORE (Committee on Racial Equality), "an organization with headquarters in New York on Park Row. . . . Its policies have been . . . supported by the usual phony Negro leadership, such as Jackie Robinson, Roy Wilkins, and Martin Luther King."[33] These leaders were accused of putting the lives of black children on the line "while they sip cocktails in the lounges of Fifth Avenue." The Muslim leaders, in contrast, do not "send our women and children into the lair of the beast. We go ourselves, but not just to sit beside him or to eat in his presence."

For the most part, Dr. King and other leaders associated with the nonviolent approach to America's racial problem either ignored the Muslims or deplored their publicly-expressed "invitation to annihilation" (as one Southern professor termed it). Those who guided the passive resistance movements felt they had nothing important to gain from answering the Muslims' charges, for they stood almost no chance of enlisting the Muslim's support. It was reasoned that no constructive communication could take place between the two groups until one or the other was ready to modify substantially its point of view. This accommodation seemed hardly likely to occur, but by the late sixties, CORE, under the leadership of Roy Innis, had become avowedly black nationalist, and black youth once committed to nonviolence as an instrument of change had become open advocates of change "by any means necessary."

## The Black Churches

At first the black churches were inclined to accept the Black Muslims as another denomination, and in at least one instance a Muslim minister is said to have belonged to a local Pastor's Alliance. The report is not incredible, for the Muslim ministers tend to be young and personable, and not much attention is paid to the theology of a church in the average American community. Further, the range of religious beliefs and affiliations among Blacks in the large cities tends to be quite wide; in the pastors' organizations, the behavior and presentability of the minister is often the chief criterion of acceptability. What a man preaches to his own church is not usually open to question, and few of his colleagues would inquire into it. A Muslim minister, therefore, would be accepted without question so long as no specific complaint was raised. And this leniency is not unusual; it is true of nearly all community organizations. It is a matter of record, for example, that a Troy, New York, Muslim was a prominent Mason and NAACP president, as well as a scoutmaster and a member of the Advisory Council of the Juvenile Court.[34]

During the period of the Movement's greatest growth (that is, from about 1955 to 1964), Muslim ministers frequently addressed Christian congregations. Although such occurrences are considerably less frequent now, they are by no means rare. One interesting recent development in invitations to the Muslim minister is a shift away from the lower-class pulpits, which once welcomed him, and toward various organizations (such as men's groups) in the upper-class churches, whose curiosity has been aroused.

Established Christian churches rarely deny newly formed congregations the use of their churches for meetings and special services. The traditional spirit of helpfulness was extended to the Muslims quite as readily as to any other religious group. After the Muslims were discovered by the national press, this practice was sharply curtailed, and it became increasingly difficult for the Muslims to obtain any accommodations in Christian churches in most cities. The following incident, reported in the *Indianapolis Times,* is a case in point:

A rally by an extremist Negro cult was cancelled yesterday when a Methodist Church locked the group out of the church sanctuary. About 50 followers of Elijah Muhammad, self-styled "messenger of Allah," milled around outside the Gorham Methodist Church, 11th and Missouri, after the church's board of trustees decided at the last minute to deny them use of the sanctuary.

The meeting was switched to Greater Zion Baptist Church, 701 N. Tremont, but then was cancelled because of the large number of police and newspaper reporters present. . . .

The Reverend G. N. Hardin, pastor of the Methodist Negro Church [*sic*], said his group decided to bar the cultists, because "the Moslems are not Christian as we see it. We do not know that what is printed [about the Moslems] is true, but it doesn't appear they are a Christian group."[3 5]

The Muslims chide the black ministers for bowing to the white man in denying the Muslims use of their sanctuaries. Why should black Christians, who themselves are not wanted in the white churches, let the white man tell them whom they may have as guests in their own sanctuaries? Yet even when the Muslims were welcomed, they often subjected their hosts to a constant and embarrassing criticism. For example:

Speaking for more than 2,000 Moslems and non-Moslems last Tuesday, Elijah Muhammad told his enthusiastic audience, "I will gladly go to prison, sacrifice my very life itself, for the freedom and rights of the 17,000,000 Negroes in America."

The spacious King Solomon's Baptist Church, 6124 14th Street [Detroit], was packed to capacity with an overflow crowd of Negro Christians and Moslems, many of whom had taken off from their jobs to see and hear the noted spiritual leader. . . .

[Said Muhammad:] "Since the Negro Church has failed to do that which we are doing, the Negro Church should be glad to join in and work with us."

He called on the Negro pastors to accept Islam and unite with the Moslems. "Let us use the Moslem Crescent, which is the sign of LIFE . . . instead of the white man's cross, which is the sign of slavery, suffering and death. Tell the white man that since he has not given the Negro Christians justice in his Christian religion, you are now going back to the Islamic religion of your foreparents . . . a religion of TRUTH, in which we get freedom, justice and equality. . . . A religion that gives us dignity, unity, and makes us FEARLESS. . . .[36]

On another occasion, in Los Angeles, three black ministers were described as having "hot-footed it out of a meeting" at which Malcolm X blamed the black clergy for "the Negro's deplorable economic condition" and charged them with helping the white man to keep the black Christian in poverty:

He said $90,000,000 is spent annually in Los Angeles in upkeeping Negro preachers and churches, while [only] $60,000,000 is spent for houses and furniture combined. . . . Malcolm X then pleaded with the Negro preachers to return to their churches and put their members' money to work "for the members" . . . building factories and supermarkets instead of [more] churches.[37]

Some churches have found themselves picketed, in effect, by pairs of quiet young Muslims who pass out literature near their doors on Sunday morning. Police in Springfield, Massachusetts, patrolled the areas around three black churches after the pastors complained of such activities,[38] and there have been similar complaints from other parts of the country.

The ministers themselves, like Christianity and the churches, have been the target of direct and vicious attacks. Muslim leaders urge the black laity to "pay no more attention to [these] black friends of the white Slavemasters [for] they have not been able to help you in all these years."[39]

> The ignorant, greedy Negro preachers . . . are the willing tools of the very ones who are responsible for our people's miserable plight. . . . [The white man] has trained these ignorant, greedy Negro preachers to parrot his religious lies to us, a pacifying religion that was skillfully designed to brainwash us and keep us in "our place."[40]

Muhammad suggests to the black clergy that they:

> *LET THE POPE OF ROME* contend with me, for you are not able to attempt to do so. You are blind to the theology of Christianity. You do not have enough knowledge of theology and scripture to contend with me.[41]

On the whole, the Christian ministers have responded with restraint. They have typically deplored the Movement's extremism and its flagrant attacks on Christianity. Yet, because of widespread segregation and other signs of racial bias within the church and throughout the Christian world, many ministers feel vulnerable. They cannot in good conscience flatly reject the Black Muslim position as a whole. Most have taken a position similar to that of The Reverend William M. James, Minister of the Metropolitan Community Methodist Church in Harlem, who repudiated black racism as unjustifiable and unavailing but pointed out that it is rooted in the persecution and the denial of common opportunities to Blackamericans. "Social disease breeds diseased leadership," he asserted, and urged those interested in eliminating Muslim-type movements to help the Black Man break out of his "ghetto encirclement."[42]

The Muslims have also exhibited some ambivalence—or at least a willingness to work with Blacks who refuse to give up their Christian faith. Even while denouncing the value of Christianity, Muhammad pleads for the cooperation of Christians and Muslims in their areas of mutual concern.

Let us lay aside, for the moment, our differences of faith and remember that we are members of the same [Black] Nation regardless of religious beliefs. Let us think of the condition of the world and of our future as a people. We can no more depend on the future of the white race, for they have no future. The time is far spent, and their sun is set.[43]

But this expediency is temporary. Muhammad's long-range goal is to win all black Christians to Islam. Some Christians are receptive, but nearly all conversions thus far have been individual. There have been almost no mass defections as far as is known.

Perhaps the only known case of a wholesale transfer of religious loyalties was that of a Baptist church in Richmond, which, after two addresses by a Muslim minister, voted to become a Muslim temple. Thereupon the minister dropped his "slave name" and became David X. It may be significant that this church was won to Muhammad during a period of extreme racial unrest, when Virginians had closed their schools rather than admit Blackamericans, and had set up segregated schools for white children in the Christian churches.

### The Black Man in the Street

In his current struggle for social dignity and a larger share in the common values of the community, the Blackamerican is generally ambivalent about means. Should he merely support his leaders, or should he take direct action on his own initiative? Increasingly he does both, for the man in the street, whether white-collar or in overalls, is generally impatient with the progress his leaders are making. Mrs. Rosa Parks, the gentle and unassuming seamstress who created the "Montgomery situation" by asserting her right to sit where she chose on a public bus, is a vivid illustration of this attitude. Mrs. Parks believed in and supported the black leadership in Montgomery; but her soul was as tired as her feet, and she could not wait any longer for deliverance at their hands.

In Memphis, some time before the public buses were desegregated, a black laborer boarded a bus in an outlying black section during the evening rush hour. Two black women who had boarded earlier were

seated midway in the bus. As the bus approached the downtown area
and more whites began to come aboard, the women were required on
two or three occasions to give up their seats and move farther back.
Finally, the black laborer could stand it no longer. Taking an old lino-
leum knife from the bag of tools he was carrying, he rushed up to
where the women were now sitting. "Ladies," he said, with tears
streaming from his face, "don't y'all move back no doggone more! If
you do, I'm going to have to hurt you. And if anybody on here tries to
*make* y'all move *just one more time,* then my life ain't worth a quarter.
We done moved back enough, and ain't none of us gon' move no
further!"[44]

When the local black leadership in Memphis could not wrest a guarantee from management that black women would be extended the same
courtesies in the downtown department stores as were white patrons,
the women began canceling their accounts of their own accord. Thereafter, those who could afford to do so did their shopping in periodic
trips to cities as far away as St. Louis and Chicago. "If I can't be 'Mrs.'
and have the use of a dinky dressing room on Main Street in Memphis,"
said one indignant black matron, "I can be 'Madame' in a State Street
salon in Chicago."

The college sit-ins were yet another illustration of the Blackamerican's ambivalence toward his established leadership—and, perhaps,
of the leadership's misjudgment of the prevailing mood in the black
community. The college students had long been among the most ardent
supporters of the relatively conservative protest organizations, such as
the NAACP. Yet the sit-ins took the NAACP by surprise, as they did
the rest of the established black leadership.

The man in the street is waiting and pushing and hoping; but he is
also looking around for alternatives. The disease of racial discrimination
has been with us longer than is reasonable in an enlightened society;
and in an atomic age, the traditional remedies make haste too slowly.
Black people want to be first class *now.* Anyone who fails to understand this has seriously misjudged the temper of the times.

Among the Blacks of the middle class, Muhammad's call for a
united front is not wholly devoid of appeal. There has been a common
notion that the black people's vulnerability has stemmed, at least in
part, from their own apparent inability to stand together to make common cause in the fight against discrimination. The superstition that

"Negroes cannot stick together, especially in a crisis," has long been accepted as a fact. The "Great Walk" at Montgomery and the sit-ins in various communities have done much to disprove this superstition and to make the average Blackamerican more receptive to proposals for group protest. Most middle-class Blacks, however, are determined to keep within the broad limits of the "democratic" and "American" tradition. They are drawn to the idea of a *united* front but not necessarily attracted to the idea of a *black* front. Similarly, the black middle class shares the increasing race-consciousness of the entire black community; but it interprets this as a unity-in-determination to resist aggression rather than anything that might be subject to an interpretation of counterracism. Blackamericans have been on the receiving end of racism as long as they have been in America, and they are sensitive to the implications of any behavior which might become a black expression of a white disposition.

Muhammad's Movement is one of rigid discipline, aimed at controlling the total behavior of the individual. This factor alone is sufficiently repulsive to dissuade the majority of the middle class from any "committed" participation, for while the middle class is highly conformist, it is oriented toward the prevailing values and taboos of the general society. The middle-class Black also refuses to identify with the Muslims, by and large, because he associates them with potential violence or because "the government is after them." (Some non-Muslims report that a visit to one of the temples has been followed by a visit from the FBI.) But above all, the middle-class black citizen is loath to add a new philosophy of racial subordination to that already imposed by the white majority. While acknowledging his hostility to the white man as both "natural" and "justified," he is not willing to give over his entire life to hatred. He is in search of freedom, not vengeance.

Nevertheless, some small businessmen and tradesmen have been forced to the conclusion that they must support a movement like Muhammad's or perish. Faced with the choice, they have joined the Movement. Muhammad has, ironically, predicted that this would happen. He has insisted that the white man will not do business with Blacks, and that integration can only weaken the black businessman's support in the black community. Only race pride, he has said, and a determination to "support your own kind" can save the black businessman from extinction.

But even among those who have joined or who favor the Movement, sympathy is generally focused not on the doctrine of racial hostility but on the issues of economic policy, race pride, and moral uplift. Such expressions as the following are not infrequent among the middle class (and they have their corollaries among the more economically and socially depressed Blacks in the slums and on the street corners):

One Chicago businessman said, "When Mr. Muhammad urges Negroes to build up solid economic holdings in the community, I agree with him 100 per cent. But I can't go along with some of his other ideas."

A Philadelphia lawyer's comment was, "He's merely trying to give the Negro the education and understanding strictly from an economic point of view, that the Jew has been getting and using for centuries. It would be a tough job, but organizing the Negro's financial intelligence into one solid buying power would be a good thing. We don't stick together and pool our capital as other groups do."

In Los Angeles, a real estate broker's comment was, "I don't know too much about the other things they want, but if they can get colored people to support colored business 100 per cent, I wouldn't be able to count all the money I'd make selling houses."

A Hartford, Conn., man said "... if ... [Negroes] want better schools, good jobs and homes they should follow the leadership of Elijah Muhammad. We need to turn to Elijah Muhammad, for he is telling the Negro to unite because unity is the key to their freedom."[45]

Finally, the chance to identify with an organization that boldly attacks social and religious conventions is for some middle-class Blacks an irresistible challenge. This is especially true of some younger Blacks who resent conformity in general, and who particularly resent the notion of conforming to a social status that implies docility and an admission of inferiority. The college students who have joined the Movement are of this class, as are many of the Muslim veterans of the armed services, who nurse their resentment of the "reward" they received for defending the nation against its enemies.

The lower-class man in the street has more immediate motivations for his attitude toward the Movement. In the crowded slums of the big cities, it is difficult to find anyone who has not heard of Muhammad and his Black Muslims. Even among those who have not joined the Movement, there is a strong admiration for the Muslim leadership and often an openly expressed identification with most of what they stand for. Typical is the statement by a Detroit youth that Mister Muhammad and his ministers are "telling the truth if they get killed for it," while the other black leaders "keep on messing around with The Man [i.e., the white man], when they know he ain't going to ever act right." In the pool halls, the barber shops, the taverns and cafes, and on the street corners, Muhammad is an inevitable topic of conversation; and more often than not, his defenders are in the majority.

To many who have despaired of ever seeing American democracy become color-blind, Muhammad represents an attractive alternative to conventional protest. The emotions of the disprivileged lie close to the surface; and the church, which managed for so long to sublimate the black resentment, finds its task increasingly difficult. Even the storefront "shouting" missions have lost much of their attraction for the man whose frustrations are choking him. The Muslims are saying bluntly many of the words he wants to hear. And the Muslims symbolize *action*.

Like their counterparts in the middle class, the Blacks furthest down are impatient with the arguments for "education and negotiation." They cannot see why people as well educated as the white man is alleged to be can't tell the difference between right and wrong. It seems to them obviously wrong that people who are not white should be treated differently from those who are, especially in a country where all are supposed to be equal under the laws of the land. They reject the half-hearted explanations about "white moderates" and "men of good will." They do not understand how "a handful of Ku Klux congressmen from Georgia and Mississippi can make the North, the East, the West, the Mid-West and all the rest of the country" conform to their style of racist practices. They are inclined to doubt the alleged good will of *any* white man, and they tend to be ready to accept Muhammad's allegation that the white man's tricknology has brainwashed the black leaders and bought them out with iced tea and worthless promises.

The followers of Marcus Garvey are represented in the Muslim temples in substantial numbers, as are the Moorish Scientists. But there are also thousands of Muslims who have had no previous contact with black nationalism. What they have had is a sustained contact with the enduring corrosion of prejudice, white hatred, and discrimination—and they are looking for a way out. Any way out.

Some potential converts in the lower class reject the Movement because of its spartan requirements. Women tend to object to the Muslim ban on cosmetics and to various other restrictions pertaining to dress. The women's liberation movement is derided in many quarters as a deceptive ploy intended to distract Blacks from vigorously pursuing their real interest, which is the liberation from racism. As a result, the women's liberation movement has had no discernible effect upon the response of black women to Islam. The requirement of strict sexual morality and the categorical prohibition of alcohol and tobacco alienate many young men for whom the Muslims' religious and racial teachings are not a formidable barrier. Those who join the Movement tend to have been so impressed with the futility of established techniques for improving their lot that they are willing to make the required adjustments in personal behavior in exchange for a new emotional outlook.

And those who do not become members may have guilt feelings because they are *not* in the Movement! In Chicago, for example, a young deliveryman was asked if he were a Muslim. "No sir," he replied, "but God knows I ought to be. I guess I just ain't got guts enough." Respectable black leadership denies that Muhammad's solution to the race problem is viable, but the lower-class man in the street is far from certain. For him it is a question of "guts," his *own* guts. He seems to take for granted that the Muslims' courage is superior to his own, and "if they take what they're doing so seriously, maybe they've got something the rest of us ought to look at. After all, it don't hurt to look."

Yet this is not the whole story. Sometimes it is easier to call oneself a coward than it is to call oneself a fool. Even in the lower class, the man in the street is loath to give up his belief that the American Creed will one day be realized, but his continuing faith has exposed him only to fresh disappointments and ridicule. In his most bitter moments, he may accuse himself of lacking the courage to give up a dream that will never come true. He has not yet capitulated. But his faith is sorely tested; and if racial oppression persists in America, the Muslims and similar movements are bound to flourish. The Muslims are confident. They have seen leaders and movements come and go. Elijah Muhammad and his program have survived and prospered. Since he has *shown* the way, then he must *be* the way. This is how the Muslims see it:

> . . . there is only one man "who is *doing* what the other leaders are talking about doing."

Almost to a man, the now dead, defunct, or potential "leaders" sat at the table of this great man at one or more times in their career and acknowledged his wisdom. These men have since basked in that wisdom, tho failing to acknowledge its source while receiving the applause of the people.

Dr. King sat at his table. Jesse Jackson sat at his table. Stokely Carmichael sat at his table, and the brood of "militants," Panthers *et al.*, Huey Newtons, Cleavers, on to the so-called leaders of "self-help," government-backed groups—all have "risen" on just a portion of his wisdom.

But all like Malcolm an arch hypocrite, who supped most often with him, who later refused to acknowledge him, eventually floundered, oft disgraced, and leave little else but rhetoric . . . behind.

But this man—The Honorable Elijah Muhammad, the Messenger of Allah—is alive and with us, and can be known and identified by his works.[46]

## II. THE JEWISH COMMUNITY

The Black Muslims deny that they have a special antipathy for Jews, and the Muslim leaders have been unable to discover a significant reservoir of hatred for Jews *as Jews* among the black rank and file. There is latent admiration for the Jewish "psychology" and for the Jew's alleged business acumen, and there is real sympathy for the Jews as a minority group who "were roasted like peanuts by the white man in Europe." On the other hand, some Muslims openly detest Jews as renegade black men and as leeches on the so-called Negro community.

Among the Muslim leaders and influential laymen, there appears to be some ambivalence about classifying the Jews as white. There is a feeling in some quarters that the Jews, as Semites, are "not quite white" and should be grouped with the Arabs as members of the Black Nation. "How can we be accused of being anti-Semitic," one Muslim minister asked, "when our Arab brothers are Semitic?" For those who accept this implication, the Jews are traitors: black men who reject their true identity, scorn their black brothers, and pass themselves off as white.

This attitude, however, is quite rare. The Muslim laity tends simply to dismiss the Jews as white, without making further distinction. "The Jew is a white man. He is accepted as a white man and that is how he wants it. He can go places we can't go." "Jews may live in ghettos, but their ghettos are in white neighborhoods, except when they are complete parasites upon the black community." Even when a Jew lives above his own store in a black ghetto, he is not really part of the black community, for he fraternizes with black men only so far as is necessary to promote his business. The Jew clings to his white identity even though he is persecuted by other white men. "The Anglo-Saxons look down on the Jew. The Jew hates the Anglo-Saxon but considers himself better than a Black Man."

The Muslims believe that certain individual behavior is determined, at least in part, by national or racial traits. For example, "the Anglo-Saxons are diplomats and statesmen; the Italians are criminals and racketeers; the stupid Irishmen are cops; the Germans are good scientists; the Jews are the brains of the white race." They are the thinkers and the writers, and they are shrewd enough to manipulate the rest of the whites—to say nothing of the so-called Negroes. "Every Jew is a born psychologist," and he uses his "psychology" to accomplish his ends. The so-called Negro begs for what he wants, or relies on the white man's Christian spirit. The white man tries to buy his way with money. "The Jew wastes neither his love nor his money: he 'psyches' his way to the top. One Jew is smarter than a roomful of 'white men.' He can spend a quarter and make a million dollars; or he can rob you blind while he's telling you a funny joke."

The Jews are believed to have a stranglehold on public opinion through their control of mass communication. They are said to own the radio and television stations, along with many magazines and newspapers. They hire gentiles to "front" for them so as not to antagonize the public; but on crucial issues, they control the thinking of the people. And they use this power to forward the Zionist cause. The late Malcolm X declared:

We make no distinction between Jews and non-Jews so long as they are all white. To do so would be to imply that we like some whites better than others. This would be discrimination, and we do not believe in discrimination. However, the Jews, with the help of Christians in America and Europe, drove our Muslim brothers [i.e., the Arabs] out of their homeland, where they had been settled for centuries, and took over the land for themselves. This every Muslim resents.

In America, the Jews sap the very life-blood of the so-called Negroes to maintain the state of Israel, its armies and its continued aggression against our brothers in the East. This every Black Man resents.

The European and American Christians helped to establish Israel in order to get rid of the Jews so that they could take over their businesses as they did the American Japanese during the war. The scheme failed, and the joke is on the white man. The American Jews aren't going anywhere. Israel is just an international poor house which is maintained by money sucked from the poor suckers in America.[47]

Muslims are especially resentful of Jews who live in the black community. "The Jew comes in and brings his family. He opens a business and hires his wife, his mother-in-law, all his brothers-in-law, and then he sends to the old country to get his father and mother, sisters and brothers—even his uncles—and he hires all of them. Meanwhile, the so-called Negroes are footing the bill, but there isn't a black face behind a single counter in the store." Soon the Jew will open another business—a laundromat, perhaps. He will then shift some of his relatives there. Still later he will open a liquor store, "because by now he's got enough money to buy off the crooks downtown." Then he follows his black customer home and buys the flat he lives in. "By that time, the Jew is providing the Black Man with his food, his clothes, his services, his home, and the whiskey he has to have to keep from hating himself. But the Jew doesn't live above the business any more. He's moved on out to the suburbs and is living in the best house black money can buy."

To the man in the black ghetto, the Jew is as highly "visible" as are the handful of Blacks who escape the ghetto and penetrate the white communities. Consequently, the negative image of the Jewish merchant is likely to be exaggerated. The Jew's presence among the Blacks—and his racial and social separation from them—make him a readily available scapegoat, an easy target for the pent-up frustrations engendered by the "place" the Blacks have been assigned by the larger society.

The Jew not only dominates the Black Man economically, the Muslims aver; he manipulates the Negro organizations as well. The NAACP, for example, is the Jews' "tiger," and from time to time they unleash it on the prejudiced Christians. But for all practical purposes, the NAACP is a *paper* tiger, since every law enforcement agency in the country is in the hands of the white man. The Jew knows this, but he keeps the so-called Negroes agitated about such nonsense as sitting beside a white man in a restaurant, or busing black children all over the countryside to be in the presence of white children that Blacks have no time to think about building factories and supermarkets and doing for themselves what they pay the Jew to do.

It is the Jew's strategy to keep the white man and the Black Man continually at each other's throats. To accomplish this, he uses the "psychology" with which Jews are inherently endowed.

"If the Jew wants the so-called Negroes to attack a white man, he circulates the rumor that the white man is prejudiced—a fact that every Negro with any sense knows to begin with." If the Jew wants to get rid of a troublesome Negro leader, the Jew does not attack him directly. Instead, he invites a *second* Negro to dinner, lets the Negro shake hands with his wife and assures the Negro that everybody is equal. "Hearing that kind of talk and being treated like that by a white man, the second Negro gets so 'hopped up' he will not only go out and organize a campaign against the Negro the Jew doesn't like, but he will kill his own mother if she gets in the way before that 'fix' he got from being invited out by the white folks wears off!" Meanwhile, the Jew sits back and enjoys the show, while remaining a "friend" to everybody.

These, then, are the prevailing attitudes the Black Muslims have adopted toward the Jews. Some of the beliefs are stereotypes held in common with the white community; some are peculiar to the black community; some are uniquely Muslim. But none of the beliefs are more virulent than those held by the Muslims about the white man in general. The Jews have not been singled out, so far, as a special target of a concentrated attack. Such an emphasis might easily occur, however, as the Black Muslims strive for a common identification with Afro-Asian Islam.

The Movement had scarcely attained wide public attention, however, before at least one United States Senator saw enough evidence of anti-Semitism in it to warrant bringing the organization to the attention of Congress. Senator Kenneth B. Keating, himself a Presbyterian, reported:

> A very disturbing development has been the emergence of a new hate group in the United States which call themselves "Moslems." [Their] leader preaches a cult of racism for Negroes and extreme anti-Semitism.[48]

Surprisingly, Mr. Keating saw the Muslims as reflecting "a new trend in Moscow," rather than domestic competitions or the machinations of international Islam. He emphasized that "the name adopted by the fanatical organization" insulted the members of the Moslem faith; and he was careful to point out that orthodox Moslems have "absolutely no relationship to this group," whereas "it obviously serves the Communist interests to promote dissensions among Negroes in this country and to incite hatred against Americans of Jewish faith."

The Jews, for their part, have begun to give official attention to the Muslim movement. They have always been sensitive to its existence, but so long as the Muslims remained a local sect without the official recognition of international Islam, the American Jew saw no reason to be concerned. Black sects and cults abound, and while they are often given to much sound and fury, they have seldom been a real threat to any other minority. On the other hand, the American Jews are also sensitive to the pressures of international Islam on the national state of Israel, and of the attempts of some segments of international Islam to enlist anti-Jewish support wherever it may be found.

The decade of the sixties saw some erosion of Black-Jewish relations without reference to the Muslims. In New York City, where both the Jewish and black populations are probably larger than in any other city in the world, a lengthening series of abrasive incidents continue to escalate tensions to the dismay of black and Jewish leaders alike. Issues ranging from "community control" of schools (in black neighborhoods—frequently involving large numbers of Jewish teachers) to clashes between Blacks and the militant Jewish Defense League headline the newspapers with increasing frequency. Jewish support of black civil rights activities has decreased sharply, and the willingness of Blacks to go it alone has bewildered and angered some Jews whose support in times past was sought and welcomed by black leaders (many of whom are now without portfolio). Some Blacks in turn feel that the civil rights cause has been abandoned by the Jews because they no longer need it—having gained their own liberation on the backs of Blacks. The decline of American anti-Semitism has opened new doors for Jews, many of which remain closed to Blacks. As a result, Blacks often tend to see Jews as identifying with "whites" in important ways not noticed before. The following observation heard at a social gathering of middle-class Blacks is illustrative:

> I'll tell you, the only difference between a Jiberal [Jewish liberal] and a Whiberal [white liberal] is what day they go to church. Both the Jib and the Whib are quick to get in the way with a whole lot of tea and sympathy when they see the Black Man roll up his sleeves and get ready to really go to work on the problem. Put them in a bag and shake 'em up, and the one that drops out first is your worst friend.

Against this background it would not be surprising if the Muslims, or the Muslim constituency, whose contact with Jewish merchants and landlords in the black ghetto is fairly constant, did not echo in exaggerated form the increased rumblings about Jews heard elsewhere in the black community. As a matter of fact, the Muslims have not attacked the Jews, but they have attacked Zionism with regularity in their official organ, *Muhammad Speaks.* The vigor and the persistence of the attacks prompted the American Jewish Committee to devote a feature article to the matter in the AJC's newsletter, *Currents:*

> Only one [black, extremist] movement remains consequential— strong, cohesive, influential. And it is *a movement that encompasses a significant strain of anti-Semitism.* These facts, including its power and potential in the black community, have made this movement potentially a greater menace to Jews today than when it first came to public attention a decade ago. . . .
> *Jews have a special reason for concern* since the Muslims' publication indulges in overt anti-Semitism and displays a pathological hatred for Israel. . . . Since it is reasonable to suppose that the level of sophistication of the Black Muslim readers about Middle East

affairs is not very high, and since the overwhelming majority have not visited Israel, the inflammatory anti-Israel material is easily translated by the reader into *hatred of American Jews,* with whom Black Muslims undoubtedly do have frequent contact.[49]

The Muslim readers may be somewhat more sophisticated about the Middle East than the *Currents* writer suspects. At least they are informed, although much may be wanting in terms of balance and perspective, the bias of a house organ being what it is. The Muslim information comes principally from "Middle East Report," a widely read column in *Muhammad Speaks* written by Ali Baghdadi, former president of the Organization of Arab Students. Other information comes from the ministers themselves. Since the Middle East is considered Arab, i.e., Muslim, the Black Muslim interest is, from their perspective, not only legitimate, but critical. Here is a typically pro-Arab, anti-Israeli item from *Muhammad Speaks:*

The Arab people are faced with a pattern of Israeli aggression, occupation of land, exiling of Arab inhabitants, annexation of Arab territories, recognition of a fait accompli and then more US arms and more Israeli preparation for new aggression.

Washington's unlimited support of Israeli militarism and expansionism is not motivated by the desire to guarantee the Jews right to live, but to preserve and expand the exploitation of the entire Arab world—which cannot be achieved except by bringing the Arabs to their knees.

The Arabs refuse to surrender. The honor and dignity of people have priority over hunger and pain. Moreover, there is no pain as intolerable to a people as the pain emanating from an attack on their national existence.[50]

The Muslims have made a cause célèbre of Israel's treatment of Black Jews, and they are particularly hostile over the resettlement of Soviet Jews in Israel. These issues are frequently linked in the Muslims' anti-Zionist posture:

The Zionists don't just come out and say this, of course. They say they are "saving" the few Soviet Jews who come to Israel (although the Jews trying to leave Israel and return to the USSR or emigrate elsewhere risk arrest to do so), and the welcomed Soviet Jews do not have to have a "visible means of support." But when it come to Black Jews, racist Israelis brings out the Jim Crow laws they learned from Hitler and the southern US militarists.

When will the Black praisers of Israel's government look into the treatment of Blacks by Zionists?[51]

And . . .

THE VALUE of a Soviet Jewish family willing to take part in the Zionist publicity campaign on behalf of US economic interests is $35,000, said Sen. Edward Muskie recently. The Maine Democrat supported a suggestion that US taxpayers' money be used to meet this cost to shift more white Jews who oppose socialism to Israel where they will be in position to participate in a civil war against the majority Black Jews and neighboring Arabs who oppose Zionism.

Black citizens in the U.S. immediately denounced Muskie's callous racism, noting that he is making no such suggestion that U.S. Blacks be compensated for encuring [sic] oppression far worse than any Soviet Jew has experienced. Muskie won "fame" by saying the US was so racist that a Black man could not win a national election. But in the Soviet Union many Jews hold national and local political offices. Obviously, while pretending to be motivated by "democratic principles" and "humanitarian sympathy," the hypocritical politician is interested only in the campaign contributions which rich US Zionists can add to his headquarters—so much so that he would take the tax dollars of US Blacks, whom he admits are oppressed, and give them to families of citizens of another country.[52]

### III. ORTHODOX ISLAM IN AMERICA

The Black Muslims are not generally accepted by the orthodox Moslem groups in America. Race is probably not a major factor in this rejection, although there is a marked clannishness among American Moslems of European descent. Some of the earliest Moslem converts in America were black followers of Soufi Abdul-Hamid, a Blackamerican who embraced Islam during his travels in Asia,[53] and black orthodox

Moslems remain scattered about the country in small numbers, occasionally augmented by the conversion of black celebrities such as Imamu Amiri Baraka (Leroi Jones), and Abdul Jabbar (Lew Alcindor). The rejection of the Black Muslims is more likely traceable to Muhammad's extreme racial views, his emphatic militancy and his unhistoric teachings about the Black Nation. American Moslems do not wish to be identified with such doctrines.

The Black Muslims, in return, assert that whatever the white man touches, he taints. Just as the so-called Negroes, in their attempts to appropriate the white man's culture, have been corrupted by its disvalues, so the American Moslems have suffered the corrosive influences of white, Western Christianity. In their yearning to gain the white man's approval, they sometimes behave suspiciously like the blue-eyed devils themselves. "No Muslim will reject another Muslim," Malcolm X argued, "except where the devils have made him forget who he is." The American Moslems who join the white man in denouncing the Black Muslims are little better than the so-called Negroes who have been "Tom-ing" for generations. When they finally see the Movement through their own *Muslim* eyes, rather than through the distorted lenses of the white Christians, they will rally to Muhammad and recognize him as the true Messenger of Allah Himself.

The Federation of Islamic Associations is the official Moslem organization in the United States and Canada. However,

> . . . the Negro society in Chicago led by Elijah Muhammad is not affiliated and it is not recognized as truly Moslem. Although he conducts the largest Arabic school in the United States, and claims to use the Qur'an as the basis for his teachings, the Federation officers . . . have remained suspicious of him.[54]

Some Moslem leaders, such as Jamil Diab of Chicago, have issued statements dissociating themselves and their followers from the Black Muslims. Diab denounced the Muslims as "a cult totally lacking in the requisites which constitute any Moslem Group." He asserted that they have "penetrated into the Afro-American society . . . [where] they propagate their views in the name of Islam. They start controversies everywhere . . . [and carry on] propaganda in an aggressive manner." Because of them, "an insidious stigma" has become attached to *all* Islamic societies in America.

Muhammad smiles mysteriously when Shaikh Diab's criticisms are laid before him, for it is rumored that the Shaikh (who is a Palestinian Arab) was once a close adviser to the Messenger and that he taught Arabic for several years at the University of Islam in Chicago. Muhammad and Diab are said to have split over questions of ritual. The Shaikh apparently sought to form the Muslims into an orthodox Moslem organization, but practically none of the rank and file followed his lead.

Another challenger to Muhammad's religious authenticity and to his leadership of Americans in the Islamic movement is Talib Ahmad Dawud, bearded leader of the Muslim Brotherhood, USA. Dawud, who was converted by Gulam Yaslum, an Ahmadiyya missionary from India, has described Muhammad as "plain Elijah Poole of Sandersville, Georgia," and "no Muslim." In an abortive bid for the Black Muslim leadership, Dawud lent his name to a series of articles in a Chicago newspaper aimed at exposing Muhammad and discrediting him with his followers. Mr. Dawud, who had just returned from his pilgrimage to Mecca, based his arguments against Muhammad's authenticity primarily upon an assertion that the Hajj Committee, which rules on the acceptability of Moslem pilgrims, would not admit the self-styled Messenger to the Holy City. Muhammad was, in fact, received in Mecca a few weeks later, and Dawud was badly trounced.

Actually, it never seemed likely that the Imam would make any serious inroads on the Black Muslim membership. His own brotherhood has only a few hundred members, many of whom are popular entertainers or musicians—Dawud's wife is jazz singer Dakota Staton—and they seem to have none of the fanatical devotion to their leader that the Muslims show for Muhammad. Nor does Dawud enjoy unqualified recognition as a leader in the American Moslem community.

Most of the authentic Moslem groups in this country have stood back from the fray, and their aloofness has strengthened rather than weakened the strategy of the Black Muslim leaders. Left to his own devices, Muhammad is able to exert a kind of papal absolutism in the direction and development of his Movement. At the same time, he has been able to cultivate the good will and respect of a significant corps of informal representatives of Afro-Asian Islam. His temples are often visited by Moslem students studying in America, some of whom address his followers or participate in the temple affairs.

Muhammad was outraged because "the Washington orthodox Muslims call us a 'cult.' This is an absolute insult to us to be called a 'cult.'" The motive for such slander, the Messenger believes, is "for the sake of being accepted by the [white] enemy." But Muhammad predicts that "The spooky-believing Orthodox Muslims [who] try to make mock of my God and of me as his Messenger . . . will come to a naught and they will be confounded and ashamed of themselves." As for being called "Black Muslims," Muhammad sets that matter at rest with: "Sure we are Black Muslims! . . . We were black in the very beginning of the Creation of the Father, who was Black. Black is what we prefer to be called."[5 5]

In Harlem, an organization called Asian-African Drums serves as an important liaison between the Black Muslims and various Moslem nationals from Asia and Africa, particularly Arab nationals. The Muslims do no proselytizing at the Drums meetings, which are kept on the level of friendly contact. The Drums organization is headed by Abdul Basit Naeem, a Pakistani Moslem, who has served as Muhammad's chief apologist and interpreter to the world of orthodox Islam. To Mr. Naeem, Muhammad is "the humblest of all important black men alive . . . extremely gentle, very courteous and kind . . . [and] the core of Mr. Elijah Muhammad's teachings is, of course, the faith of Islam. . . . The book of Mr. Elijah Muhammad is the book of ALL Muslims, known as the Holy Qur'an." Further, "his work and teachings are not entirely unknown to other Moslems . . . Including the beloved president of the United Arab Republic, Gamal Abdel Nasser."[5 6]

As for the late President Nasser, Muhammad met him while on a trip to the Middle East in 1959. Apparently they got on well together, for Muhammad reported that Nasser "wanted me to teach in Africa. . . . He offered me a home there in Cairo, Egypt—a 75 room palace." Muhammad declined the offer because "Allah would not approve my going out of the United States to teach anyone until this mentally dead black people in America had been given the knowledge of self and kind." On the occasion of Mr. Nasser's death in 1970, Muhammad wrote in *Muhammad Speaks:* "We in the Nation of Islam have lost a great friend in the death of President Nasser, but Allah is the Best Knower."

Not all the contacts with extranational Moslems in America have been through Black Muslim-sponsored organizations. The Black Muslims have participated in various Moslem affairs held on the campuses of some American universities, such as the celebration of Pakistan Independence Day at the University of Southern California,[57] and they have been represented at conferences concerned with the interests of various Moslem states. At one such conference, held in Hollywood and sponsored by Dr. Mohammad T. Mehdi of the Arab Information Center in San Francisco, Malcolm X boldly demanded attention for the Black Muslims as a potential power in the sphere of international politics. "The Arabs, as a colored people," he said, "should and must make more effort to reach the millions of colored people in America who are related to the Arabs by blood. These millions of colored peoples would be completely in sympathy with the Arab cause!"[58]

### IV. WHITE AMERICA

One might expect—from the Muslims' diatribes against the white man and from their commitment to retaliation—that there would be constant open conflict between the Muslims and the white community. But few open battles have been joined thus far. The Black Muslims do not pretend to love the white man, but they avoid overt antagonism. They shun the white community entirely, except for requisites of work or business, and they do not seek the white man's social acceptance. Muslim women particularly are forbidden contact with either sex of the white race, on the theory that "no white man has honorable intentions toward any black woman" and that white women are "immoral by nature." The white women are said to corrupt the minds of the black women, who then try to imitate them by "displaying their bodies, neglecting their children, and abandoning their men."

In his communication with the white man, the Muslim tends to be both polite and direct, a technique which helps to avoid tension and misunderstanding. Speaking to a white group, Malcolm X declared:

I don't want you to think I'm being disrespectful to you as white people. I am being frank, and I think a frank statement will give you a better insight into the mind of the Black Man than statements you get from people who call themselves "Negroes," and who usually tell you what they want you to hear, . . . [in the interest of creating] a better possibility of getting some of the crumbs you may let fall from your table. Well, I am not looking for crumbs, so I am not trying to disillusion you. . . . Diplomacy fools people. Diplomacy misleads people. It is better to be frank. . . .

The white community is constantly assured that the Muslims are not anti-white simply "because they tell you what they think, nor anti-American because they say that America made our fathers slaves and refuses to give us civil rights." Malcolm assured the white man that "you can go anywhere among us and receive more courtesy and real respect than you can among the so-called Negro leaders who lick your hand for crumbs." But the white man must wake up, for "the Negro you used to know is dead."

According to Malcolm X, much of the white man's ignorance of the Black Man's true nature "results from his habit of picking Negro leaders who, since their jobs depend upon his pleasure, only report to him what will make him happy. But these leaders don't have things under control. And they can't control this generation with anything less than freedom and justice." The white man's educational system also contributes to his unrealistic view of things.

The educational system . . . is designed to make you think you are God. . . . There is no one else like you and everyone else is below you. . . . You can't blame the American [man in the street] for looking down on the Black Man when every day he is brainwashed by the movies, the television, radio and the newspapers. . . . He is taught in school that he is the best, and that anyone not as white as you cannot be on your level.[59]

The white man is urged to treat the Black Man with respect and to provide an opportunity for him to learn "something about himself." Only then can there be any hope of peace between the races. When the Black Man learns the truth about himself, he will not seek integration with the white man; he will be proud to associate with his own kind. When this happens, "the white man will no longer have to worry about the Negro becoming his brother-in-law," and each race will respect the other for wanting to maintain racial purity. As things are now, the so-called Negro has not been educated: he has been trained.

He is like a dog—a watchdog. You don't give him credit for intelligence, you give him credit for being well-trained. You sic him on the Japanese and tell him to bite them, and he will run out and bite the Japanese. You tell him to bite, and he will bite the Germans, the Koreans. He will bite anyone you say bite. Now you don't give him any credit for having done a good job. You give yourself credit for having trained him so well. Now when he comes back from biting the Germans and the Japanese, you can hang his mother on a tree and have his wife before his eyes and he will stand there whimpering with his knees knocking and his tail between his legs. Why? Because he's waiting for you to say "sic 'em!" That's what he's been trained to do.[60]

The white men in America are like diners at a banquet table. The Black Man is there, too, but the white men pass the dishes back and forth in front of him without ever letting him be served. The Black Man is not a diner; he is simply at the table looking on. The white men think he should be satisfied with being present: "To be in the presence of so many fine people who are enjoying themselves at such a sumptuous feast—you'd think he would be grateful." But the Black Man has got knots in his stomach because he is hungry; and since he helped to kill the game, he thinks it's his right to eat. Now.

In the same way, the white man tries to pacify the Black by telling him that he is a citizen. But the Black Man is waking up to that. He has learned that he is a full-fledged citizen in wartime and at taxtime, but at no other time.

They tell us that we are all citizens, that we were born in this country. Well, a cat can have kittens in an oven but that doesn't make them biscuits! The Black Man in America can never be called an American until he is enjoying what America is offering to everybody else. . . . Twenty million black people here in America today are called "second-class" citizens. We don't accept that. You are either a citizen or you are not a citizen. No country has citizenship by degrees.[61]

In the summer of 1960, Muhammad broke precedent and allowed whites to attend some of his public rallies. Until then, no whites had been admitted to any group addressed by the Messenger; and whites are still barred from the temples themselves. The sudden change in policy was partly inspired by criticism which likened the "crepe-black" Muslim organization to the "lily-white" white citizens councils. But it was equally inspired by Muhammad's certainty of mass support from the black people of Chicago and Harlem, and his desire to demonstrate his strength to any whites who cared to come.

In Harlem, where one of the "open" rallies was held, Malcolm X announced that "because of the grave race crisis that faces the Western world [and] to which white America is trying to blind itself, these white people need someone to tell them what time it is." In the audience of seven thousand people was a sprinkling of whites, scattered throughout the hall. Some of these whites joined in the Muslim prayers, facing east with their palms upraised, and some even applauded parts of Muhammad's address. Most, however, simply sat and took notes or stared in unbelief.

While the white man in the street has not commented, the Movement has often excited his attention. On learning of its existence (but almost never with any detailed knowledge), some individuals and groups have regarded it with a degree of approval. A white woman in Boston applauded Malcolm X's extended interview on radio station WMEX and opined that "this Movement will do more for the Negro and the whole country than anything the Negroes have tried so far." A well-known Texas millionaire, perhaps not unsympathetic to Muhammad's advocacy of racial separation, is alleged to have shown his approval of the Movement by an outright gift of several thousand dollars. But most white people who learn of the Movement tend to consider it a preternaturally extreme and dangerous social aberration. They are anxious to be reassured that it "has reached its peak" and that "most Negroes do not really feel like that."

The Movement has caught the attention of researchers in colleges and universities across the country. Professors and graduate students in such widely separated schools as Harvard, Radcliffe, Union Theological Seminary, and the Universities of Chicago, Missouri, and Michigan are studying the Black Muslims. Interest in the Black Muslims in French-speaking Canada (where the issue of national separation has escalated) is strong. At least one thesis for the Master's degree has been written on the Muslims at the Sorbonne in Paris (1970), and a doctoral dissertation on the Muslims (researched in America), was approved by the Sorbonne in the spring of 1972. Law enforcement agencies and their libraries in many cities across the country are amassing data on the Movement.

The tendency in the white-controlled mass media was at first to ignore the Movement, but its importance in the current racial crisis has warmed the microphones and loosened the typewriter keys. Apparently these media now feel that the people have a right to know about the Muslims. Since 1959, extensive coverage has been given the Muslims in *Time,* the *New York Times,* the *Christian Science Monitor, Reader's Digest,* the *Reporter, U.S. News and World Report, Chicago's American, Providence Bulletin,* the *Denver Post, Chicago Sun-Times, Springfield* (Massachusetts) *Daily News, Columbus* (Ohio) *Dispatch, New York Post,* the *Detroit Free Press,* the *Boston Herald,* the *Minneapolis Tribune,* the *Boston Globe,* and many other newspapers and periodicals.

What do they say, the writers in these "white" media, which mold opinion for millions of Americans? What is their image of the Black Muslims? Most of the news stories are essentially descriptive; almost all turn hopefully to the established black leadership for interpretation of the Movement. However, some editorial comment has appeared.

*Time* refers to Elijah Muhammad as a "scowling, incendiary speaker . . . pouring out his scorn upon all 'white devils,' 'satisfied black men,' the 'poison' Bible, Christianity's 'slavemaster doctrine,' and America's 'white for white' justice." *Time* considers Muhammad to be a "purveyor of . . . cold black hatred . . . calmly feeding the rankling frustration of urban Negroes." The Muslim leader is held to be "well beyond the run-of-the-street crackpot Negro nationalist groups . . . [and] of rising concern to respectable Negro civic leaders, to the [NAACP], to police departments in half a dozen cities, and to the FBI."[62]

The *Christian Science Monitor* is more positive in its views. While finding that "Mr. Muhammad's counsel is not entirely free of animosity," it suggests that out of Muhammad's guidance "appears to have come an environment which . . . has made possible a degree of middle-class respectability for many Negroes whose lives before had been crude at best." Yet the *Monitor* recognizes the Black Muslims as "one of the most controversial and curious organizations of Negroes"[63] and generously estimates that the Movement has gathered "some 200,000 of the 20,000,000 non-whites into its fold in the last three years."[64]

"It was inevitable," says the *Denver Post* "that some Negroes would prove unable to keep their heads as the struggle [over racial discrimination] continued." And it warns that "the excesses of a Negro hate group can poison the whole integration movement in the United States and jeopardize the progress that has already been made."[65] The *Providence Bulletin* observes that "thousands of Negroes are turning their backs on Christianity and embracing a highly nationalistic religion that takes Islam for its spiritual basis." The *Bulletin* believes that "the Movement has weight" and that "Muhammad cannot be laughed at as Father Divine has been. . . . The Black Muslim Movement is a force to take seriously, . . . [for] the Messenger isn't just a-whistling 'Dixie.' "[66]

In Boston, the *Herald* deplores Muhammad's "black supremacy" doctrines and declares them to be "as disgraceful and inflammatory as those of the Ku Klux Klan." It points out that "on a Harlem street corner where a member of the Temple harangues a group it is wise for a white man to pass by quickly"—a circumstance which is, "of course, deplored by the best Negro civic leaders."[67] The *Detroit Free Press* asks, "Is the [Muslim] cult dangerous?" and then assures its readers that "Detroit police keep an eye on it. State Police routinely pick up lists of students attending the University of Islam. The FBI watches."[68]

On September 3, 1959, Bill Stout of CBS-TV in Los Angeles reported that "the Negro group called Moslems, a religious sect dedicated to black supremacy and the destruction of the white race," had mushroomed from 300 members to "more than 3,000" in Los Angeles in six months. He quoted "a Los Angeles leader of the Moslem group [as saying] at a recent meeting, 'No torture of the whites—just annihilation.' " The TV newscaster called the Los Angeles temple "the biggest in the country," and he marveled that there had been "no public notice of the Moslem sect in this area." What Mr. Stout probably did not know is that in Los Angeles, as in many other cities, there is (or was) a tacit agreement between law enforcement officials and the major news media to bar publicity about the Movement. Without the aid of the press, it was hoped, the movement would soon wither.

That hope persists, and *The Reporter* magazine found it "difficult to see how a militant movement like the Temples of Islam can attract a wide following." It quoted with apparent finality the sentiments of a Negro integration leader who told that magazine, "I don't think they'll get much stronger," but who then immediately asserted that "We

[Blacks] have a right to our crackpots as you do to yours." *The Reporter* predicted that "Malcolm X may yet be an executive in the Urban League, but Elijah Muhammad is more likely to end as Marcus Garvey did—with little left but pictures of himself addressing huge crowds years before."[69] Pulitzer Prizewinner Harry Ashmore, writing in the *Boston Globe*, predicted that the Muslims "are not themselves going anywhere. But as long as they are around and talking it is a reasonable assumption that the great mass of American Negro people are not going to be content to stand still."[70]

A dozen years after the Muslims were uncovered by the white press, the Movement had not "withered," although ironically, many of the journals which were vigorous in 1959, had. Malcolm X was dead, and the possibility of a mutual embrace with the Urban League was, in consequence, mooted. Whether the Muslims were "themselves going anywhere" was still being debated, but the evidence that black people were "not going to be content to stand still" was everywhere apparent.

In his detailed apologetic on Elijah Muhammad (*This Is The One*), Bernard Cushmeer reviews the attitude of the white news media from the perspective of a practicing Muslim:

> Back in 1959, the white press, as if on signal, launched a furious attack on Messenger Muhammad and the Nation of Islam, following the dishonest portrayal of us entitled "The Hate that Hate Produced." Through such publications as "Time," "U.S. News and World Report," "Newsweek," "The Reporter," "Esquire," "Confidential," "True," "Saga," and a host of other magazines and newspapers, white America spewed forth a flood of articles, both superficial, spurious and poisonous in nature. A few among them did a creditable job, as far as they went. But the bulk of what was written was insidious and rotten to the core. But it did not hurt us.
> . . . . . . . . . . . . . . . . . . . . . . . . . . . . . . . . . . . . . . . . . . . . . .
> The white people—newscasters, commentators, etc.—have lied in concert. The television newsmen were not, and are not, above editing their films in such manner as to actually tell lies to their viewers. They conspired to deceive the public regarding Messenger Muhammad. . . .
> Messenger Muhammad and his followers have been lied on by

whites for 40 years. Whites lie on us and then react to their lies as though the lies are true, by charging us with being guilty of their lies. They continue their persecution in various ways, such as through their brute police force. Their "peace" officers have desecrated our places of worship in Los Angeles, California; Monroe, Louisiana; and Newark, New Jersey. This has led to the death of some of the Messenger's followers. So to some degree, everyone of you who have slandered and libeled Messenger Muhammad and his followers, are responsible for and accountable to Allah for what you have done.[71]

White America seems to have a marked ambivalence regarding the Muslims' separatist ideologies. In Alabama, for example, where involuntary racial separation has been a way of life for centuries, when the Muslims attempted peacefully to farm a piece of land they had bought near Pell City, the *New York Times* reported that "2,300 grim faced white persons crowded into the gymnasium of a high school . . . to vow that Black Muslims will not be allowed to keep the land they have bought to farm." The crowd represented 10 per cent of the white population of St. Clair County. In the emotionally charged meeting, a white Baptist minister announced his readiness "to lay down my life for the cause." Sixty-three of the Muslims' prize dairy cattle were either shot or poisoned. There were rumors that the Muslims were recruiting a thousand men to send to Alabama to protect their property there; the Ku Klux Klan began leasing farmland surrounding the Muslim holdings, and local Blacks were arrested and jailed on suspicion of being "un-registered Muslims," in violation of an Alabama law requiring Muslims to register with the police if they remain in the state for more than five days.

Muslim clashes with the police in many large cities, and their frequent involvement in prison agitations, contribute to the aura of menace with which many white Americans view the movement. Undoubtedly, white harassment, through the police or other agencies, contributes to the self-fulfillment of somber prophecy, but the Muslim ideology itself offers little comfort to whites who may be looking for reassurance. The Armageddon must still be faced. Bernard Cushmeer writes:

We are faced with the final phase of the war of Armageddon. This war has already started. . . .

The outcome of the scrimmages between white and Black in this country are not usually presented in a way that indicates the true nature of the conflict. However, . . . it is clear that the explosiveness of our day must be seen in terms that include Armageddon. If this is so, it manifests the faultiness of every analysis of the "race" problem except that given by Messenger Elijah Muhammad. If Armageddon has started, this means that the issue is not how to get white and Black together. If Armageddon has begun it is not merely the issue of improving the Black man's condition while he remains under white rule. If Armageddon has begun, the question is not how to make integration or civil rights a reality. . . . For the only place where white and Black will be together in a few more weeks is in the Lake of Fire![72]

Freedom is what the Muslims say they want from the white man. "Nonwhite people all over the earth," says Cushmeer, "include in their definition of freedom the freedom from the white man's corrupting guidance." But "the white man is not in position to decide anymore for our future. He doesn't have a future."[73]

# 7 Tensions: Inside the Movement

HAIL TO ELIJAH MUHAMMAD

I

Who is The One the scriptures meant?
                  Elijah Muhammad!
Who is The One Allah has sent?
                  Elijah Muhammad!
Who leads where others fear to tread
Who raised us from the living dead
Who put a crown upon our head?
                  Elijah Muhammad!

II

The Planet Earth is our design
                  Elijah Muhammad!
The Star and Crescent is our sign
                  Elijah Muhammad!
Long may our great Black Nation rise
Long may we praise him to the skies
The truth he taught us never dies!
                  Elijah Muhammad!

III

Our Messenger—without a fault
                  Elijah Muhammad!
Through him we live the life we ought
                  Elijah Muhammad!
He raised us up from low degree

He gave us strength through unity
May Allah bless him graciously!
                    Elijah Muhammad!


                    IV


All hail the Crescent and the Star!
                    Elijah Muhammad!
All praise is due our God, Allah!
                    Elijah Muhammad!
He sent us One who made us free
Peace, Justice, and Equality—
One Aim, One God, One Destiny!
                    Elijah Muhammad!
                    *A Believer**


The characteristic demeanor of the Muslims presents a monolithic face to the outside world. They are on the upswing, rapidly gaining power, and their resultant excitement and self-confidence breed a natural sense of unity. They feel beset by a powerful enemy—a threat which impels them to minimize internal conflicts and pull together. And they are genuinely unified in their dedication to Elijah Muhammad, the Messenger, whose force of personality is a strong deterrent to divisiveness and internal bickering.

Yet some tensions are perceptible within the Movement, and these seem likely to increase with time. There are problems both of definition and of control. As the Movement solidifies, it will have to make more and more explicit its relationship to both the white American and the international Third World. For the moment, the Muslim leaders are purposefully vague on these points. When they must declare themselves, the present quiet disagreements within the leadership will most likely become sharp and bitter factionalism. And as the Movement grows in size and influence, it will become more and more a tempting prize for those who covet power. Rivalries within the leadership already exist,

---

*From an anonymous letter to the author.

and there has been some violence. These rivalries may erupt quickly when Muhammad dies; or they may not wait so long.

The future of the Movement—and of the world on which it has an impact—will be greatly affected by these internal tensions. They are, of course, extremely difficult to pin down precisely; they are the Movement's best-guarded secrets. But a certain amount of information is available, and from this a broad outline of the internal tensions can be fairly accurately sketched.

## I. THE CONCENTRATION OF POWER

### The Long Road from Sandersville

"And after these things I saw another angel come down from heaven, having great power; and the earth was lightened with his glory. And he cried mightily with a strong voice, saying, Babylon the great is fallen, is fallen, and is become the habitation of devils, and the hold of every foul spirit. . . ."

*The Supreme Wisdom,* sacred text of the Black Muslim Movement, teaches that this angel having great power (mentioned in the eighteenth chapter of Revelation) was "no other than Master W. F. Fard Muhammad, the Great Mahdi." The Mahdi came for the express purpose of enlightening the so-called Negroes and pronouncing judgment on the white devils, who had enslaved the Black Nation and still hold them in "mental slavery." The Great Mahdi "announced the immediate doom of America," for "America committed suicide when she brought the so-called Negroes into slavery." He urged all black men to resume their true religion, Islam, and their true identity. Each black man who took this momentous step he blessed with a holy name of Allah's—on written application and for a ten-dollar fee. This name was the applicant's "true name," concealed from him by the slavemasters and restored through Fard's divine knowledge. The restoration of this true name at once identified the Muslim with the Black Nation and provided him with an Afro-Asian history. "The name," the Muslims say, "is everything."

As the Bible teaches us that He Will Accept those who are called by His Name. And some of us are so foolish as to say, "What is in a

name?" Everything is in a name. The Bible teaches us that all of
these Names of Allah (God) is more valuable than fine gold, because
in the Judgment it will save your life from being destroyed.

ALL people who do not have a Name of the God of Righteousness and Justice will be destroyed.[1]

Among those blessed by the Mahdi during his sojourn in the Wilderness of North America was the son of a Georgia preacher for whom
the devil-ridden city of Detroit had proved to be less than the Promised
Land. This convert's "slave name" had been Elijah Poole; the Great
Mahdi rechristened him Elijah Karriem and later, to show his increasing
favor, Elijah Muhammad, a name meaning "one worthy of praise."

Poole (who has also been known as Gulam Bogans, Muhammad
Rassouli, Elijah Muck Muhd, and various other aliases) was born in
Sandersville, Georgia, a rural hamlet[2] midway between Macon and Au-
gusta, on October 7, 1897. He is one of thirteen children born to Wali
and Marie Poole. His father was a Baptist preacher—a fact which is
doubtless reflected in Elijah's charismatic gifts—and both parents had
been slaves of a white family of the same surname. Elijah completed the
fourth grade. At sixteen he left home. Ten years later, in 1923, he and
his wife Clara (Evans), with their two children, moved to Detroit. Poole
had heard rhapsodic praise of the city from Blacks of his own home
town who had moved there after the end of World War I, but the
rhapsodies turned out to have been exaggerated. He worked in factories, holding several different jobs, until the Depression set in late in
1929. A year or so later he came under the spell of Fard, who, he
recalls gratefully, took him "out of the gutter in the streets of Detroit
and in three and a half years taught [him] the knowledge of Islam."

From the start, Muhammad's relationship with Fard seems to have
been a close one. One old-timer remembers Muhammad as "doing er-
rands for the Prophet" (as Fard himself was then known) and helping him
"put out some kind of paper." In 1932, Muhammad established the
Southside Mosque—later called Temple No. 2—in Chicago and apparently ran it for some time. The following year, when Fard was trying to
elude the police, he sought refuge with Muhammad in Chicago. A Detroit Muslim had been convicted in 1932 of a sacrificial killing of one of
his "brothers."[3] Thereupon, says Muhammad:

He [Fard] was persecuted, sent to jail in 1932, and ordered out of

Detroit, Michigan, May 26, 1933. He came to Chicago in the same year, [was] arrested almost immediately and placed behind prison bars. He submitted himself with all humility to his persecutors. Each time he was arrested he sent for me that I may see and learn the price of truth for us (the so-called Negroes).[4]

Muhammad's willingness to conceal Fard and brave the law for his sake must have cemented their mutual trust and respect, for Muhammad soon became Fard's chief minister and gradually took over the leadership of the Detroit temple. Before long, he was charged by Fard with full administrative responsibility for the Movement and was being groomed as Fard's successor.

Not all of the Black Nation in Detroit took kindly to Muhammad's favored position with the Mahdi. Some of his antagonists rejected his second rechristening (from Elijah Karriem to Elijah Muhammad). When Fard disappeared in June 1934, with Muhammad as his logical successor, they immediately spread rumors that Muhammad had induced Fard to offer himself as a human sacrifice. Fard was still considered a prophet, not an incarnation of Allah, and it was a common belief among his followers that a Muslim who immolated himself could become "Savior of the world." The rumors were never substantiated, of course, and they do not square with anything that is known about the relationship between the two men. Still, it is interesting to note that Fard is honored by Black Muslims everywhere as the "Savior" and is celebrated as such every year on his birthday, February 26.

Whatever its merits, this unsparing hostility to Muhammad split the Movement into factions. After Fard's disappearance, Muhammad withdrew to Chicago and designated Temple No. 2 as the new headquarters of the Movement. His faction became known as the "Temple People" and their meeting places as "Muhammad's Temples of Islam." Fard was deified and was thenceforth referred to as Allah; Muhammad took upon himself the mantle of Prophet and presented himself as the sole Messenger of Allah. Human sacrifice was never again mentioned as a Muslim doctrine. But the most important change was an expansion of the horizon of ambition: Muhammad was determined to bring into the light of the divine knowledge every black man in America.

As his chief minister—a post roughly analogous to the one he had held under Fard—Muhammad appointed a Haitian, Theodore Rozier, who had never known Fard. The dissident factions repudiated Rozier on the ground that he "never saw the Savior" and that his "second-hand revelation" was not sufficient qualification for the role. Their real objection, however, seems to have been to Muhammad's audacity, for he was already beginning to identify himself as the only channel through which Fard's truth could be brought to the sleeping Black Nation. In any case, Rozier was not a successful proselytizer; he could not capture the imagination of the people. Muhammad gradually won back most of the dissidents, but the Movement made only small inroads on the Black community. Not until the late 1940s, when "the Big X" became the right hand of the Messenger, did the Movement begin to catch fire.

Muhammad's association with Fard, "the Supreme Being among all Black Men," invests him with a status and power that have never been successfully challenged. The Muslim lay brother often expresses the wish, gravely and wistfully, that he might have seen Allah (that is, Fard), much as the devout Christian wishes he might have known Jesus when he was on earth. But Muhammad proclaims in *The Supreme Wisdom:* "I know Allah, and I am with him." And in Chicago he informed some ten thousand followers and curiosity seekers:

> I am not trembling. I am the man, I am the Messenger. . . . I came directly from God. I am guided by God. I am in communication with God, and I know God. If God is not with me . . . protecting me, how can I come and say things no other man has said and get away with it?[5]

The Messenger assures his listeners that the world will soon know who sent him, and he admonishes the black Christians that "God is here in person; so stop looking for a dead Jesus and pray to HIM . . . who is ALIVE and not a spook."[6]

Muhammad is known not only as "Messenger" and "Prophet" but also as "Spiritual Head of the Muslims in the West," "Divine Leader," and "The Reformer." His ministers most often refer to him as "The Honorable Elijah Muhammad" or as "The Messenger of Allah to the Lost-Found Nation of Islam in the Wilderness of North America." Occasionally the less formal reference "Brother Elijah Muhammad" is used.

Muhammed is a slight, brown, quickly energetic man. He often works an eighteen-hour day, pausing for his one daily meal at six in the evening. In his private life he is calm and temperate—a sharp contrast to his writings and to the fanatical intensity he inspires in the tens of thousands who call him the Messenger. His face is rather lean and angular, although his receding hairline broadens his forehead in a suggestion of strength and intelligence. His lips are thin; his eyes quick and penetrating. He has no features that are pronouncedly within the Negro stereotype. One recent writer has described him as "a slight man with a zealot's intense solemnity . . . [and] a quick, intuitive intelligence."[7] He lives on Chicago's South Side and has an unusually large family, six sons and a daughter.

For the most part, Muhammad speaks, writes, and directs the activities of his movement from his Chicago headquarters, Muhammad's Temple of Islam No. 2. Administrative policy is set chiefly through written directives and conferences in Chicago and enforced through a few lieutenants of demonstrated loyalty. But as the Movement gathered momentum, the Messenger himself had to travel extensively. The response his presence evokes in the black masses is phenomenal, especially in the light of his difficult-to-follow delivery. Wherever he has gone, his visits have been followed by spurts in the temple membership, but advancing age and administrative responsibilities now keep him close to Chicago. For more than a decade Malcolm X was Muhammad's presence in the scattered enclaves of the Nation of Islam. Today, Minister Louis Farrakhan is his National Representative (for spiritual matters), while Raymond Sharrieff, son-in-law and Supreme Captain of the Fruit of Islam, shuttles about the country to look after the Nation's business. Yet, the Messenger himself is far from idle. Sister Anne Ali offers a portrait of Muhammad on a typical working day:

Rising in the morning after a couple of hours sleep, he is at his desk when the secretaries and laborers report in. He is there already working on the problems of the 30 million Black People.

The phone rings—and it continues at the rate of from 30 calls a day. Perhaps it is a business executive requesting an appointment with Messenger Muhammad. . . .

The doorbell rings, perhaps it is a banker, or lawyer, or Laborer, or perhaps it is a follower with some personal problem—big or small, in the Messenger's tremendously busy schedule, he has to solve them all. The appointments continue throughout the day, at the rate of approximately ten cleared by noon. . . .

Through all of Messenger Muhammad's busy schedule, he never forgets his prayers. And, he will excuse himself to say his prayers. And, we do likewise, praying that Almighty Allah (God) blesses us to please the Messenger in our work; knowing that if we please His Last and Greatest Messenger, we do please Him.

The mailman has now delivered the mail, at the rate of 800 pieces a week. All of which Messenger Muhammad looks into daily and gives answers to as many as he possibly can before the next appointment or call interrupts him.

By this time, Messenger Muhammad has singed [sic] several salary contracts, ordered several hundred head of cattle to be fattened for the market, instructed 10 varieties of pies to be baked by our bakeries, advertised for several sales at YOUR SUPERMARKET and special dinners at SALAAM RESTAURANT, made both spiritual and business National broadcasts, dictated both spiritual and business articles, answered all mail possible, cleared ten business appointments, answered at least thirty business calls, ranging from truck drivers and editors to cattle raisers and architects. Besides this he has dispatched work to his more than fifteen secretaries, not to mention guiding and instruction countless Laborers.[8]

The announcement that the Messenger is to visit a particular temple is a signal for feverish activity on the part of the members. Cleanliness, always emphasized in the teachings at the temple, is given additional stress. In the Muslim homes, the best furnishings and utensils are brought from under wraps and put on display. The Muslim restaurants and other businesses are given new coats of paint, and pictures of the Messenger are prominently displayed. All this despite the fact that Muhammad rarely sees the results. He almost always remains in seclusion at his hotel or in the home of the host minister until it is time for his address, and he seldom misses the first flight available after his public appearance.

Several days before the Messenger is scheduled to arrive, members of the FOI security corps cover every inch of the route he is to travel from the airport to the temple. On the day of his arrival, Muslim guards are posted at strategic points along his route several hours in advance. Each guard is briefed as to precisely what he should do in the event of an emergency. The penalty for carelessness or error is severe.

The Messenger always travels with a personal security force, comprised of three or four members of the FOI from Temple No. 2. This guard is usually headed by Supreme Captain Raymond Sharrieff in person. When Muhammad deplanes, he is always preceded and covered from behind by this personal guard. As soon as he is on the ground, the local security force takes over. The Messenger is immediately surrounded by a force of from twelve to twenty men, and other Muslims are scattered inconspicuously among the crowds at the airport. An additional force in several automobiles takes over as he leaves the airport, some preceding and others following the car in which the Messenger is riding. The FOI captain of the local temple, riding in one of the lead cars, exchanges signals with individual guards previously stationed along the way. Should the guard not return the proper signal, the entire force is put on "emergency alert" and an alternate route is chosen.

Muhammad's arrival at the temple or auditorium causes much excitement. The crowds usually begin arriving two or three hours in advance. By the time Muhammad arrives, those who can be accommodated in the hall have been searched and seated—men to the right, women to the left. The Muslim women march in as a separate group and occupy a section of the hall reserved for them. They are dressed in flowing white gowns and shawls, and wear no makeup. Scores of Muslim brothers are on security duty inside the building—at the doors and in the restrooms and hallways. The hall will have been thoroughly searched at least twice before the public is admitted, and roving patrols are constantly on the lookout for trouble. As many as a hundred men may be assigned the task of securing the inside of the building and searching each member of the audience.

Outside, Muslims are on constant patrol on foot or in cars, ranging several blocks around the area. In a meeting held in Atlanta, the FOI even placed a patrol on the roof of the Magnolia Ballroom, where the Prophet was to speak. In Boston, the FOI set up a counterwatch on what they took to be FBI agents watching them from an office building across the street from the John Hancock Hall, where Muhammad was speaking.

When the Messenger finally arrives outside the hall, an Honor Guard escorts him along the sidewalk down a double row of Muslims and so into the building. (At a meeting held in the Uline Arena in Washington, D.C., in the summer of 1959, Muhammad marched from his car down an aisle of eight hundred Black Muslims, standing shoulder to shoulder all the way from the street to the rostrum.) As he enters the hall and comes before his audience, there is a quiet stir, an excitement compounded of awe, pride, and reverence. This decorous intensity of response is maintained throughout his speech, punctuated only by the usual affirmations: "That's right! That's right!" But the Messenger's charismatic presence seems to cause a vibrancy in the air—a vibrancy that lingers long after he has finished his speech and departed, quickly and quietly, from the hall.

In the informality of his home, Muhammad conveys the impression of an almost wistful gentility and kindness, and the visitor is immediately impressed by his deep feeling of responsibility for his people. He is peculiarly sensitive to attacks by black leadership and is perplexed that "the educated ones who should know more than the rest of us cannot see the truth of what I am teaching." He attempts to avoid controversy with other black leaders, believing that eventually all will recognize that "the salvation of the so-called Negro in this country depends upon the unity of all Black Men" and that this unity can come only when Blacks are willing to "see the white man for what he is" and reject him.

Muhammad has a personal antipathy toward white domination that borders on the pathological, and it is almost exclusively in this reference that his passions are likely to escape restraint. Yet he denies teaching hatred.

They say that I am preacher of racial hatred, but the fact is that the white people don't like the truth, especially if it speaks *against* them. . . . It is a terrible thing for such people . . . to charge me with teaching race hatred when their feet are on my people's neck and they tell us to our face that they hate the black people. . . . Remember now, they even teach you that you must not hate them for hating you.[9]

Muhammad enjoins his followers never to initiate violence but to retaliate if they are attacked. He ridicules the whites for demanding that black men turn the other cheek, when they themselves will kill even without provocation.

It is against the law of nature. The Christian government of America can't do it. The Pope of Rome can't do it. If you and I don't wake up to that knowledge and execute the law of an eye for an eye, we might as well be dead and forgotten.[10]

The white man's greatest fear, Muhammad believes, is that the Black Man will know the truth about him and will unite against him. As a result, the white community slanders the Muslims and treats them like criminals. The white men "claim the truth to be subversive and hate-teaching. . . . They tap our telephones, eavesdrop and follow us around . . . use tape-recording machines [and] the hypocrites and stool pigeons among us to keep up to date on what we say and do. They are even bold enough to ask [our own] relatives to help them do [us] evil!"[11] This accusation is hardly exaggerated. The FBI and local police *do* keep Muhammad and his Movement under close scrutiny, from outside and probably also from within.

Muhammad seems to live comfortably in this atmosphere of hostility and counterhostility, but he is rarely without an awareness of danger. He observes characteristically:

I have it from the mouth of God that the enemy had better try to protect my life and see that I continue to live. Because if anything happens to me, I will be the last one that they murder. And if any of my followers are harmed, ten of the enemy's best ones will be killed.[12]

The Messenger has already tangled twice with the law—and lost. In 1934, when he refused to transfer his child from a University of Islam to a public school, he was found guilty of contributing to the delinquency of a minor and was placed on six months' probation. In 1942 he was arrested by federal authorities in Chicago and this time was obliged to serve time in prison. In a story headlined "12 Negro Chiefs Seized by FBI in Sedition Raid," the *Chicago Tribune* gave the following account:

Arrest of more than 80 Negroes, members and leaders of three organizations, on charges of sedition, conspiracy, and violation of the draft laws was announced by the Federal Bureau of Investigation here.

Twelve of those arrested are considered leaders in the groups. They were charged with ... conspiracy to promote the success of the enemy, making false statements to those about to be inducted into the armed forces, [and] disrupting morale and causing mutiny.
... The three organizations are known as "The Peace Movement of Ethiopia," ... "The Brotherhood of Liberty for Black People of America," and an organization known as "The Temple of Islam."
... Elijah Poole, who calls himself Elijah Muhammad, was [among those] arrested. ... Elijah is also known as Elijah Muck Muhd, and is known as "The Prophet."[13]

Arrested with Muhammad was Lenzie Karien, identified as one of the Ministers of Islam. Both Muhammad and Karien admitted sympathy for Japan, but Chicago FBI Chief Johnson said "no definite connection had been found by his men between Negro organizations and Japanese activity in this country."[14] Nonetheless, indictments were drawn on the ground that the three organizations were "alleged to have taught Negroes that their interests were in a Japanese victory, and that they were racially akin to the Japanese. ... J. Albert Woll, U.S. District Attorney, ... said the defendants made statements 'as vicious as any ever uncovered by a grand jury.' "[15] For these "vicious" statements, Muhammad went to federal prison at Milan, Michigan, until 1946. He apparently was able to direct the Movement even while in jail, for it gained strength during those years.

After his release, Muhammad repeated and elaborated on the sentiments that had brought him to jail. He taught that the white man is—and has been since his creation—the oppressor of all who are not white; and he asserted that all who are not white are, by the white man's own social definition, black. Consequently, he reasoned, it made little sense for black people in this country to fight against the Japanese, who are equally victims of the white man's hatred and color prejudice. World War II was not a battle in which American Blacks ought to have been forced to participate. The Black Man's war is "the Battle of Armageddon," which will be fought "in the wilderness of North America." It is, in Muhammad's words, "a battle for freedom, justice and equality—to success or to the death."

Muhammad is ostensibly not troubled about what direction the Movement will take when he returns to Allah, or about who will succeed him. "Allah will see that the work is carried on," he insists with conviction. Yet Muhammad, more than anyone else, must recall the schisms that rent the Movement after Fard disappeared in 1934, and it would be hazardous to take his apparent naivete at face value. He must sense, as many observers do, that the struggle for succession is already on and that the image of the united front that the Black Nation has labored so hard to build will once again be fractured when the Messenger's voice is heard no more. It will be interesting to see who, if anyone, will be able to pick up the pieces and fit them together again.


### Malcolm X: First Plenipotentiary

No one man could carry alone Muhammad's immense burden of responsibility. In directing the complex affairs of the Black Nation—coordinating its program, managing its economic enterprises, founding new temples, and so on—he relies heavily on the closely knit inner circle of Muslim leaders. Foremost of these was his chief aide, Minister Malcolm X Shabazz, once minister of the powerful Temple No. 7 in Harlem, and one of the few ministers granted an "original" (that is, an Arabic) surname.[16] One observer has described Malcolm as "the best thing that ever happened to Muhammad."[17]

Malcolm was an indefatigable organizer and speaker. Whereas Muhammad speaks almost exclusively to the black masses, Malcolm frequently appeared at colleges and universities, and he was a popular radio and television discussant. He also visited temples in every part of the country with the regular frequency of a salesman. He organized new temples, pumped spirit and encouragement into the missions or newly founded cell groups, conducted rallies and fund-raising campaigns, and served as Muhammad's general trouble-shooter and spokesman.

The New York minister was a tall, powerfully built, light-skinned man. Much of his youth was spent on the streets of Harlem as "Big Red"—a nickname he earned during a career of petty hoodlumism, which he blandly attributed to his early training as a Christian and to the white man's habit of making it difficult for the so-called Negro to earn a decent living in a respectable way.

Like Muhammad, Malcolm had his difficulties with the police, though for different reasons. He explained with great bitterness that, since his delinquency as a youth was caused by social conditions for which the white man is responsible, the white man should thank him

for trying to change those conditions. While in prison, he was attracted
to the daring disclosures about the Black Man in Muhammad's teachings, became a Muslim, and turned back from his criminal career. Malcolm credited his rehabilitation entirely to the "knowledge of self"—
and its corollary, "the truth about the white man"—as taught him by
Elijah Muhammad.

> All I have learned has been from the Islamic influence of Mr. Mu-
> hammad. . . . I am what you would call an ex-convict. I am not
> ashamed of this because it was all done when I was a part of the
> white man's Christian world. As a Muslim, I would never have done
> these awful things that caused me to go to prison.[18]

Malcolm X was born Malcolm Little in Omaha, Nebraska, about
1925. He was one of eleven children and, like his acknowledged master,
the son of a Baptist minister. While he was very young, the family
moved to Lansing, Michigan, where the father—Malcolm called him "a
race man" and "a little too outspoken for Lansing"—soon incurred the
hostility of the whites. When Malcolm was only six, the family home
was burned by the Ku Klux Klan. "The firemen came and just sat there
without making any effort to put one drop of water on the fire. The
same fire that burned my father's home still burns my soul." But the
worst was yet to come. "A typical Garveyite," the father "was making
his first step toward economic independence by building his own store.
At the time we were the only Negroes in the block." His initiative drew
a swift reprisal—"my father was found with his head bashed and his
body mangled under a streetcar." Malcolm was certain that this was a
calculated murder.

The bitterness over his father's troubles with the white people of
Lansing never left Malcolm X. On the contrary, he seems to have nurtured and fed it, so that it structured and oriented most of his interper-
sonal and professional relations. "There is no white man a Muslim can
trust." Yet, ironically, it was a white woman whose kindness Malcolm
remembered most vividly.

After his father's death, the Little family fell upon evil days. His
mother boiled dandelion greens every day to try to keep the children
from starving to death. "We stayed dizzy and weak because we stayed
hungry," Malcolm recalled. What he and his brothers could pilfer aug-

mented the wild greens his mother picked along the roadsides. They fought desperately to remain together; but eventually the family broke up, and Malcolm was sent to an institution for boys. There, he recalled with a rare touch of tenderness, "when everybody else at that school was kicking me around, the housemother took up for me. She was good to me, and I followed her around like a puppy. I was a kind of mascot." Soon it was arranged for Malcolm to attend a nearby school. He was the only black student at the school, and he stood first in his class often enough to incur resentment from teachers and pupils alike.

He was asked in the eighth grade what he wanted to become. He preferred law but was told that law was not a suitable profession for a Negro and that instead he should think of a trade such as carpentry.[19]

"This," said Malcolm, "was the turning point in my thinking."

Eventually he left the school and moved East to what became a life of juvenile delinquency. "By his late teens, Malcolm was operating successfully on the fringes of the Harlem underworld."[20]

Admitted to the underworld's fringes, sixteen-year-old Malcolm absorbed all he heard and saw. He swiftly built up a reputation for honesty by turning over every dollar due his boss ("I have always been intensely loyal"). By the age of 18, Malcolm was versatile "Big Red." He hired from four to six men variously plying dope, numbers, bootleg whiskey and diverse forms of hustling. Malcolm personally squired well-heeled white thrill-seekers to Harlem sin dens, and Negroes to white sin downtown. "My best customers were preachers and social leaders, police and all kinds of big shots in the business of controlling other people's lives."[21]

Malcolm sometimes earned as much as $2,000 a month. He "paid off the law from a $1,000 roll from the pockets of his $200 suits." But eventually a less suceptible "law" caught up with him, and "Big Red" went to prison—not once, but several times.

In 1947, while in the maximum-security prison at Concord, Massachusetts, Malcolm was converted by one of his brothers who had become a member of the Detroit Temple. After that, the Movement claimed all his energies and all his loyalties until he broke with Muham-mad seventeen years later. During his long ministry, his personal loyalty to his mentor seemed unshakable, but in spite of this there did come a day when Malcolm and the Messenger went their separate ways. As the Messenger's messenger, Malcolm enjoyed great popularity with Muslims across the country and abroad. In 1959, for example, he visited several of the Moslem states in the Middle East as Muhammad's emissary. He was the guest of minor officials of several governments, but refused the invitations of those of higher rank on the grounds that such honors should be reserved for Muhammad himself. On the other hand, Mal-colm's impatience with some of the older ministers' "softness" toward the white man was seldom disguised.

The Big X was undeniably a leader of great charisma. His formal schooling ended at the eighth grade, but experience taught him after that. He more than held his own, in numerous radio and television appearances, against men with far better formal educations. In the Massachusetts prison, the minister's son read "thousands of books be-cause I wanted to know what made people the way they are." He was confident of his own abilities, yet he credited Elijah Muhammad with "teaching me everything I know that's worthwhile." Whether address-ing the masses on a Harlem street corner, the Muslim faithful gathered in any one of the Messenger's scattered temples, or a university seminar, his important statements were inevitably prefaced with "The Honorable Elijah Muhammed teaches us. . . ." And there was pride and confidence in his voice.

The onetime hoodlum considered himself "completely reformed by the teachings of Elijah, for knowing the truth, I don't need the crutches I used to think I had to have. When I was in the world of the Christians, I behaved as they did; I did what the white man did because, like everybody else, I thought his was the best possible thing to do."

Following the assassination of President John Kennedy in Novem-ber, 1963, Malcolm X, in a characteristic flight of rhetoric, indicted white America for creating the climate of hatred and violence in which such an outrage could occur. In a meeting in New York, Malcolm expressed the opinion that Mr. Kennedy's murder was a matter of "chickens come home to roost." "Being an old farm boy myself," he added, "chickens coming home to roost never did make me sad; they've always made me glad."[22]

The next day Malcolm was suspended by Muhammad for ninety days, during which he was to exercise none of the functions of a minister, nor was he to make any public statements. Ostensibly, Muhammad's move was to counter in advance the negative attention the Muslims were bound to receive as a result of Malcolm's intemperate statement, but beneath the surface scenario there seemed to be evidence that a rift had already developed between the two men, and that the "chickens statement" merely provided an occasion for what had already been determined. Muhammad trusted Malcolm, having appointed him National Minister only a few months before—to the extreme distaste of some factions who felt that Malcolm already had too much power. The degree to which jealousy and intrigue on the one hand and disaffection and willful independence on the other contributed to the rift will probably never be known completely. What is known is that once the cleavage became public, the chasm could only grow wider. That is what happened.

Early in March of 1964 Malcolm X withdrew from the Black Muslims and formed his own organization, The Muslim Mosque, Inc., followed by its secular counterpart, the Organization of Afro-American Unity. During 1964 he traveled extensively in Africa and the Middle East. Shortly after his return to the United States he was assassinated (February 21, 1965). Inevitably, his erstwhile Black Muslim brothers were accused of his murder, although the convicted assassins denied being a part of any Muslim conspiracy. The CIA was also a popular suspect in the murder, especially among black nationalists who felt embarrassed that the killers were black. Apparently, Malcolm knew he was going to die. Several other attempts had already been made on his life, and just four days before his death he promised to speak at Brown University the following Tuesday, *"if I am still alive on Tuesday."* When asked why he did not inform the police of his impending death, he answered cryptically, "They know it already."

A Malcolm X cult sprang up immediately after his death. Strangely, the cult cut across racial and class lines. Thousands who had denounced or ignored Malcolm in life suddenly identified with him in death. Malcolm X buttons, medallions, tee shirts, plaques, busts, and pictures appeared everywhere, as did a vast literature from a host of "interpreters" who had never bothered to hear him speak or seek his presence. In short order, Malcolm was projected in a thousand different images by a thousand different experts who suddenly discovered after his death "what he was *truly* like," and what his intentions were.

The Malcolm X affair shook the Nation of Islam, and although Muhammad's programs went on as before in the economic sphere, Malcolm's charisma, his organizing genius, and his polemical ability were sorely missed for a time. Beyond that, although the organizations he founded did not survive, the Malcolm X *cult* did, and apparently it continues to plague the Nation of Islam. In a double-page editorial on Malcolm, *Muhammad Speaks,* the official organ of the Black Muslims, declared:

> Some people want to build a backward movement by goading unstable youths to violence. . . . Such people are attempting to use Malcolm to mislead his sincere admirers. His good qualities—the long hard study put in under the guidance of Mr. Muhammad—are ignored. And what youths are really being told is that by being a degenerate, hustler, and quick-to-kill, they are being "revolutionary" like the "real Malcolm," the pre-Muslim Malcolm. Other young Blacks are being told that Malcolm discovered some great, abstract . . . "humanistic" "Truth" in the last eleven months of his life. This nameless, mystical abstraction they would have impressionable Blacks substitute for a program of real social progress . . . for dignity bestowed on hard work . . . which are consistently advanced by Messenger Muhammad year in and year out.[23]

The following week Raymond Sharrieff himself took up the cudgel in a second double-page article to declare:

> YOU must remember that Malcolm's greatest desire was to get people to think about fighting. We never have learned how much fight Malcolm had in *himself.*
>
> BUT, this is the greatest thing that Malcolm was trying to show-off in—in saying that he would like to have an army to be taken and killed, while going to war to kill the white people in the South for their mistreatment of us.
>
> THAT is insane thinking! That is not the thinking of the scholars and the scientists of our Black Nation of Islam.

. . . . . . . . . . . . . . . . . . . . . . . . . . . . . . . . . . . . . . . . . . . . . . . . . .

IN worshipping Malcolm, you are hated before God and before His Angels. . . .

I only want to acquaint you with the basic meaning of what you are actually trying to carry into practice, and that is a worship of a dead Malcolm. . . .

Malcolm, goes to MECCA. He makes a pilgrimage, and for the first time Malcolm gets a chance to eat out of the same dish with the devil. This excited Malcolm, lover of the devil.

Malcolm, came back from MECCA, worshipping the devil because this was the closest that he had ever gotten to be in the society of the devil. Malcolm all but wanted to swear at your God and my God, and Mr. Muhammad, for not teaching him to love white folks.

Malcolm, saw white people in MECCA and he dined with them and ate out of the same dish with them. Judas Iscariot ate out of the dish with Jesus, but Judas was not a Jesus. Judas was a betrayer.[24]

If his newspaper has been generous in its public attention to the lingering spirit of Malcolm X, the Messenger himself has not. In a rare interview in February of 1972, Muhammad dismissed a request for "an assessment of the life of Malcolm" with a terse:

No, I would not lose any time with a man that has been talked and talked about for years. If the people do not have a knowledge of him after these many years, I am not going to waste my time with going into Malcolm's history. Malcolm, I do not have any time to waste with him. . .[25]

That is where the matter seems to lie. The appointment of the very personable Louis Farrakhan as National Minister has proven to be good strategy. Since Farrakhan was trained by Malcolm X and was very close to him at the time he left the movement, Muhammad has dramatically demonstrated his disdain of any influence Malcolm may have left in the Nation; and Farrakhan's popularity as a spokesman has risen steadily among black youth, and in the community as a whole. Twelve thousand people turned out to hear him address Harlem's Black Solidarity Rally in October of 1971. But Farrakhan has already let it be known that

"the Messenger has very big shoes; and my feet are small." It is unlikely that history will repeat itself.

### Near the Center

So far as is known, the Muslims do not have a rigid hierarchical
structure of administration. Muhammad is the "Messenger" by reason
of having caught the mantle from Fard, founder of the Movement. But
apart from Muhammad, no one has an inherent claim to any office.
Farrakhan serves as Muhammad's aide at the Messenger's pleasure; by
the same token, Muhammad could summarily banish him to outer darkness. Presumably the same is true of Raymond Sharrieff, who is Muhammad's son-in-law and the Supreme Captain of the secret paramilitary organization, the Fruit of Islam. Sharrieff has long been a Muslim,
but he is hardly known outside of the organization. Even the Muslims
know little about him except that he is Muhammad's chief aide in
managing the sect's commercial enterprises and overseeing the FOI.
Some police authorities suggest that Sharieff also collects tithes from
delinquent members and, through a hand-picked corps of lieutenants,
effectively silences any defectors from the Movement who may wish to
cooperate with the police in exposing its secrets. The Muslims say only
that Sharrieff "sees that the wishes of the Messenger are carried out."
Nevertheless, someone tried to kill Sharrieff by firing a shotgun at
him five times in October of 1971.[26] Muhammad disclaimed any notion as to why anyone would want to kill his son-in-law, "an innocent
man, sitting behind the wall in his own office." Speculation outside the
Movement is that young insurgents who want to see some change occur
in the Nation's priorities have been frustrated in their attempts to gain
access to the Messenger, and hold Sharrieff responsible. Others see Sharrieff as the likely successor of the lion's share of Muhammad's wealth
and power. But Muhammad has six sons, five of whom must be reckoned with when the day finally comes for the Messenger to yield his
scepter. Says Muhammad in answer to questions about a successor: "I
would say this: I am not going to come back and look over the staff to
see who is on it."
Internal bickering spilled over into public notice over Muhammad's
intention of building a mansion for himself in Chicago at a cost of half
a million dollars, with four other mansions for certain of his top ad-

ministrators and members of his family to cost $350,000 each.[27] A scathing editorial in *Muhammed Speaks* entitled "When the Envier Envies"[28] was the first official notice that internal opposition to such a lavish expenditure was developing:

As the holy flame of divine success grows stronger ... the unholy flame of envy grows in its intensity. But what a price the envier pays for his envy.... Envy and jealousy is one of the earliest and most common emotions that the Black people have ever known, here in America. Envy is so degrading to the person who envies; from the time of slavery, if a Black brother was able, through his hard striving to purchase ... a new pair of shoes, an evil brother looked on with envy. Envy is such a disease among our Black people.... Evil is the envier, and evil is his envy. Whenever you find a person who envies, know that you have found an evil person. Know that you have found an opposer, know that you have found an enemy.[29]

Some of the faithful were outraged that Muhammad's intention "to build himself a home"—at whatever cost—was even so much as questioned by his followers. For months, *Muhammad Speaks* published letters and articles denouncing the "enviers" and affirming support for the Messenger:

He is the kindest, most sympathetic, most generous leader that the Blackman in America has ever known.... He is not like the preachers and politicans who are all for self.

. . . . . . . . . . . . . . . . . . . . . . . . . . . . . . . . . . . . . . . . .

Our humble Messenger doesn't wear expensive clothes or jewelry.... He has bought beautiful homes for some of you ... better dwellings than some of his own children [have].

Perhaps some clue to who the "enviers" are can be seen in the following excerpt from an article by "A Believer."

He has sent you to schools of higher learning, here and abroad.... However, upon returning with your degrees some of you turned your back on him.... You are trying to hinder our poor Black

brothers and sisters from coming to our sacred mosques . . . you try to block our people from attending our annual convention.
. . . . . . . . . . . . . . . . . . . . . . . . . . . . . . . . . . . . . . . . . . . . . . . . .

Some of you criticize his use of good homes and luxury cars; while others of you are so foolish to believe that Islam deprives you of having the better things in life. We who follow the Honorable Elijah Muhammad benefit personally from following him with money, good homes and friendships in all walks of life. The money which is donated to him by his followers, he gives right back to them. He helps his followers to have, and is happy to see us have. We who follow the Honorable Elijah Muhammad, want him to have all of the best of comfort available to him for in the work of leadership which he is doing with the hard headed and rebellious people that we are. Anything to make the physical workings of life easier for him, we are happy to help him to have.
. . . . . . . . . . . . . . . . . . . . . . . . . . . . . . . . . . . . . . . . . . . . . . . . .

Wouldn't you agree that after forty long years of suffering for our causes that this meek, humble, most kind, and generous man, now in His declining years, doesn't He at least deserve a beautiful home built to his own desire? It's no wonder why Allah said that no one wanted us but Himself, and that our Messenger has the worst task ever put on any man.

As for the Messenger himself, he remained majestically aloof to the controversy. The houses, he told the press, would cost somewhat more than the figures reported (indeed, he wished he could build them so cheaply!). But at the same time, he was negotiating with the city of Chicago for a tract of land on which to build one hundred low-income houses for some of his followers. Good homes are hard for black people to find, no matter who they are. "My greatest desire," confides the Messenger, "is to build better homes for the Black Man on the South-side of Chicago. Again, my greatest desire is to put him up a hospital, which he sorely needs."

### Trouble on the Horizon

Elijah Muhammad is a hale, energetic, and mentally vigorous man, capable of sustaining a grueling workday under very nearly spartan self-discipline. He celebrated his seventy-fourth birthday in 1971 and seems likely to remain in firm control of his Black Nation for some years to come. While he does so, any aspirant to power within the Movement must be immensely cautious and far-sighted, for rivalry—or even open disagreement—with the Messenger is not tolerated.

Muhammad does not proclaim himself divine, but he is invested with quasi-divinity as one who knew Allah (W. D. Fard), and has carried Allah's revelation down the years and across the continent. Muhammad's people know well that he has raised them from a small cult, nearly shattered by police harassment and factional in-fighting, to a potentially powerful force in America's social and political economy. Their unquestioning devotion to Muhammad is further intensified by the unique emotional cathexis of the true believer. And Muhammad himself does not discourage this flow of gratitude and adoration. In the early years after Fard's death, he asserted his claim as the sole Messenger of Allah, in whom the Movement must thenceforth be concentered. There is no evidence that he has ever seen reason to abate that claim.

Yet flesh is mortal; and even to the Messenger of Allah, death must one day come. So far as is known, Muhammad has not yet named his successor, and we may assume that a struggle for that honor is already under way. The two leading contenders would logically have been Malcolm X and Raymond Sharrieff. Malcolm was Muhammad's chief lieutenant in the open affairs of the Movement and his emissary to the Islamic nations of Africa and Asia. He was its most articulate spokesman and its most indefatigable organizer, infused with the Messenger's authority and admired by the ministers and the laity alike. But Malcolm X is dead. Raymond, on the other hand, is Muhammad's son-in-law and his chief lieutenant in the secret affairs of the Movement, manager of its business enterprises, and Supreme Captain of the secret army, the Fruit of Islam. And Raymond Sharrieff is very much alive. But attempts have been made on his life; and they are likely to be repeated. Such is the price of prominence when power is up for grabs.

By the time of Muhammad's death, the Black Muslim Movement will presumably have continued to prosper. What with active tithing and the burgeoning growth of Muslim commercial enterprises, there will be a wealthy empire at stake. The political force of the Movement will also be a rich prize—not to mention the immense personal prestige and sense of command that will be inherent in the position of leadership of so potent and monolithic an organization.

During the last ten years, the factionalism predicted for the Movement has in fact appeared. As the Movement gained vested interests—real estate and commercial enterprises, as well as economic and political weight in the black and white communities—one bloc of the Muslim leadership has become increasingly conservative. It will urge the case for maintaining a stable status quo, rather than risk the loss of so much that will have been so arduously gained. This bloc will very quickly realize that the Muslim gains can be protected only while there is a fairly stable white society in America. Racial separation—and especially an economic or political weakening of the dominant white community—would place severe strains on the Muslims' dependent economy and would render meaningless their political balance of power. An extended outreach to the Third World would jeopardize more parochial interests, and, more important, the door to a different kind of power arrangement would inevitably be opened. The conservatives will almost certainly seek a status quo in revelation, asserting that Fard's original divine knowledge has been given its perfect and ultimate expression by his Messenger, Elijah Muhammad.

A successful Movement, however, almost always runs the risk of attracting to itself an element of believers whose zeal and vision transcend the horizons of the tried and true. This element will attract to itself a cadre of others who will inevitably share their fiery, aggressive spirit. This second bloc will be scornful of mere material and negotiable gains. Clinging to the spirit of the original revelation and holding it capable of continual renewal in each generation, it will demand a relentless war on the detested status quo, with its entrenched white domination. Given sufficient time and numbers, this bloc may split further into purists, who abide by Muhammad's injunction to shun violence, and radicals, who demand war and victory at any cost.

A ruler who is not considered divine. A rich prize for anyone who succeeds in wresting the position of command away from the incumbent. And built-in tensions that *must* create conflicting blocs, each of which will feel morally impelled to control the course of the Movement. . . . How can there help but be bitter and vicious struggles for power? Even the sense of a common enemy will not rule out such struggles, as the history of the Russian Communist movement shows all too well.

Indeed, the struggle for succession that will erupt at the Messenger's death is already in progress. Evidence is at times ambiguous, for the

Muslims' central organizational problems are closely guarded secrets. The few ex-Muslims who can be found are *very* reluctant to discuss Muslim affairs. But occasionally a development becomes known which casts a penetrating light into the darkness in which these rivalries and power-plays are wrapped.

The internal struggle seems to be centered in Chicago—in Temple No. 2, the very seat of Muhammad's power, and the symbolic Mecca for the whole Movement. Persistent rumors of attempts on Muhammad's life abound, but such rumors do not seem to disturb the Messenger:

> For forty years, I have been a target for assassination, but I do not pay any attention to that kind of talk. That does not annoy me, because I know if God is on my side to protect me . . . I am not afraid about anyone making threats. . . . I do not believe our people are that foolish as to think they can take it over. There may be some people that think, "If such one and such one is out of the way, I could get his place." That may be in the minds of some of the people, but I do not believe actually they really believe it themselves. . . . I do not ever look at the people who are talking about assassinating me, because I know they are not going to be successful.[30]

Muhammad plays down the possibility of his being assassinated by dissidents in his Movement, but he is not unaware of their presence. In an open letter in *Muhammad Speaks* addressed simply to "Hypocrites," the Messenger denounced these purveyors of "venomous poison" and promised to be "hard against such people" as required by the Holy Quran:

## HYPOCRITES

The HYPOCRITES who have and who are now set in THE NATION OF ISLAM, must be removed out of our way.

No people nor organization, regardless to what it is, religious or political, can be successful with HYPOCRITES on its panel.

HERE IN CHICAGO, the die has been set. And, the material has been made according to the die. I hope that Allah will Cause you to see, for I most certainly hope to get you removed out of our Temple No. 2, which is full of DISBELIEVERS as well as in other Temples where they go from one to the other carry venomous poison of hatred against Brother and against Sister and those who are trying to live the righteous life with the Truth that will bring them into a HEAVEN AT ONCE.

## DO NOT BEFRIEND HYPOCRITES

Being FRIENDS with the HYPOCRITES is dangerous. The Holy Qur-an warns you against taking them for friends, and the Holy Qur-an teaches you and me their disbelieving actions so that you may recognize them, if they be in your family or home, you cannot be successful trying to befriend one who is against your God and the Truth, for he is against you for believing it.

He becomes your enemy, regardless, if it is your husband, wife, sons, or daughters. So, remember how the Holy Qur-an teaches us that the Messenger must be hard against such people; and I AM. I just hope the day will come that I can weed them out, by the help of Allah, BECAUSE YOU (HYPOCRITES) ARE A GREAT HINDRANCE TO YOUR OWN SALVATION AND THE SALVATION OF OTHERS.

*Elijah Muhammad,*
*Messenger of Allah*[31]

### The Fruit of Islam

"The day must come," says Muhammad, "when we will be separated from our natural enemies, the blue-eyed devils of the white race." While overt hostility toward whites has been markedly deemphasized in the Movement in the years of economic consolidation, separation from the white man and the inevitable "Armageddon" remain central tenets of Black Muslim teaching. The Muslims "have been mistreated" in Chicago, New York, Los Angeles, and other places. "They go to prison and the federal penitentiary to serve time that the government put upon them . . . but that is all given to us [i.e., we expect it]. But the trial of the Black Muslims in America must come to pass. We must be tried."[32] Exactly what the Messenger meant by "trial" is not precisely clear, but early in January of 1972, a band of young Blacks purporting to be Black Muslims appeared in Baton Rouge, Louisiana, and offered themselves for a trial of sorts. When the shooting was over and the smoke had cleared, two Blacks and two white policemen were dead, and thirty-one other people had been wounded.

The drama began when a caravan of young Blacks converged on Baton Rouge in late December. They checked unobtrusively into several motels, made contact with the black youth of the city, and promised to show them "how to get their city back" from the whites. January 10 was the day set. At noon, the "Muslims," about fifteen strong and wearing dark suits and bow ties, blocked a major traffic artery (North Boulevard near 14th Street) with two cars. Then, standing shoulder to shoulder with arms folded, they quietly waited for the police to arrive. The police came, armed with riot weapons. A shot was fired, and in the ensuing melee four men were killed. The "Muslims" were unarmed, and official autopsy reports revealed that all the men killed were shot with .38 caliber revolvers such as those carried by the police. The "Muslims" relied on karate, chanting all the while: "Allah is the Greatest! Allah is the Greatest!" A bystander reported that: "The police came to bang a few heads, but the Muslims were karate-chopping the hell out of them. The whole thing was just mind-blowing to the cops. Here were some Blacks who were not running. The cops could do nothing but pull their guns and shoot. They lost face!"

Young black militants across the country were impressed by the "cold courage" the self-styled Muslims displayed at Baton Rouge. Elijah Muhammad was not. They were not registered at any of his mosques as "good Muslims," he reported. A "good Muslim" he defined as "one who observes and obeys the laws of the religion of Islam." As for the Baton Rouge militants, "we did not know these people in the beginning. Their names, some of them are foreign to us altogether."

Whether the young Blacks who confronted the police at Baton Rouge were Muslims or not is of more than academic importance. If they were, the Black Muslims may begin to look more like the logical successor to the moribund Black Panthers, at least to the more revolutionary-oriented black youth looking for "action" rather than "talk." This was the image the Muslims had ten years ago in the heyday of Malcolm X. If they were not "good, registered Muslims," the Movement itself may be in deeper trouble than appears on the surface. *They looked and behaved like Black Muslims and they were accepted as such.* The possibility that other such groups acting independently of Chicago may exist would seem to pose a problem for Muhammad, whether they are registered or not. The Mayor of Baton Rouge may have said more than he knew when he said: "This Elijah Muhammad, whoever he is, better watch out for these people. He doesn't know it yet, but this splinter group is out to kill him."

Muhammad dismissed the Baton Rouge incident with the remark that: "We do not consider a Muslim is a Muslim who is running around over the country trying to start trouble." True, the Muslims are taught to avoid trouble, but trouble seems to have a way of finding Muslims, even when they run from it. The fact is that every Muslim represents a potential threat to a society whose doom he has predicted and fully expects to occur. Further, while Muhammad urges his followers never to initiate a battle, every Muslim is expected to fight if attacked and to lay down his life, if necessary, for the Black Nation. The entire Movement is, in short, a kind of reserve fighting corps—a phalanx of black men ready to wage open war against the entire white community in case of white provocation.

The nucleus of this force—its vanguard or officer cadre—is the secret army known as the Fruit of Islam, which was established as a protective unit in the early years of the Movement. Beynon reported laconically in 1937:

> Fear of trouble with the unbelievers, especially with the police, led to the founding of the Fruit of Islam—a military organization for the men who were drilled by captains in military tactics and the use of firearms.[33]

Since then, the FOI has flexed its muscles and become the most powerful single unit within the Movement. It now has a section in every temple, and its local officers report not to the minister but to the Supreme Captain of the FOI, Raymond Sharrieff, at the Movement's headquarters in Chicago. This virtually autonomous body is an elite group, carefully chosen, rigorously trained, aware of its own distinction and responsibilities, admired (and very likely feared) by the rest of the Muslim brotherhood. It is entrusted with top security assignments and remains on constant alert. Most ominous of all, it shrouds its activities in nearly absolute secrecy—a tactic that has aroused the deepest suspicions of observers like the FBI.

The FOI no longer dedicates itself solely to guarding the Black Nation against trouble with the unbelievers, or with the police; it now acts also as an internal police force and judiciary—or, more exactly, a constabulary and court-martial—to root out and punish any hint of heterodoxy or any slackening of obedience among the Muslims themselves. Possibly this enforcement of internal discipline has become the FOI's primary function. No outside observer is yet able to say with certainty.

The Fruit of Islam is comprised of the best physically and psychologically conditioned males in the Black Muslim Movement, though the criteria for admission vary slightly to meet local conditions. In some of the larger temples, only the best qualified men under the age of thirty are admitted. In some small temples, every male Muslim is considered eligible. (Obviously each section is urged to reach a specified minimum size, even at a possible temporary sacrifice in quality.) A few temples have as many as three distinct FOI groups: a Junior FOI for youths up to sixteen, a prime group for men sixteen to thirty-five, and a third group for men over thirty-five. No reliable estimate of the total membership of the FOI is available.

The chain of command is simple and strictly maintained. The FOI sections are divided into squads, each of which is under the command of a lieutenant. The lieutenants of each section report to a captain, who heads the section and reports (according to informants) directly to Muhammad. In practice, the captains undoubtedly report to Muhammad's deputy in this area, the Supreme Captain of the FOI, Raymond Sharrieff. One of Muhammad's sons, Elijah, Jr., is second in command and serves as captain of the FOI section in Temple No. 2, the Chicago headquarters temple, from which Muhammad's personal security force, or honor guard, is drawn.

As part of their tactic of respectability, the Muslim leaders present the FOI as an ordinary physical training program, like those of the YMCA, CYO, Masons, or Boy Scouts. Its members do, indeed, engage in body-building and physical hygiene activities; they also receive training in judo, military drill, and karate. There is no evidence that the FOI sections still receive small-arms training—as Beynon reported in 1937—or that the FOI high command is gathering an armory for emergency use. Such activities are not beyond possibility, however, for the FOI looks forward to playing an heroic role in the impending Battle of

Armageddon, even though Muhammad insists that Allah will do the fighting.

The FOI's duties fall under two broad headings, *security* and *discipline.* As a security force, the FOI stands guard in the temples, checks visitors at all Muslim meetings, and provides a personal guard for all ministers and traveling officials, including the Messenger and Louis Farrakhan. As a disciplinary force, its supervises the "trials" of Muslims charged with such offenses as adultery, the use of narcotics, misuse of temple funds, not attending meetings, sleeping during meetings, failing to bring "Lost-Founds" (visitors) to meetings, reporting temple activities to outsiders, using unbecoming language before female Muslims, eating or selling pork, failing to pay extra dues for being overweight, allowing anyone to enter the temple under the influence of liquor, or stating an unwillingness to die for Allah.

At the trial, the offending Muslim is placed in the custody of the temple's FOI. The proceedings are conducted jointly by the FOI captain and the minister, with the entire FOI section in attendance. (In the case of lesser infractions, all regular members of the temple may be admitted.) The defendant is not allowed to offer any defense: the charges against him are read, and the verdict is thereupon pronounced—by the minister in case a religious issue is involved, by the FOI captain in all other cases. This verdict is final; there is no appeal.

At least three types of sentence are known to be imposed as the result of these FOI trials. For minor violations there is a "Class C" sentence, under which the convicted Muslim is required to perform labor at the temple or some other designated place for a period of time. A more serious but not infrequent punishment is the "Class F" sentence, or suspension, under which the convict is isolated from all Muslim contacts for a period of time ranging from ninety days to five years. During this time he is barred from all Muslim temples, enterprises, and businesses; and other Muslims are forbidden to talk with, visit, or otherwise associate with him. The more serious sentence—and it is apparently rarely invoked—is formal and permanent expulsion from the Movement. Both Malcolm X and Muhammad Ali came under suspension. Malcolm eventually left the Movement of his own accord. Ali has waited patiently for reinstatement. In 1969, Muhammad issued a statement to "tell the world we are not with Muhammad Ali . . . in his desire to work in the sports world for the sake of a 'leetle' money."[34] Three years later he characterized Ali as "a good believer [though] full of sport . . . [who has] done nothing that cannot be forgiven if he repents."[35]

Recruits to the FOI are carefully screened before admission, for they are expected to set the highest possible standards of character and dedication. Each candidate is required to pass oral examinations on certain levels of knowledge about the Movement and its history—examinations in which the candidate must recite long memorized passages verbatim, without a single error. Candidates are also required to take a secret oath on admission.

From that point on, the men and officers are held rigorously to the most demanding Muslim ideals, for the Fruit of Islam are considered the living exemplars of the Black Nation. They must be "absolutely independent in every respect"—a phrase which means that they must be self-reliant and able to protect themselves against any form of attack. They must be perfectly obedient to all "constituted" authority, black or white, and they must promote complete unity and harmony within the group. They must respect and protect black womanhood; there can be no deviation, for the "era of disgrace for the black woman has come to an end, even if it costs her life and the lives of her defenders." They must reassume the position of leadership and guidance in their own homes. And they must examine and question everything they see and hear, accepting nothing as sacred or certain except on its intrinsic merits unless, of course, it is a teaching of Muhammad.

As a result of its power and secrecy, its high standards, and strict discipline, the FOI has drawn about itself an especially glamorous aura. Its military aspect appeals directly to the pent-up militancy of the true believer; and many Muslims who may not join the FOI act out their militancy by adulating it. To these true believers, the FOI is the vanguard of Muslim destiny, the glorious army of the Black Man's revolution that is now gathering its strength. But the FOI also has a certain aura of mysticism. "Fruit," the Muslims explain, is the "final product of any tree"; it is the purpose for which the tree exists. Yet in the fruit is the seed: the beginning of a new tree. The Black Muslims see themselves as the fruit of the American system of slavery and oppression, bearing within themselves the seed of the coming Black Nation. The Fruit of Islam, therefore, symbolizes the inner meaning of the Movement as a whole. It is the liberating element of the Nation of Islam.

Yet the structure and role of the FOI—indeed, its very existence—

suggest that it may soon become the focus of profound tensions inside the Movement. For example, when a struggle for succession breaks out at Muhammad's death, as it inevitably must, to whom will the FOI throw its support? And if the FOI is recognized as a key weapon in that struggle, will there not be increasingly tense intrigues among the leadership for control of the secret army? Surely it is no accident that Muhammad has appointed, as the two chief officers of the FOI, his son-in-law and his son.

Again, the FOI trials reveal clearly that discipline in the Muslim ranks is less than perfect. The Muslim leadership has chosen to notice even minor infractions and to punish them through the FOI. But if "loyalty" and "obedience" are so narrowly defined, they *cannot* be maintained; and if the inevitable infractions are punished highhandedly, the Muslims' spontaneous loyalty and obedience to the Movement must eventually give way to resentment and rebellion. In that case, the FOI might easily degenerate into a strong-arm elite keeping a restive membership in line. Such a development would mean trouble not only within the Movement but also between the Muslims and the community at large.

Above all, there is the curious paradox that a divine black nation, outraged by the injustices of a class-structured white society, has now deliberately created an elite of its own. How will the mass of Muslims react as they come to realize that, after all the bright promises, they are second-class citizens again, even in the Black Nation of Islam?

### III. THE SEARCH FOR RESPECTABILITY

*Violence and the Christian Tradition*

The private image of the Movement has changed considerably since the days of Wallace Fard, and it continues to be modified as the Muslims search for respectability and acceptance.

The Detroit Muslims of the 1930s had a number of bizarre excesses charged against them, including, as we have seen, human sacrifice.

On November 21, 1932, the people of Detroit became conscious of the presence of the cult through its first widely publicized human sacrifice. A prominent member, Robert Harris, renamed Robert

Karriem, erected an altar in his home at 1249 Dubois Street and invited his roomer, John J. Smith, to present himself as a human sacrifice, so that he might become, as Harris said, "the Savior of the World." Smith agreed, and at the hour appointed for the sacrifice—9:30 a.m.—Harris plunged a knife into Smith's heart.[36]

Other reports of sacrifices or attempted sacrifices were current in Detroit as late as 1937.

In Chicago in 1935, two hundred Muslims rioted in a courtroom and attempted to storm the bench while one of their members was on trial. Before the melee was over, one policeman was dead and eleven had been injured. Two of the Muslims were shot in the clash, and forty were sent to prison.[37] In 1958, Muhammad made a special trip to Detroit to quiet his followers, who were having trouble with the police.[38]

In 1960, in a case involving Muslims in New York City, the presiding judge cleared the courtroom before the jury's verdict was read, fearing that "the Muslim followers who packed the hall every day of the seven-day trial might demonstrate if a verdict of guilty were issued."[39] The Muslim defendants had been charged with assaulting two policemen who entered their homes without a warrant; they were found not guilty, and the anticipated trouble did not develop. The *Los Angeles Herald-Dispatch* reported, however, that fifty Muslims, "led by Minister Malcolm X, silently patrolled the corridor of the court building while the jury carried on its deliberations" and that "outside the court building in a small park across the street, some 400 male followers of the Muslim faith were gathered. They were silent, well-disciplined, ominous." Malcolm X was described as "a disturbingly intent figure as he sat on a corridor bench munching dried raisins . . . pondering the explosive factors largely in his command."[40]

In spite of such incidents, however, Muhammad prefers to disassociate his Movement from violent activity of any kind. His followers are forbidden to carry weapons, and they are cautioned not to carry any instrument that might conceivably be considered even a potential weapon, should they be searched by an overzealous police officer. But the Muslim leader is caught on the horns of a dilemma, for he has taught his followers not only to avoid precipitating violence but also to defend themselves and each other if they are assaulted.

We must take things into our own hands. We must return to the Mosaic law of an eye for an eye, and a tooth for a tooth. What does it matter if 10 million of us die? There will be 7 million of us left, and they will enjoy justice and freedom.[41]

The constant threat of violence is implicit in the basic doctrines of the Movement, and this fearlessness before the white man is one of the Movement's strongest appeals.

Much is made of the "Battle of Armageddon" that is expected to take place right here in North America. But this battle—until recently a prominent feature in Muslim literature and teachings—is more and more relegated to the realm of the eschatological, where such battles usually are fought. It belongs to a future in which the present believers are not likely to participate. *Unanticipated* violence, on the other hand, may occur at any moment. The Muslims display a kind of contained aggressiveness, which may occasionally provoke violence without actually initiating it.

Muhammad does not wish to alter the self-image of the Muslims as "men among men." Yet he does wish his followers to be accepted as peaceful, law-abiding, religious individuals. There may be no logical inconsistency here, but there are serious emotional obstacles which prevent the black community at large from accepting him and his Movement on the terms of his stated proposals. First of all, most Blackamericans have known no religion other than Christianity, and the Christian faith—with its emphasis on charity and long-suffering—has perhaps been more meaningful to the older generation of Blacks than to the young who have not been the victims of such absolute rejection. Consequently, any new religion not strongly conditioned by the Christian traditions of meekness and love may expect to find the black masses generally unreceptive, although there has been decisive change in the way many Blacks interpret their Christian obligations to whites. New concepts in "black religion" and "black theology" have challenged the place of meekness and nonviolence in the "responsible" response to white oppression.

But Muhammad's peculiar brand of Islam at once snatches away the comforts of heaven, which have been earned at so great a price on earth, and substitutes a supreme black man for the sure and comforting presence of an omnipotent father. Those educated in the Christian spirit believe that patience and loving-kindness on earth will earn the sweetest of all rewards: eternal life in a kingdom where all men love their brothers and live as equals in the nearness of God. In exchange for this gentle faith, the Muslims offer the black Christian only the taste of violence—the chance to vent his hostilities here on earth and then to die forever. This exchange is not generally acceptable, at least not in theory, although, again, the notion that whites can respond positively to patience and loving-kindness has suffered some erosion. In short, although some Blacks are increasingly ambivalent about how their Christianity applies to white people in practical, day-to-day situations, they remain reluctant to adopt an official dogma which conceives whites as nonhuman (devils) and commits them to a race war, the Armageddon.

In an attempt to bridge the gap, Muhammad has recently modified and hushed some of the Movement's most strident assaults on Christianity itself. The "debunking" of the virgin birth of Jesus, for example, was a standard dramatic feature of every temple lecture a few years ago. Today it is seldom mentioned unless the issue is raised by a non-Muslim. The Muslim denunciation of the Bible as a "poison book" has been radically reinterpreted. The Bible, the ministers now say, is both true and accurate when "correctly interpreted." It was "poisoned" by the white man, who wished to use it to justify his wicked behavior. Finally, Blacks are cordially invited to attend lectures—and even formally to join the Movement—while remaining active members of the Christian church.

The Muslims have thus softened their derision of Christian symbols but not their contempt for the Christian faith. They are clearly gambling that the symbols have become empty of meaning, that the black Christian clings to them only because they are familiar and comfortable and a badge of religious respectability. The Muslims are willing to let the black Christian cherish these "meaningless" symbols, at least for a while, if he will become a Black Muslim at heart. And new developments in the black Christian community seem to be nurturing this prospect. The earthly rewards of meekness and a gentle faith are slow in coming, perhaps too slow for the prevailing mood of urgency. Black Christians, like white ones, are rapidly learning to modify their faith wherever secular advantage is at stake. Even among the devoted apostles of nonviolence, Christian love may at times become a technique rather than a way of life.

### The Race Issue

The Black Muslim leadership's search for respectability—a concomitant of its desire for rapid growth—may also force an internal showdown on the vehemence and bitterness with which the race issue is to be pressed. Muhammad still openly denounces the white man—the entire white race, without exception—in the most scathing language ever heard in the white-dominated nations of the world. These denunciations attract and delight the true believer, but they repel many potential black converts, who themselves are daily victims of extreme and irrational racial generalizations. The average Blackamerican feels that anyone who publicly participates in the categorical denunciation of any race must be either insane or a troublemaker or both. The victims of racism are chary of becoming racists.

Yet Muhammad is aware of the paradox that the less respectable he is, the more he is respected. His boldness in "saying for millions what millions fear to say for themselves" has elevated him to a recognized position of leadership in the black ghetto. Even more important, it may have earned him the respect of the white man, who admires solidarity and determination. And the respect of the white man is the key to respectability, for "whom the white man respects, all others hasten to embrace." Thus, ironically, Muhammad may have won by extremism a position of power and prestige he could never have won by moderation. This society still values the ability to deliver over what is being delivered.

In playing this gamble, Muhammad risks incurring the fate that befell Marcus Garvey: tagged as a hatemonger, Garvey could not consolidate the black masses under his standard and so was easily toppled by a combined action of white pique and black envy—at the top. Perhaps for this reason, Muhammad is especially distressed by charges that he is hatemongering. He asserts that hate would be morally justified, for "the white man has hated the Negroes . . . ever since they have been on this planet earth,"[42] and that hate is given divine approval in the Christians' own Bible:

> God, Himself, hates: see Malachi 1:2-3: "Was not Esau Jacob's brother? saith the Lord: yet I loved Jacob and I hated Esau. . . ." St. Luke 14:26, no man could be the disciple of Jesus unless he hated his father, mother, wife, children . . .[43]

Yet his own racial teachings, he insists, are not hate but the simple truth.

> I am here with the truth for you to accept or be the losers. I am not afraid to speak the truth regardless. . . . Let those who accuse me of teaching hate point out that portion of my teaching which constitutes hate. . . . Is it hate to call upon you to unite?[44]

Muhammad presents himself as a man who is dispassionately revealing the truth about an enemy—an absolutely ruthless enemy, who has skillfully camouflaged his character by distorting the facts of history and intimidating all who are unwilling to accept the distortion. The Messenger claims to preach not hate but simply "the truth which is capable of setting the Black Man free."

If this gamble pays off, Muhammad may gain respectability for his Movement without retreating an inch on the race issue and without having the Movement destroyed by internal dissensions. If it fails, the result may be a tug-of-war between those who cling to respectability and those who cling to hatred. In either case, the Messenger has made his own position clear: "I will never, after having knowledge, love nor befriend the enemies of . . . my Black Nation, whether my people believe as I do or not."[45]

# 8 This Side of Orthodoxy

A major goal of the Muslim leadership a decade ago was the general acceptance of the Movement as a legitimate religion—specifically, as a legitimate sect of orthodox Islam. This is no longer considered necessary: the Muslims' self-respect does not hinge on such acceptance. Muhammad has stated that the Muslims *are* legitimate and Islamic, and so far as the Muslims themselves are concerned, this settles the matter. Nor is it an expedient directed at the black community any longer, for the aegis of orthodox Islam means little in America's black ghettos. So long as the Movement keeps its color identity with the rising black peoples of Africa, it could discard all its Islamic attributes—its name, its prayers to Allah, its citations from the Quran, everything "Muslim," without substantial risk to its appeal to the black masses.

In pressing their demand for complete acceptance as a legitimate religion and a Moslem sect, the Muslims had their eye primarily on the white community. In many ways, America does live up to its democratic ideal in the elaborate safeguards it provides for freedom of worship. Religious groups in America are unfettered; only in the most extreme cases is certain behavior in the name of religion construed as against public policy and, as such, prohibited.[1] The Black Muslims know that, as they prosper, they will encounter repression and reprisal. The more swiftly and securely they could become acknowledged as a legitimate religion, the more securely they could rely upon the counter-pressures of democratic toleration and constitutional immunity to protect them from harassment. Malcolm X was a strong advocate of the internationalization of the Nation of Islam. Elijah Muhammad never was. While he may have wanted the legitimacy of orthodoxy, the possibility of his black nation losing its identity in the vast configurations of international Islam was not a notion he ever entertained seriously. What he wanted was recognition as a legitimate religious leader presiding over a legitimate religion.

The Muslims have generally been given the benefit of the doubt. They have been treated, if only provisionally, as a legitimate religion. Except in prisons, their meetings have never been barred by any agency of the government. The Universities of Islam are legally approved as parochial schools. And the temples and school properties are tax exempt in all states where they exist, under the same regulations that govern the church properties of all other religious bodies.

But this provisional acceptance is not enough. The Black Muslims are not generally included in the national gatherings of religious leaders, and Muhammad, who frequently equates himself with "the Pope of Rome," resents being snubbed. Beyond that, the FBI keeps the Movement under as close surveillance as it would a political terrorist organization. And in some instances, the Muslims' status as a religion has been flatly denied by government officials. Perhaps the most significant of these denials to date have occurred in prisons, which are among the Muslims' most fertile recruiting grounds. In some prisons, the Muslims are permitted to hold services, but in others they are denied the right of assembly. A case in point is Clinton State Prison at Utica, New York, where four inmates were allegedly placed in solitary confinement when they sought to practice their new faith. (The warden described three of the prisoners as "Protestants a year ago"; the fourth had been a Catholic.) Prison officials did not dispute that discipline improves markedly among those converted to Islam, but they protested that the Muslims have "ulterior motives," aimed at "forcing supremacy over whites, although they do not express it."[2]

To defend themselves against such harassments, now and in the future, the Muslims are pressing hard for complete recognition as a legitimate religion, on equal terms with the reigning triumvirate of Protestants, Catholics, and Jews, but they do not want to be identified with "white orthodox" Islam. The orthodox Muslims are denounced for currying favor with the (white) enemy. The Asiatic origin of the Nation is now down-played: "The Black African, the Aboriginal Black People of the earth are our real brothers," says Muhammad. "The Black Man of America and the Black Man of Africa must unite again. We are a part of, and belong to each other."[3] Hence, the Muslims want to be "Islamic" but not "orthodox," because orthodoxy is contaminated with the implications of whiteness. Just how this goal is to be accomplished is not exactly clear, but Muhammad speaks of a "New Islam" to be ushered in after his death:

> It will be a New Islam to what the old Orthodox is today. It will be altogether a New One. . . . The Old Islam was led by white people, white Muslims, but this one will not be. This Islam will be established and led by Black Muslims only.[4]

Who will rule over the new Black Islam? Allah. Once the truth has been established, there will be no need for human intermediaries:

> There will be no successor. There will be no need for a successor when a man has got the divine truth and has brought you face to face with God. . . . When we are face to face with God, that is the end of it, and so what would another one do? There is nothing for him to do.[5]

In fact, Muhammad sees himself as the last Messenger the Black Nation will ever have, or need. He has brought his people to the point where they, if his teachings are followed, will be able (to use his own famous aphorism) to go for self. As for the material wealth gathered by the Nation, it will be looked after in terms of instructions already laid down. The whole Nation will be responsible:

> That will be carried on by the Nation. After setting up the Nation on the right way, or right path, to take care of themselves, they do not need anymore instruction on that. They will follow it as the Constitution of America will be followed.[6]

It is commonly accepted among the faithful that in lieu of ordinary death, Muhammad will "go away for a period," after which he will return with Allah himself—"in the person of Fard Muhammad." Hence the Messenger's reference to bringing them "face to face with God." Following the Messenger's lead, the Black Muslim rank and file have taken up the task of distinguishing between themselves and the "spooky-minded" orthodox Muslims. Orthodox Muslims are "spooky minded" because "they believe that Allah is some immaterial something, but yet he made a material universe!" (Alas! Most Christians must also be "spooky minded!") The Blacks are the true Muslims:

> . . . every Black Man under the sun is born a Muslim by nature. . . . There are some of the white race who are Muslims by faith. The white race is the only people on Earth that are not real Muslims, or Black Muslims by nature. . . . These poor Orthodox or Conventional Muslim brothers fail to understand our Leader. . . the Honorable Elijah Muhammad. . . . 99% of our Muslim brothers from the East have been deceived one way or another. . . .[7]

The notion that Black Muslims are seeking indiscriminate solidarity with the world of orthodox Islam is further shattered by Ali Baghdadi's attack on Iran in his column "Middle East Report" in *Muhammad Speaks:*

> The 2500 year birthday celebration of the so-called Persian empire, destroyed by Alexander the Great, is just one of the many reasons for which the Shah of Iran, "King of Kings, Light of the Aryans, Shadow of God, and Center of the Universe," should be brought to trial as one of the most wanted world criminals. This party unmatched in history cost the impoverished people of Iran over $80 million. Some say the total cost is closer to $2 billion.

Iran's foreign policy fares no better:

> The Shah's reactionary policy, which is in agreement with the Nixon doctrine, simply means that Asians equipped by the U.S. government will be used to suppress other Asians seeking national liberation and progress.
> The Shah has made it clear that he intends to secure the colonial interests of the United States and to guarantee the flow of oil to his imperialist masters.[8]

At the moment, orthodox Islamic groups in the United States do not acknowledge the Black Muslims as in any way related to world-wide Islam. The response from Arab and other Moslem nations is more ambiguous. There seems to be no good reason to doubt that the Black

Muslims will eventually find the acceptance they want in international Islam, and this despite their insistent parochialism. In rejecting orthodoxy, Muhammad has been careful not to reject Islam, nor for that matter does he reject all Moslems who are orthodox. His adulation of the late President Nasser of Egypt is undiminished, and apparently the whole Arab bloc (which is considered "black" by many Blackamericans, Muslim and non-Muslim) is excluded from the worst implications of the "spooky minded."

### A Legitimate Religion?

The line that separates a purely social organization from a purely religious communion is seldom well defined. Religion is, in part, a facet of man's social life; and social concerns are at times invested with an almost religious aura. Some great religious movements developed originally out of social concerns (Methodism is a well-known example), and social movements ranging from communism to the Townsend Plan have exhibited marked religious overtones.[9] An incipient mass movement such as the Black Muslims, therefore, may be *both* "social" and "religious," though its emphasis will be weighted in one direction or the other.

America has always been wary of definitions which claim to draw a precise line between the religious and the secular. Such definitions tend to be either too nebulous or too subjective; in either case, they are unreliable guides for a democracy intent on safeguarding an absolute freedom of worship. The American public, as a result, eschews all rigid criteria of orthodoxy and maintains an historically unique tolerance of religious deviation. Americans may reject and even combat an organization which claims to be a religion, but they are not likely to deny that it *is* a religion.

Within the American tradition, then, it is not necessary for the Black Muslims to prove that they are a valid religious communion. The question is whether it can be proved that they are *not*. If the negative cannot be proved, a general acceptance of the Movement as a legitimate religion is assured.

Emile Durkheim, one of the most critical observers and students of the sociology of religion, insists that any attempt at a definition of religion must derive from the existential phenomenon, from "the reality itself . . . for religion cannot be defined except by the characteristics which are found wherever religion itself is found."[10] At an irreducible minimum, he suggests, these characteristics are *beliefs* and *rites.*

> Religious phenomena are naturally arranged in two fundamental categories: beliefs and rites. The first are states of opinion, and consist in representations; the second are determined modes of action.[11]

A religious rite is distinguished from its secular counterpart by the sacred nature of its object. A moral rule or a legal statute, for example, may prescribe behavior identical to that of a religious rite; but the religious prescription refers to a different *class of objects.* The religious object is "sacred"; the secular object, even when of the highest social value, is "profane." There is no necessary relationship, however, between the sacred and either "deity" or the "supernatural." Neither the divine nor the supernatural is necessary to a religion.

> The circle of sacred objects cannot be determined . . . once for all. Its extent varies infinitely, according to the different religions. That is how Buddhism is a religion: in default of gods, it admits the existence of sacred things, namely, the four noble truths and the practices derived from them.[12]

Indeed, the "circle of sacred objects" cannot be rationally defined at all. That is sacred which the believers of a particular faith *feel* is sacred. And this feeling is at once the most subjective and most widespread, the most familiar and most elusive of phenomena. It evades definition, yet its presence is the identifying mark of a legitimate religion. In pragmatic terms, wherever a body of men shares the feeling that a specific group of objects is sacred and has elaborated this feeling into specific beliefs and rites, there a religion must be said to exist.

It must be granted, then, that the Black Muslim Movement constitutes a legitimate religion within the definition of the sociology of religion.[13] But there are many kinds of religion; and while all enjoy a nearly unrestricted freedom of worship in America, they are not all granted equal deference and respect by the community at large. Mere cults, for example, like the followers of Father Divine and "Daddy

Grace," are not taken as seriously as Presbyterians, say, or as Jews. But the Black Muslims want and are determined to achieve the respect of all Americans, even of the "blue-eyed devils." Their success will depend, in large part, on the *kind* of religion they are—that is, on the degree of religious stability and respectability they can be said to have achieved.

Perhaps the best known analysis of religious groups into broad categories is that developed by Ernst Troeltsch and refined by J. Milton Yinger. This system of categories, like all others familiar to Americans, is based on Christian groups, and there is no real assurance that it is valid when applied to non-Christian religions such as the Black Muslims. It is, nevertheless, the system by which the Muslims will be evaluated by most Americans; it is the scale against which the Muslims will actually be measured in their demand for deference and respect.

Troeltsch divides religious groups into two types: the *church* and the *sect.* The leader of a church is characteristically a "priest"; the leader of a sect is characteristically a "prophet." In broader terms:

> The Church is that type of organization which is overwhelmingly conservative, which to a certain extent accepts the secular order, and dominates the masses; in principle, therefore, it is universal; i.e., it desires to cover the whole life of humanity. The sects, on the other hand, are comparatively small groups; they aspire after personal inward perfection, and they aim at a direct personal fellowship between the members of each group.... Their attitude towards the world, the State, and Society may be indifferent, tolerant, or hostile since they have no desire to control and incorporate these forms of social life; on the contrary, they tend to avoid them; their aim is usually either to tolerate their presence alongside of their own body, or even to replace these social institutions by their own society.[14]

The church, in short, attempts to include the whole society in its outlook and thus inevitably becomes an integral part of the social order. It may even become a determining force, providing stability and sanction; but to the same extent it becomes a captive of the upper classes and dependent on them. The church may thus defeat its own ends, for as the lower classes find themselves abandoned, schisms will occur, and the social order will again be threatened. New religious groups, or sects, will then coalesce in response to various middle- and lower-class needs not met by the church—needs which center at times on theological or ritual disagreements but more often on questions of economic or political enfranchisement, racial or ethnic status, social mobility or social change. The church, to the extent that it is a balance wheel of the status quo, is impotent to cope with such revolutionary tensions.

The sect, by contrast, draws primarily upon the disinherited, the unchampioned, and those opposed to the existing social order. It repudiates the compromises the church has made with secular institutions, and it resents the church's failure to assert itself against social abuses. The sect may respond to worldly evil by withdrawing from society, hoping to avoid present injustice and ultimate perdition, or by embracing a radicalism intended to establish in the social order its own ideals and sense of justice.

Not all sects (as Yinger points out) originate in the lower classes. The Methodist movement, for example, "remained throughout its history in the control of men who had been born and bred in the middle class,"[15] although it was substantially a lower-class movement until recent times. The Bahais, Christian Scientists, Theosophists, and numerous other familiar sects have been predominantly middle class from their inception. Middle-class sects are not characteristically in protest against the social order, for they have usually been favored by it. They are more often disenchanted with the institutionalized churches, which seem to them to be neglecting essential human values.

Lower-class sects, on the other hand, are most often spawned in poverty, disprivilege, depression, and despair. They are the refuge of those who are without power and who lack even an effective advocate in the circles where power resides. The existing society has been unjust to them, so they will reorganize the social order—usually along lines that those in power construe as "radical." But sects of this type tend to elicit concerted opposition and are thus predisposed to failure. They incur the hostility not only of the power elite but also of the less radical sects, which are potentially more mobile and which stand to suffer if the power structure, feeling threatened, becomes more rigidly exclusive. The usual history of a radical sect is therefore short.

The Black Muslim Movement is clearly a sect, in Troeltsch's broad definition of that term. Appealing to an almost exclusively Christian black community, the Movement repudiates the Christian church not only in particulars but *in toto.* It insists upon the separation of black men from white society, leaving that corrupt edifice to crumble under the weight of its own iniquity. And where the Movement is forced into contact with the white community, it reacts with a radicalism which is—from the Muslim point of view, at least—idealistic and just. But to categorize the Muslims as a sect is not quite so simple as Troeltsch's terms suggest, for Yinger's modification introduces a new element that must be carefully reckoned with.

As part of his refinement of Troeltsch's categories,[16] Yinger points to the existence of a third type of religious group which, while it somewhat resembles the sect, is in fact quite dissimilar. This type is the *cult,* a small group of people unrelated to any other religious institution and "tied together only by common religious emotions and needs."[17] Yinger seems to consider the Black Muslims a cult, pure and simple:

> Pure cult types are not common in Western society; most groups that might be called cults are fairly close to the sect type. Perhaps the best examples are the various Spiritualist groups and some of the "Moslem" cults among American Negroes.[18]

The cult, as Yinger defines it, is characteristically organized around a charismatic leader (such as Muhammad), in whom are centered the loyalties of the rank and file. As a result, the cult usually is confined to a small area and dies with its founder: problems of succession are not effectively anticipated, and the bereaved cult disintegrates into splinter groups, which eventually fade into oblivion. But while it exists, the cult deviates even more sharply than the sect from the dominant church and the established social order, and its "implications for anarchy are even stronger."[19] It takes individual problems, especially the "search for a mystic experience,"[20] as its total concern and shows little or no interest in problems of social justice. Cult members are typically indifferent to their status and prospects in the enveloping society.

On the surface, the Black Muslim Movement might seem to merit Yinger's designation of it as a cult. It is (1) a relatively small group of people, (2) under strong charismatic leadership, (3) deviating sharply from the established social order and, (4) diverging absolutely from the dominant church of its society. But on close inspection, a number of significant differences appear. (These differences were perhaps not familiar to Yinger when he wrote in 1957, for there had been no serious published study of the Black Muslims in almost twenty-five years.)

The Muslims originated as a small, local group, but in their period of greatest growth—the middle 1950s to 1964—their membership may have reached between 50,000 and 100,000. No one outside the movement can be certain, and only the inner circle of the inner circle of the Chicago headquarters of the Nation would have the inside information on membership. There are still more than fifty mosques stretching across the country and many of these have satellite units identified only as "A," "B," "C," etc. While still relatively small compared to the nation's major religious bodies, they are larger than *most* American denominations, sects, and cults. More than fifty Protestant denominations, for example, have fewer than ten congregations each, and more than half the sects in the nation have only 7,000 members or less.[21]

The impressive cohesion of the Black Muslim Movement today is certainly due to the charismatic leadership of Elijah Muhammad. True, he is not the founder of the Movement but only the Messenger of Allah; the Muslims passed through their first crisis of succession when, under extremely divisive conditions, the mantle was passed down from Wallace Fard to Muhammad. Yet the Muslims' absolute loyalty to Muhammad and their uncritical faith in his wisdom and leadership suggest a simple continuity of charisma, which has postponed the problem of succession without really solving it. On the other hand—and perhaps of decisive importance—the Movement is rapidly developing a firm organizational structure. Under the direction of an aggressive clergy and inner council, the Movement continues to expand vigorously in all parts of the country without the physical presence of the Messenger.

The Muslims do deviate sharply from the established social order, and their call for separation in some ways resembles the withdrawal characteristic of the cult. The Muslims consider futile any attempt to reform American society; they plan simply to retire from it, cultivate the Black Nation, and wait. The white devils, lacking black victims, will then presumably turn on each other and destroy themselves, and the Black Man will inherit the earth. Yet the driving force of the Movement is not separatism *per se*, but a sense of the unique manifest destiny Allah has decreed for the Black Man. In the Black Muslim's understanding of ultimate reality, the white man simply *isn't!* His present temporary existence is an anachronism, a physical and social aberration foisted upon human society by a mad devil named Yacub. The devils now have the upper hand over Allah's Black Nation; hence, the torrent of racial condemnation which fills its sermons and publications is undeniably social protest, all the more so for its bitter rejection of any hope for reform. There is no trace among the Muslims of that mystical absorption and indifference to social injustice which mark a cult.

Finally, the Muslims are unequivocal in their repudiation of the dominant church in American society. Their beliefs and rites are almost totally deviant from those of the Christian tradition, and within this frame of reference a case might be made for labeling them a cult. But the Muslims do not claim to be a Christian sect. They have declared themselves an integral part of Islam, which they consider the church of the Black Nation. Muslim leaders are now working skillfully and hard to establish the Movement's authenticity as a legitimate Moslem sect. If they succeed—and it seems virtually certain that they will—the last realistic argument that would relegate the Movement to the status of a cult will have been answered.

The massive weight of all available evidence, in short, suggests that the Black Muslim Movement is not a cult but a sect.[22] It is not local, ephemeral, or isolated; it will be shaken by, but will probably not collapse at Muhammad's death; and it may soon be able to draw upon the vast prestige and power of international Islam to defend it in case of harassment by the white community, despite its repudiation of orthodoxy. To shrug it off, in the manner of some observers, as "just another cult" would be a tragic error. The Muslims today are powerless children of despair and poverty in revolt against a social order they have found unjust. But they will not remain powerless, and it is likely that they will be with us for a long time to come.

## A Moslem Sect?

The Muslim dream is to have a solid Black Muslim community in the United States, recognized and supported by Moslems throughout the world as an accepted part of Islam. This is not sheer expediency: from the earliest days of the Movement, the Black Muslims have considered themselves devout adherents of the Moslem faith. They recognize Allah as the one true God (though they see Him not as a unique deity but as the Supreme Black Man among Black Men, all of whom are divine). They base their services on both the Quran and the Bible, and they are learning Arabic so as to be able to rely entirely on the original Quran. They observe the classic Moslem prayer ritual and dietary laws, and they hold in high esteem the traditional pilgrimage to Mecca.

On certain fundamental points of doctrine, however, the Black Muslims have departed widely from the orthodox Moslem tradition. Partly for this reason, and partly from an instinctive militancy toward newcomers, the official representatives of orthodox Islam in the United States have refused any recognition of the Black Muslims. The Movement has not been admitted as an affiliate of the official Federation of Islamic Associations in the United States and Canada, nor has it been recognized as legitimate by any affiliate of the federation. It has, in fact, been vigorously denounced by several Moslem groups, including the rival Muslim Brotherhood of America.

Muhammad readily admits that some of the teachings and practices of his Movement are at variance with those of other Moslem groups, but he presents these as differences of *interpretation* within a unity of belief. Blackamericans, he argues, have been the victims of a harsh and cynical oppression, and the Islamic faith in its pure orthodox form is not appropriate to their needs:

> My brothers in the East were never subjected to the conditions of slavery and systematic brainwashing by the Slavemasters for as long a period as my people here were subjected. I cannot, therefore, blame them if they differ with me in certain interpretations of the message of Islam.[23]

He is not troubled by the rejection of the handful of orthodox Moslems in the United States; his hopes are staked on recognition by the more important (and more flexible) officials in the Moslem nations of Africa and Asia.

Two of the Black Muslims' basic doctrines are at the heart of the controversy: their insistence that the Black Man must separate himself from the abhorrent and doomed white race, and their belief that it is the manifest destiny of the Black Nation to inherit the earth. These doctrines are in flagrant contrast to the orthodox Moslem ideal of an all-embracing brotherhood of man. Moslems have, throughout their history, shown a rare and admirable indifference to boundaries of race; and any tinge of racial bigotry in an acknowledged Moslem group would cause the orthodox acute embarrassment and anguish. The Black Muslims, however, refuse absolutely to moderate or compromise their racial doctrines. Muhammad is convinced that a belief in panracial brotherhood would leave his followers with no more dignity and hope than they can now find in the Christian church.

Are these contradictions so extreme that the Black Muslims must be said to have excluded themselves from Islam? The question will have to be answered, of course, by Moslem theologians, but it seems likely that they will find the Black Muslims to be within the pale—a legitimate if somewhat heretical Moslem sect. Every faith has its deviates, and every international faith makes broad allowances for interpretations of doctrine to fit local conditions. The fact that orthodox Moslems in America reject the Movement has no real significance: most Christian sects and denominations were likewise spurned by the orthodox in their founding years. And a clear precedent exists in Islam itself for the ultimate recognition of heretics as a sect despite major doctrinal differences. This precedent is the Ahmadiyah movement, a small Moslem group of India and Pakistan,[24] with an increasing number of black adherents in the United States.

The "prophet" of the movement was the pious Mirzā Ghulām Ahmad (1839-1908), . . . [who] was accepted by many, including orthodox religious, as a great [Moslem] reformer. Suddenly, in 1889, his popularity gave place to extreme denunciation, when he announced that he had received a revelation authorizing him to receive men's allegiance as the promised Messiah and *Imām Mahdī;* that is, Jesus returned to earth and the apocalyptic saviour who [Moslem] tradition has held will appear at the last day. The general [Moslem] community, and particularly the divines, outraged by this blasphemy, attacked him relentlessly. . . . Despite intense persecution, the community grew, in numbers and in faith.[25]

There are still intermittent quarrels between the Ahmadiyah and the orthodox, but the Ahmadiyah are now generally accepted as a legitimate sect of Islam.

The open assertion by the Black Muslims that it is their destiny to inherit the earth and that the present rulers of this world will soon fall upon evil days is certainly not unique in the history of religions. Such a religious philosophy is at least as old as the ancient Hebrews and at least as recent as the newest adventist Christian sect. The characteristic orientation of all religions has been the expectation that God's first pleasure is His own elect, the elect being those who are pure in doctrine, correct in ritual and, oftentimes, racially or ethnically select. The multiple fractures within the Catholic and Protestant communions respectively, and the sects which elaborate every other major religion, provide ample if disheartening evidence of this universal assumption.

Islam itself, although it claims no significant racial bias, does share this pronounced intolerance for the nonbeliever. To this extent, the ground is prepared for understanding and perhaps even tolerating the Black Muslims' racial exclusiveness. A Christian writer, while praising Islam's record of racial inclusiveness, has suggested that racial lines might be drawn and held even by orthodox Islam, "if it got a foothold in Europe or America, where the deeper racial prejudices seem most to flourish." He cites the case of a Moslem missionary in this country meeting separately with white and black members "because of the Christian background of the white people."[26]

Racial hatred, wherever it is taught or practiced, reflects a social depravity. It debases the hater, alienates the hated, and usually impairs the creative capacities of both. Yet history offers almost no instance of a religious subgroup being expelled from the parent communion because it teaches hatred of the outsider. The Christian church, for example, was divided in its early years over the issue of whether to admit gentiles; today it is in controversy over the status of its black members. Yet never, in all its turbulent history, has the church developed a tradition of excluding those whose racial views are repugnant to the mainstream of Christian thought. Instead, the church has sought to preserve its ties, hoping that time and circumstance, interpreted through the spiritual emphases of the church, might work reform.

The most pertinent example, perhaps, is the split within American Protestantism over the question of slavery. The Southern churches taught—and many still teach—that some races are superior to others and that men's social destinies are divinely predetermined by race. These churches formally withdrew from communion with the Northern churches when they could reach no agreement on the slavery issue, yet their status as Christian churches was never in dispute. Even today, a number of Southern Protestant churches proclaim the inferiority of black people whose role as "hewers of wood and drawers of water" is said to be preordained by God Himself; and in the Mormon Church, racial bias categorically excludes Blacks from full membership. Yet these churches have not been expelled from the Christian communion, nor are they even held in suspicion of heresy by their brothers in Christ. Shall we expect any other religion, even Islam, to be more insistent on brotherly love than we are ourselves?

In 1959, Malcolm X made a special trip to Egypt and other Moslem countries to test the acceptability of the Black Muslim Movement abroad. He was received cordially as a "Moslem brother." Later that year, Muhammad and two of his sons made a tour of several Moslem countries. The Messenger was recognized as an important leader and was permitted to make the traditional Moslem pilgrimage to Mecca. He wrote to his followers in the United States:

> On my arrival in Jeddah, Arabia, December 23, 1959, it was almost a necessity that I go to Mecca. The next day . . . the authorities made ready a car to take me and my two sons over the forty-mile distance from Jeddah to that ancient city which is the glory of the Muslim world of Islam.[27]

In Cairo, Muhammad reported that:

> Here . . . I met the Great Imam. He invited me to visit him, and I have experienced great happiness . . . with him. He is over all the Imams in . . . Egypt. He placed a kiss upon my head, and I placed a kiss on his hand.[28]

Back in the United States, the Muslim leader described his Islamic tour to some ninety-five hundred Blacks who gathered to hear him in Los Angeles. In Boston and New York, meanwhile, Malcolm X announced that the question of the Muslims' orthodoxy is "a closed issue," because "those who are not orthodox do not go to Mecca."

### The Political Implications

Like Christianity and Judaism, Islam is more than a religion: it has served also as a political force, drawing together coalitions of states for various purposes at various times. Today it is dynamically important in shaping political alignments among Moslem nations from Morocco to Indonesia—that is to say, across the entire span of the African-Asian land mass. If Islam could establish a large and influential body of believers in the United States, the Moslem brotherhood would circle the earth.

Apart from the followers of Muhammad, there are scarcely 33,000 Moslems in the whole of North America—compared with 345,000 in South America, 12½ million in Europe, and more than 400 million in Africa and Asia. This disproportion is due not so much to the vitality of the Christian church as to America's immigration policies, which discriminate against Africans and Asians. To build an effective bloc in the United States, therefore, the Moslem states would have to convert large numbers of American citizens to Islam—and this the Black Muslims are doing with evident success. The orthodox Moslem bodies in America are dwarfed by Black Islam, and their cries of protest are likely to fall upon apathetic ears in the important Islamic capitals of the East.

Much has been made of an alleged link between the Black Muslims and the United Arab Republic. The Muslims are accused of accepting financial support from the Egyptians and of being "pro-Nasser." There is no known evidence to support the allegation of financial support, and Muhammad has vigorously denied these allegations:

Now it has been charged that I am receiving aid from some alien government or ideology. These charges, of course, come from those who resent the progress we have made toward enlightening our people. I want to say here and now that these charges are absolutely false. I do not receive any aid from the United Arab Republic; I do not receive aid from the Communist party; there is not one dime that comes to us from any source other than our own followers.[29]

But political favors do not always turn on money. The UAR has shown little public recognition of the Movement, but Muslim leaders have been welcomed enthusiastically abroad, and the Movement has received important encouragement and advice from Egyptian nationals in this country. The Muslims have responded by considering themselves specifically "anti-Zionist" rather than "anti-Semitic," and they were proud to identify themselves with President Nasser, whose picture still graces the walls of many Muslim homes and temples.

Malcolm X made a frank bid for UAR support, offering the growth potential of the Movement as a prime incentive. "The Arabs," he asserted, "as a colored people, should make more effort to reach the millions of colored people in America who are related to the Arabs by blood." The Arab leaders' response to this appeal is not known. But Malcolm's pledge that "these millions of colored peoples would be completely in sympathy with the Arab cause" was undoubtedly received with quiet appreciation.

In January 1958, Muhammad sent the following cablegram to President Nasser, who was then host to the Afro-Asian Conference:

*Lt. President Gamal Abdel Nasser*
*President of the Egyptian Republic, and*
*Host to the Afro-Asian Conference*

*In the name of Allah, The Beneficent, The Merciful.*
*Beloved Brothers of Africa and Asia:*

*As-Salaam-Alaikum. Your long lost Muslim Brothers here in America pray that Allah's divine presence will be felt at this historic African-Asian Conference, and give unity to our efforts for peace and brotherhood.*

*Freedom, justice and equality for all Africans and Asians is of far-reaching importance, not only to you of the East, but also to over 17,000,000 of your long-lost brothers of African-Asian descent here in the West. . . . May our sincere desire for universal peace which is being manifested at this great conference by all Africans and Asians, bring about the unity and brotherhood among all our people which we all so eagerly desire.*

*All success is from Allah.*

*As-Salaam-Alaikum:*

> *Your Long-Lost Brothers of the West*
> *Elijah Muhammad*
> *Leader, Teacher and Spiritual Head of*
> *The Nation of Islam in the West. . . .* [30]

The *Pittsburgh Courier* carried President Nasser's purported reply:

*Mr. Elijah Muhammad:*

*Leader, teacher and spiritual head of the Nation of Islam in the West.*

*I have received your kind message expressing your good wishes on the occasion of the African-Asian Conference. I thank you most heartily for these noble sentiments.*

*May Allah always grant us help to work for the maintenance of peace, which is the desire of all peoples. I extend my best wishes to our brothers of Africa and Asia living in the West.*

*(Signed) Gamal Abdel Nasser*[31]

In the summer of 1959 came Malcolm X's visit to the United Arab Republic. The invitation was originally extended to Muhammad, who then appointed Malcolm to make a preliminary tour as his emissary. Malcolm was warmly received in Cairo and Saudi Arabia by Arab officialdom, and he met all of the important people in the Moslem Congress, thus insuring Muhammad's impending visit against embarrassment. The Black Muslims were taken as Moslems, and the Egyptians were delighted by the throngs of black worshipers they saw on the 11″ x 20″ photographs Malcolm carried in his briefcase. They were also properly appalled at his descriptions of the oppression of the Black Man in America.

During his tour, Malcolm found that:

The people of Arabia are just like our people in America . . . ranging from regal black to rich brown. But none are white. It is safe to say that 99 per cent of them would be jim-crowed in the United States of America.[32]

From Africa, he wrote:

Africa is the land of the future . . . definitely the land of tomorrow, and the African is the man of tomorrow. . . . Africa is the New World, a world with a future . . . in which the so-called American Negroes are destined to play a key role. . . . Like the Asians, all Africans consider America's treatment of Negro Americans the best yardstick by which to measure the sincerity of America's offers on this continent. . . . The veil of diplomatic art does not obscure the vision of African thinkers when abuse of black Americans still obtains.[33]

A few months later, Elijah Muhammad went to Cairo and thence to the Holy City. Muhammad is not fluent in Arabic, but on the counsel of his advisors, he learned the various Moslem prayers and creedal affirmations before setting out on his trip. On his return to America, he declared: "The whole world of Islam is behind me. I was received as a brother and a leader. I did not have to ask for a visa to make the Hajj [pilgrimage] to Mecca, the Holy City. They asked me to go."[34]

That these visits of top Muslim leaders to the Islamic countries have political implications is taken for granted by most observers. The precise weight of these implications remains open to speculation. However, it is reasonable to conclude that the controversial Muslim leader could hardly have been admitted to Mecca in the face of the opposition of American Moslems unless he had powerful friends abroad to sponsor and receive him. Because of his heterodoxy, that sponsorship is unlikely to have been primarily religious. It seems possible that some Moslem leaders, at least, found the political possibilities sufficiently impressive to overbalance the religious risk.

Thus does the Messenger maintain his spiritual liaison with the wider world of international Islam. They have their Mecca; and they have Medina. But Elijah has Chicago. And New York. And Los Angeles. The block lettering on the facades of his many temples always proclaim: *MUHAMMAD'S* MOSQUE OF ISLAM, or *MUHAMMAD'S* UNIVERSITY OF ISLAM. *Elijah* Muhammad is what is meant—not some other. And wherever his name appears, *he* is the Leader, the Teacher, the Prophet, the Messenger, the One-Who-Knew-Allah (in the Person of Master Fard Muhammad), and who raised the Dead Nation, indeed, the *Lost* Nation from low to high degree, bringing them face to face with their own black destiny. Muhammad does not want orthodoxy. Paradoxy will do.

# 9 The Spectrum of Black Protest

### I. THE PERSISTENT PROBLEM

he American conscience is like a Georgia mule drowsing under a mulberry tree. It will twitch where the fly bites —now here, now there, and so to sleep again. This moral lethargy is the persistent problem of America. Possibly we are no more guilty of social indifference than the other supernations of the world with whom we share the distribution and administration of power, for there seems to be a certain callousness for the concerns of the individual citizen built into the national character of great political states. Nevertheless, there is a certain irony in the fact that this nation was born of what was intended as a humanitarian response to entrenched political principles which were patently non-humanitarian. We had before us the model of evil. We knew what kind of society we did not want. Yet we managed to create a political Frankenstein because we opted for a society in which our humanitarian ideals were held to be racially restrictive.

As a result, the history of our nationhood has been a history of racial strife. It has been a history of the postures and the maneuvers of a Christian democracy officially dedicated to the equality of all people, while at once intent upon the establishment of the inequality of non-white people in theory and in practice. The matter of his equalness was never a question in the Blackamerican's mind, but because there was seldom effective communication from mind to mind between black people and white, the black protest organization developed as a concrete expression of the black rejection of the white man's peculiar notions about the prerogatives of color.

### The Erosion of Faith: The Desiccation of Hope

Once it could be said with confidence that the Black Man's hatred of the white man existed only syllogistically—only in the sense that given the white man's own hatred and abuse of black people, black hatred would be the logical consequence. That there was little evidence of the "logical consequences" ever displayed in the black response to white oppression intrigued the social scientist and gave reassurance to the vast majority of white people who found it comforting and necessary to believe that the Black Man's love and fidelity were consistent expressions of his natural slavishness. The white man's comfort was in large part the cold comfort of self-delusion, a condition brought on by a selective rendering of history which ignored the David Walkers, the Henry Highland Garnets, and the Nat Turners whose voices and exploits might have cautioned men less taken with their own fantasies. And if, as the social scientists so confidently explained, the Black Man's hatred was inverted and turned against himself and his kind, never reaching its true and "logical" target, it seems that mere prudence would at least consider the possibility that sooner or later the apple would fall down instead of up. By the end of the "Savage Sixties" that day had in fact arrived, and the sounds of anguish and betrayal were heard in the land. "The Negroes," it was charged in bitter disbelief, "have become bitter. They hate us!"

If the allegations were true, their truth was not total. There are millions of Blackamericans who have not indulged themselves with hatred but, nevertheless, whose impatience with white racism leaves no room for love. The values for which the white man stood or, more precisely, the values with which he was traditionally identified have lost much of their appeal, either because they have been practically unattainable, or because they have been dishonored by the white man himself. There was a time, for example, when merely being identified as "American" was for most Blacks a value as far beyond price as it was beyond practical experience. It was a yearning for acceptability, for being included, for being considered a part of a great civilization. It was a wish to deny the ugly implications of color and prejudice in America; to give the white man the benefit of the doubt: to persist in the faith in the American Dream. It was not that Blacks ever lost the feeling that America was a white man's country and that all others enjoyed it by his sufferance. It was rather the hope that the white man would outgrow his childish assumption of prerogative and mature into a reasonable expression of his humanitarian pretensions. The Black Muslims represent the erosion of faith and the desiccation of hope that white America ever intends to include black America with full force and meaning under what is implicit in "American."

It seems ironic that at a time when so many white Americans have disavowed their country and fled from it to avoid serving it, or even being associated with it, Blacks in America are still intent upon establishing their identity as "Americans," but there is a difference. They want to be *Blackamericans,* enjoying at once the freedom to celebrate their peculiar cultural heritage as *black* people along with the rights, privileges, and responsibilities incident to being an integral part of a great nation they helped to build and develop.

From time to time, the trusting Blackamericans sought to prod the white man's moral sense indirectly—through the churches, the labor unions, and various interracial organizations—and by personal appeal. There was always a willingness to give the white man the benefit of every doubt. But nothing changed; and after a hundred years of waiting and hoping, the black people finally lost patience with the white man and confidence in his integrity. The black offensive finally took on a new character. Where he had been willing to accept "consideration," the Blackamerican now began demanding his rights—his rights to work, vote, buy a home, eat a meal, see a movie, worship in a church, ride a bus, sit in a public park, and send his children to school on the same terms as all of America's other first-class citizens. But the courts are slow; litigation is expensive; and the implementation of court rulings seems to be peculiarly uncertain in the area of civil rights.

There developed, in the last decade or two, a wide and dramatic spectrum of extralegal black protest. The passive Blackamerican, who trusts that God and the good white people will salvage his dignity while he concentrates on avoiding trouble, is rapidly becoming extinct. Those Blacks who still believed in the possibility of peaceful change developed a bold but gentle technique to quicken the white man's conscience. They simply ignored restrictive laws and went wherever they knew they had a moral right to be—on trains and buses, in restaurants and stores, public beaches, and houses of God. These were not "angry young men"; they were not "bitter." They were just tired of waiting.

At the opposite end of the spectrum are the Black Panthers. They *are* angry; they *are* bitter; and they are also tired of waiting. Their response to white nationalism is black nationalism and their militancy is barely restrained. America can benefit from the lesson they seem intent upon teaching *if* America can tolerate their presence long enough to hear what they are trying to say. But the Panthers have created an hysteria which hardly insures their survival.

### Group Identification: The Corporate Response

In Chapter II, we noted three types of response to pressure and discrimination: avoidance, acceptance, and aggression. These represented the attempts on the part of individuals to adjust to social hostilities directed against them. These same channels of response may also find a corporate expression.

People organize in the face of a persistent threat. The plantation "folk Negro" is adjusting to social hostility when he goes out alone to steal the white boss's corn or potatoes on Saturday night. He is no less adjusting when he loses himself "beyond the Jordan" in company with his neighbors on Sunday morning. One response is a personal expression of resentment and counteragression; the other is a corporate escape. Each kind of response, personal and corporate, has its special advantages in relation to the situation that excites it.

Minorities are created by pressures exerted by the majority. If the majority did not choose to exclude a group, the group would not be a minority; it would be an indistinguishable part of the whole social body. In the same way, the sense of unity and cohesion which we call group identification develops in response to outside pressures. It is a way of ensuring not identity (the majority has seen to that) but the survival of the members and their most cherished values.

Professor Arnold Rose believes that "group identification is the minority's major defense against discrimination and prejudice from the majority."[1] This major defense seems to be clearly effective. Wherever men have exhibited a corporate unity in the face of social oppression, they have had respect and ofttimes an abatement of persecution. The desegragation of eating facilities in the South is a classic example. In six months of concerted effort, black students (supported by some whites) caused the desegregation of lunch counters in about seventy Southern communities.[2] To be sure, organized resistance seldom maintains the "good will" of the prejudiced majority; but only a diseased good will depends on discrimination for its existence. Indeed, the very presence of social abuse is *de facto* evidence of the absence of a healthy good will. What the minority group loses by organization is not so much "good will" as an artificially maintained rapprochement.

But group identification also has its hazards.

> Group identification . . . may create foolhardiness and a tendency to martyrdom without securing the gain that risk-taking can secure. It creates a group pride that may become satisfied with mediocrity. It frequently promotes chauvinism and nationalism, which voluntarily separates the group from the broader opportunities and contacts that it presumably is fighting to secure.[3]

It may, in short, militate against the very aims it seeks to achieve. A group which becomes enamored of its own achievements, real or mythological, or which blinds itself to the accomplishments of other groups closes the door to its own improvement. And the image it presents to others may be so threatening as to increase tensions or cause outright alarm.

Most ethnic minorities in the United States can look forward to eventual assimilation, for their distinguishing characteristics are cultural rather than biological.[4] Consequently, their organizations tend to exist primarily for sociability rather than for defense or protest. Such organizations come into being as temporary expedients, until the organizational life of the majority is opened to their members, and the least severely excluded minorities show the least incidence of in-group associations. European immigrants, for example, have a very low incidence of such associations (except those related to their churches), while American Blacks probably have more in-group organizations than all other minorities combined. It is interesting to note, however, that the new black ethnicity, which became pronounced in the "black is beautiful" syndrome of the late sixties and early seventies, did have the effect of creating a culture-wide scramble for ethnic identity. Some ethnic groups which had long forgotten the reasons and the need for ethnicity suddenly rediscovered their ethnic past and demanded its celebration.

A few years ago the Common Council for American Unity estimated that there were only 155 fraternal organizations, with fewer than three million members, for all the different nationality groups in the United States.[5] But this figure did not include racial groups. It would probably have been doubled by the inclusion of black fraternal groups alone, not to mention the black defense and protest organizations which span the entire spectrum from the ultraradicalism of the Black Panthers to the ultraconservatism of the National Urban League.

Jews, like Blacks, have developed a large number of voluntary associations, though most Jews do not belong to them.[6] "When Jews find themselves unwanted in fraternities, country clubs, or other sociable organizations, they form their own in great numbers to 'demonstrate' that they can enjoy themselves without benefit of admission to the majority's sociable groups."[7] Neither group does so without resentment; but the Jew, who has a unique, well-defined, and clearly remembered cultural heritage to sustain him, probably suffers less from exclusion from the common life of the majority group than does the Blackamerican, who has opted for the cultural heritage of the group which excludes him.

Moreover, some Jews can and do pass into the dominant white group, often through the simple expedient of changing their names. Like Blacks, some may pass temporarily in order to enjoy advantages or avoid discrimination in business or social life. In a New York suburb, for example, there is a Jew whose legal name is John Smith; and as Dr. John Smith he has a good dental practice. How he would fare if he practiced as Jacob Goldstein is problematic. Dr. Smith himself has no doubt but that, in the community where he lives, there is a considerably larger practice available to Dr. Smith than there would be to, say, Dr. Goldstein.

America has never been a land of unlimited opportunity for Jews. As soon as they arrived on our shores, they found themselves confronted with the same bigotry and hatred that had driven them from Spain, from Russia, from every corner of the globe. But the Jews fought back. They organized for the protection of the group. First, the Independent Order B'nai B'rith, or "Sons of the Covenant," was founded in New York City in 1843. Three quarters of a century later, in 1913, the Anti-Defamation League was organized as a unit of B'nai B'rith specifically for the purpose of combating anti-Semitism. It does so primarily by investigating and exposing anti-Semitic groups.

The American Jewish Committee, the American Jewish Congress

(which uses legal action, educational propaganda, and social research as weapons against bigotry), the Jewish War Veterans, the Jewish Labor Committee—these and a substantial number of other national, state, and local organizations serve the Jewish community in two ways. They stand guard against prejudice and discrimination, keeping a watchful eye on such areas as civil rights, immigration laws, American foreign policy in the Middle East, politics, and interfaith relations. And they caution the Jewish community itself against yielding blindly to a false acceptance. In many communities, Jews can be accepted warmly by the majority if they will simply give up their Jewish identity and cultural values. This is, of course, an indirect anti-Semitism, and the organizations seek to meet it by acting as rallying points for the preservation of Jewish values.

The recent development of the Jewish Defense League, a kind of vigilante organization of young Jewish militants, has divided Jewish sentiment and caused some embarrassment to the more respectable Jewish organizations. The JDL is conceived by some Jews as the Jewish answer to the anti-Semitic stance of some black militants. However, most of the JDL's public energy has gone into harassing Russian diplomats associated with the United Nations, and their wives and families—to the intense embarrassment of the U.S. State Department. The League, founded and led by a New York City Rabbi (Meir Kahane) considers its major work to be that of calling attention to and protesting the treatment of Jews in the Soviet Union.

Except for these Jewish groups and the comparable black groups, there are in America few widely known minority protest or protective organizations. One such organization exists among the Japanese-Americans, who, like the Blacks, suffer from high social visibility. Most Japanese-American groups are social and mutual aid societies (such as the *kenjinkai,* or organizations of families originating in the same *ken,* or prefecture). For many years, however, the Japanese Association of North America sought to protect Japanese-Americans from discrimination and was active in many legal cases on their behalf. Unfortunately, unlike its counterpart, the NAACP, the JANA was neither broadly based nor successful: all its members were Japanese, most of them alien, and the group lost nearly every case it entered. Eventually it confined its activities to promoting social welfare and Americanization among its members.

A far more effective social action group, the Japanese-Americans

Citizenship League, developed out of the old JANA. Unlike the parent organization, the JACL admits only American citizens to membership. It has an able and energetic leadership, and like many black organizations, it has the support of some liberal whites. The JACL is both a political and a community service organization; it has entered the courts in a number of cases with conspicuous success. However, a curious fallout of World War II and the postwar Americo-Japanese alliance seems to be a reduction of prejudice against Japanese nationals and Nisei in this country.

Spanish-speaking Americans, the second largest unassimilated ethnic group in the country,[8] have organized a number of local or regional groups which concern themselves with problems arising from discrimination. The largest of these is the United League of Latin American Citizens, commonly known as ULLAC.[9] Most of the 3½ million Spanish-speaking minority, however, is concentrated in the Southwest (almost a third of them in Texas),[10] and ULLAC necessarily confines its major activities to state and regional problems. In New York City a local organization of Puerto Ricans called Young Lords is an active advocate of the Puerto Rican poor.

It is the Blacks, then, more than any other minority, who find a corporate release in social, protective, and protest organizations. It is the Blacks who give decidedly the most emphasis to protest organizations and whose protest finds the widest range of corporate expression. But all black protest groups, across the entire spectrum, have one thing in common: a new sense of *urgency,* which has begun to stir similar responses in other minorities.

Every black protest organization today is, in its own way, impatient. Each is learning to seize the moral or political initiative. Each is preparing to force America to a showdown. And sooner or later, America will have to yield—if not to reason and persuasion, then to some unpredictable expediency. In short, the alternative is between more freedom for the still unfree, or more repression for those who object to existing oppression.

## II. SEPARATIST ORGANIZATIONS

With significant exceptions, most contemporary black protest organizations restrict their membership to black people. The "Black-and-white together" chant which symbolized much of the protest activity of the early 1960s has not been heard in recent times. Since 1965 there has been an increasing inclination on the part of Blacks to go it alone, and, on the part of their erstwhile white supporters, to let them. The reasons are many and complex. A rapidly maturing, more broadly based black leadership is one. The new-found security inherent in black ethnicity is another. The bewilderment and confusion of some whites over the unaccustomed experience of black people wanting to direct their own affairs is another. And the white American's commitment to the efficacy of what Daniel Patrick Moynihan calls "benign neglect" as a way of controlling the Blackamerican's movement through social and economic space is yet another. In short, just when the Black Man is saying let me take the wheel, the white man seems to be saying let's slow down and cool the engine.

## The Black Church

The black church was the one significant mitigating organization which stood between black people and the utter hopelessness of slavery, and it has remained the prime source of strength and leadership for black dissent ever since. To some extent the Church is and was escapist. E. Franklin Frazier observes that it "has two roots: one in the efforts of the free Negroes in the North to escape from their inferior position in white churches and assert their independence, and the other in what has been aptly called the 'invisible' institution on the plantations during slavery."[11] Benjamin Mays concludes that "if the Negro had had greater freedom in the social, economic, and political spheres, fewer Negroes would have been 'called' to preach, and there would have been fewer Negro churches."[12]

Dr. Mays' conclusions are everywhere buttressed by the facts. Black people with talent were "called to preach" because there was no place for them in the professional life of white America. Except for a handful of black colleges, the academic world was closed to them. Politics was not an option; Blacks had been excluded from the political world since Reconstruction. The world of business and high finance was not available to them. They could not become the administrators of public (or private) institutions. They could not become diplomats or government officials. They could become preachers. And they did. Every black pastor was a politician, an administrator, a financial wizard, an educator, and a leader of his people. Being "called to preach" meant being called to exercise in one office all the talents and all the expertise the self-confident individual has at his command. And then some. The "call to preach" may have been escapism, but only in the sense of accepting the reality of a closed white society which made no provision for the Blackamerican of unusual capacity. One of the little ironies of fate is that Malcolm X who stood at the head of his class was advised in good conscience by his white teacher to study carpentry—so he could be certain of getting a job. Malcolm, like countless others of similar experience, chose to preach.

Religious escapism took other forms. Sometimes it meant security in an age where security for Blacks was hard to come by and doggedly defended. A few years ago a national news magazine reported the following:

> Racial segregation should be continued in the Methodist Church for the foreseeable future . . . a Methodist Commission reported last week. There was no minority dissent to the report. . . . Moreover, leaders of the 360,000 Methodist Negroes . . . agreed with the decision. The reason for this extraordinary state of affairs [is that] . . . this segregation [has] brought some advantages for Negro Methodists in terms of representation and influence in the Church. . . . There are four Negro Methodist bishops in the [all Negro] Central Jurisdiction, for instance, while the theoretically non-segregated Protestant Episcopal Church in the U.S.A. has none at all in the continental U.S.[13]

The Methodist Church eventually got rid of its segregated Central Jurisdiction in 1968, and now assigns its bishops without official notice of race. However, black Methodists now fear a steady decline of black representation in the episcopacy and in high-level administrative appointments. After a hundred years and more of segregation, they had learned to cope with it and make the best of a bad situation. If you are a tiny minority in a vast superdenomination, how do you cope when the rules are suddenly changed to make you "equal"? One day all Blackamericans may have to face that possibility.

The black church has not, of course, been entirely escapist:

The [Negro] churches have sometimes been charged with providing an escapist philosophy and so diverting the Negro protest. There is, no doubt, considerable truth in this charge, especially with respect to the revivalist churches to which many lower-class Negroes belong. But the all-Negro church was probably the very first protest organization under slavery, and . . . many Negro ministers [today] take their texts from those sections of the Bible which favor equality and fraternity.[14]

Black protest and black leadership are something more than the selection of a text or sermon topic. Black religious leaders from Nat Turner to Martin Luther King have left their Bibles in the pulpit and laid their lives on the line in the streets for what they believed in.

Not all black clergymen, and not all black churches, however, have involved themselves in the struggle for black rights. The black clergy has yielded a considerable amount of its influence in recent years to business and to other professions. Only lately are there some indications of a renaissance in clerical leadership; and even now, the most significant social leadership is offered by those denominations that lack institutionalized hierarchy. "For the most part, black churches have contributed to the perpetuation of the American racial system through the reinforcement of the extant mores."[15] In spite of its estimated ten million members,[16] the black church has sponsored comparatively few programs against the discrimination it exemplifies.[17] But this is changing. There are "black caucuses" in every major denomination, both Protestant and Catholic, and they tend to be embarrassing to the notion of a Christian brotherhood oblivious of race. They not only call attention to the more obvious practices of racism in the church, but insist on a more equitable sharing of the church's economic interests, i.e., jobs and the use of church facilities such as summer camps, homes for the aged, educational funds, etc., and on black representation on the faculties of seminaries, church-related colleges, and the governing boards of church-owned agencies. The emergence of a school of black theologians has increased the appeal of a black church considered to be the true expression of the Christian church in contradistinction to the "white American" church where Christianity has been hopelessly distorted by racism. There is a strong belief among many black churchmen that the black church may well be the "saving remnant" by means of which Christianity in the West will recover its vitality and its relevance.

### Black Fraternal Organizations

The Blackamerican has traditionally relied upon various types of fraternal organizations to assure him comfort and companionship while he lives and often to bury him (or at least to dignify his funeral) when he dies. His lodges and orders have frequently been the only arena in which he could exercise his political interests; and in many communities, except for his churches, they have been the only social and recreational outlets available to him. In recent years the fraternal orders have diminished in importance, yet even today one rarely encounters a black community without an order of Masons or Elks. As a general rule, however, neither politics nor social protest has been a prime concern of the fraternal orders, and they have had little influence on the lightening of the Blackamerican's racial burdens.

Black fraternal organizations date back to 1775, at least, for on March 6 of that year, fifteen black men were initiated into a British lodge of Freemasons at Boston. After the Revolution, the white American Masons refused their black brothers permission to set up a lodge, but the Blacks applied directly to the Grand Lodge of England and were immediately granted a charter. The first black lodge was established in Boston in 1787. Through much the same procedure, the Odd Fellows were chartered in New York City in 1843 under direct warrant from England.

The Colored Knights of Pythias was probably unique in its origin. In 1870, a group of black citizens petitioned the Supreme Lodge for membership. When the petition was denied, several fair-skinned blacks, passing as white, infiltrated the order and learned its ritual. They then set up a Supreme Council and organized a lodge of their own in Vicksburg, Mississippi. It is ironic that the order from which they were excluded had itself been created "to extend frendship, charity, and benevolence among men." Black lodges were soon organized throughout the country.

One of the most important of the older fraternal and benevolent associations is the Improved Benevolent and Protective Order of Elks, founded in Cincinnati in 1898. Through judicious investment in war bonds and other commodities over the years, the Elks amassed a substantial treasury. Hundreds of thousands of dollars are said to have been spent on scholarships for black youth. Other support has gone to Meharry Medical College and to the Howard University Medical School.

Eight college-based Greek letter societies for Blacks represent a membership of perhaps 150,000 men and women.[18] These societies, like the older fraternal organizations, grew out of the exclusion of Blackamericans from participation in the normal social life of the community to which education and status would have normally entitled them.

The first black fraternity—not a college society—was organized by a group of men of similar interests and social status in Philadelphia in 1904. Sigma Pi Phi, now more commonly referred to as "the *Boule*," has traditionally conceived itself as an "aristocracy of talent" and has, in fact, included among its members some of America's most distinguished Blacks. E. Franklin Frazier describes it as apparently "governed still by that [outlook] of the 'isolated aristocracy of talent' which comprised its membership 40 or more years ago. . . . But the spirit of social exclusiveness has persisted while the emphasis on intellectual and professional attainment has disappeared."[19] In recent years, the *Boule* has waned in prestige and membership.

The first black college fraternity, Alpha Phi Alpha, was organized at Cornell University in 1906, when, "because of race prejudice these students were not eligible for membership in white fraternities and were excluded from general participation in the social activities of the University."[20] Five years later, the same experience gave birth to a second fraternity, Kappa Alpha Psi, at Indiana University. Two others followed at black colleges in 1911 (Omega Psi Phi) and 1914 (Phi Beta Sigma), as did four sororities during the same general period.

Unlike the *Boule*, the college fraternities (mainly through their graduate chapters) have participated vigorously in the fight for full citizenship and have shown a constructive overall concern for the welfare of the black community. For several years, these organizations jointly supported the American Council on Human Rights (ACHR), a Washington-based organization concerned with minority-group protection. One sorority, Alpha Kappa Alpha, maintained a lobby in Washington to influence legislation affecting Blacks; it has also spent thousands of dollars sponsoring an extended Health Project to provide medical and dental care for poor Blacks in the rural South. Another, Delta Sigma Theta, has a comprehensive program including support of child welfare and aid to delinquent girls. Kappa Alpha Psi fraternity has an extensive "Guide Right" program for counseling black high school youths and encouraging them to prepare themselves for creative participation in American vocational and professional life. All the Greek letter societies have contributed important financial support to the NAACP.

In the black community, these societies have a community-wide responsibility that is not paralleled by their white counterparts. They began as social clubs, and they remain so; but their very existence is a sobering reminder of the unusual responsibilities that devolve upon educated Blacks in terms of leadership and example. The societies are controlled by black intellectual and professional leaders, rather than being centered on the college campuses; and while they represent a certain exclusiveness (only college men and women of acceptable academic performance may become members), they are dedicated to a creative concern for the entire racial group.

## SNCC

In the past, the Greek letter societies functioned as important screening devices in the determination of social status. The black youth of today are impatient with the class pretensions and claims of status. As a result, the fraternities and sororities have never completely recovered from the World War II era when most of the men were drafted. Today's black college students frequently see the "Greeks" as irrelevant at best, and divisive or "part of the problem" at worst.

Two of the most militant organizations growing out of the civil rights struggle of the sixties were the Student Nonviolent Coordinating Committee (SNCC), and the Black Panther Party. SNCC began as an organization of black college students concerned with coordinating student efforts to desegregate lunch counters and other places of public accommodation in the South. At the height of the movement the SNCC group was augmented by perhaps 100,000 black and white students from across the country. Many were arrested; some were beaten; others were dismissed from their colleges. Despite all this, more than a hundred cities in the South and in the border states were forced to alter their age-old customs of segregating people by race in places of public accommodation.

Begun as a nonviolent adjunct to the Martin Luther King movement, as new leadership emerged SNCC adopted an increasingly militant stance. White students attached to the organization were invited to leave and to address their efforts to problems of racism in their own communities. In 1966, under the leadership of Stokely Carmichael, SNCC became identified with the "black power" movement, an undefined,[21] amorphous political allure which proved inordinately threatening to conservative black leadership and white liberal supporters. "Black power" was never more than a hackle-raising slogan, but the cry on the lips of militant young Blacks produced an unsettling effect upon the society at large which was reflected in the swift withdrawal of support from any organization associated with it. By the end of the decade, the lack of a financial base aggravated by a series of internal squabbles had effectively silenced the Student Nonviolent Coordinating Committee.

## The Black Panther Party

The Black Panther Party for Self Defense was founded in California in 1966 by Huey Newton and Bobby Seale. Seale became Chairman of the Party while Newton became Minister of Defense. As the movement worked to clarify its ideals, "Self Defense" was dropped from its official designation. The membership of the Panthers is limited largely to militant black youth committed to armed revolution as the inevitable strategy for social change in America.

The Black Panthers' policy of appearing in public bearing arms and patrolling black communities to protect Blacks from police harassment quickly earned them the enmity of law enforcement agencies; and the toll of Panthers killed by the police under questionable circumstances finally alarmed even those civil libertarians who deplored the Panthers' existence. During the late sixties and early seventies, police-Panther clashes in the large urban ghettos were commonplace, and the incarceration of Black Panther leaders was routine.

The Black Panthers believe all Blacks in America to be "colonialized" and oppressed by the white establishment, and their program calls for an independent black community based on socialist principles. The decimation of the party ranks by violence has been augmented by defections and internal dissension. Stokely Carmichael, former head of the Student Nonviolent Coordinating Committee (SNCC), resigned from the Panthers in a dispute concerning party alliance with white radicals. By 1971 the Party had split into two factions: one, headed by Eldridge Cleaver (living in Algeria to avoid a prison sentence), had its headquarters in New York; the other faction, led by Huey Newton, maintained its headquarters in Oakland, California.

### III.  INTEGRATIVE ORGANIZATIONS

Since the term "integration" produces, in many people, an excruciating anxiety,[22] a few definitions may be in order. *Integration,* for our present purposes, refers to participation in the total life of the community without necessarily merging with the majority group. In an integrated society, social acceptance, civil rights, political freedom, etc., are not negotiable in terms of race or color. But one is free to retain his own identity and cultural values. *Assimilation,* on the other hand, refers to the merging of a minority into the general community and the gradual loss of its identity and its unique cultural values. In an assimilated society, a minority group does not cling—and is not forced to cling—together. Its members are dispersed into the general community, accepted and fully mobile in every area of social and cultural intercourse.[23] The values of the assimilated are the prevailing values of the overculture. Some ethnic groups like the Jews tend to resist complete assimilation, but the increasing number of Jewish youth who prefer assimilation is a matter of great concern to Jewish traditionalists.

Unlike the Jew, Blacks need not be troubled by the possibility of assimilation into the mainstream of American life. Even those who consider it desirable know that it is not soon to be achieved. "Assimilation," Gunnar Myrdal has warned, "is likely to occur only when the majority accepts the idea." Other observers are more specific: "When the combined cultural and biological traits are highly divergent from those of the host society, the subordination of the group will be very great, their subsystem strong, the period of assimilation long, and the process slow and painful.."[24] The Blackamerican does not seriously address either his efforts or his hopes to such a goal.

But if he is unexcited about assimilation, he is intensely serious about integration, although not in the sense of what integration was once understood to mean—amalgamation and loss of cultural identity. Few contemporary Blacks want that. They do want the personal options that a truly integrated society ought to provide.

## NAACP

Probably the best-known organization commonly associated with Blacks is the National Association for the Advancement of Colored People. The NAACP was created by liberal whites and militant Blacks, largely in response to the increasing outrages against Blacks in the South early in this century. J. Saunders Redding reports that:

> In the first decade of the [present] century, nearly a thousand of them [Negroes] were lynched in public spectacles that outmatched the Roman circus for savagery and obscenity. No appeal to conscience was effective. Civil, legal, and moral rights meant nothing.[25]

White supremacy and a white disposition to violence followed the Blacks as, in terror and despair, they migrated north and west. In the summer of 1908, a race riot—precipitated by a false accusation of rape, and led by a white woman who was already under indictment as a criminal and out of jail on bond—focused the attention of the nation on Springfield, Illinois. "Here in the home of Abraham Lincoln, a mob containing many of the town's best citizens raged for two days, killed and wounded scores of Negroes, and drove thousands from the city."[26] In the wake of the riot, the city of Springfield discharged more than fifty Negro employees, although their efficiency and fidelity were not in doubt. The state of Illinois dismissed still others. A thousand disheartened Negroes, "many of them substantial and respected citizens, left the city for parts unknown."

It was against this background that the NAACP came into being. In an article in the *Independent,* the prominent Southern journalist William English Walling declared:

> Either the spirit of the abolitionists, of Lincoln and Lovejoy, must be revived and we must come to treat the Negro on a plane of absolute political and social equality, or [Southern demagogues] will soon have transferred the race war to the North.[27]

Walling was moved not so much by the riot itself as by the implications of such terror for the national welfare. If unchecked, such behavior could destroy the political democracy and the unity of a nation only two generations emerged from civil strife. "Who realizes the seriousness of the situation," he appealed," and what large and powerful body of citizens is ready . . . to aid?"

As a result of Walling's article—and through the good offices of Mary White Ovington, a wealthy white social worker in New York City—a call "for a national conference on the Negro question" was issued on Lincoln's birthday of the following year. The response was indicative of the concern of men and women of stature over the unhappy state of affairs. To the meeting came such notables as W.E.B. Du Bois, Jane Addams, John Dewey, Moorefield Storey, Oswald Garrison Villard, Rabbi Stephen Wise, William Lloyd Garrison, and J.G. Phelps Stokes. Fifty-three persons signed the statement, and the NAACP was formally incorporated in 1910, committed to an uncompromising policy of racial equality.

The NAACP today is a large membership organization, with some 500,000 members located in every state. Both the membership and national staff are multiracial, although the percentage of black membership has increased in recent years. All presidents of the NAACP have been white. The executive secretary, Roy Wilkins, and the chief legal counsel, Nathaniel Jones, are black. Jack Greenberg, who succeeded the famous Thurgood Marshall as Chief Counsel of the Association's Legal Defense and Education Fund, is an American Jew. Mr. Marshall is now a member of the U.S. Supreme Court.

In the sixty years of its existence, the NAACP has done much to loosen the collar of caste that has chafed the Blackamerican's neck for so long. It has made a triple-threat attack—legal, legislative, and educational—against disprivilege and discrimination. Its legal efforts have included numerous appeals to the United States Supreme Court, most of which it won. Among the victories have been court rulings that racial segregation is unconstitutional in public schools and colleges, in public parks and playgrounds, in intrastate buses, and in interstate travel accommodations of all kinds. The NAACP has won Supreme Court decisions invalidating the enforcement of racially restrictive covenants in housing; it has more firmly established the Blackamerican's right and opportunity to vote; it has enabled him to escape the indignity of eating in segregated dining rooms or waiting in segregated waiting rooms when he travels beyond the borders of his state. It has been a major factor in the passage of fair employment legislation and has been successful in some of its efforts to eliminate discrimination in public housing. It championed the student sit-in movement and provided expert counsel for students who were jailed in the course of such demonstrations.

The effectiveness of the NAACP can perhaps be seen most clearly through the attempts that have been made to destroy it. In 1956 alone, Louisiana, Alabama, and Texas banned the organization by court decree, and the Virginia legislature moved to halt its activities in that state. Several Southern states passed laws which made it impossible for public servants such as teachers to belong to the organization and still retain their jobs. The list goes on and on, for the NAACP has made more important enemies than any other organization with which black people have ever been associated. This could well be the best index of its success.

### The Urban League

Like the NAACP, the Urban League is meticulously biracial. Until the early sixties, the league had always had a white president and a black executive secretary. And like the NAACP, the league looks to the combined efforts of Blacks and whites to find some workable solutions for the country's racial problems. The Reverend J.A. McDaniel, former executive secretary of the Memphis Urban League, interprets the philosophy of the national organization as follows:

The Urban League is an interracial organization, and it strives to work within the framework of interracial cooperation. We [Negroes and whites] are interdependent—one upon the other. We of the Urban League do not believe that the Negro can resolve his problems alone; nor can the white man [resolve his] alone. But working together in the American philosophy of teamwork, we can resolve our differences and our problems.[28]

But here the similarity between these organizations ends.

"If the NAACP was too radical to merit the support of the philanthropists who gave to Negro causes," observed J. Saunders Redding, "the National Urban League was not."[29] In this distinction lies the answer to much of the present confusion about the roles of these organizations. The NAACP receives the greater part of its financing from membership fees, individual contributions, and foundation grants. The Urban League is heavily dependent upon local resources, such as community chests. The league's program and philosophy, therefore, must remain within certain conservative limits; it must remain acceptable to its local sources of support. Yet the league is governed by national policies; its program emphases vary according to local needs and conditions, but even in the South it hews closely to its founding commitments.

The league was born as a coalition of three social agencies in New York City in 1910. Around 1905 or 1906, two interracial groups—the Committee for Improving the Industrial Conditions of Negroes in New York City and the League for the Protection of Colored Women—were organized by certain white philanthropists in an attempt to ameliorate social conditions among Blacks in New York. In 1910 a similar group, the Committee on Urban Conditions Among Negroes, made its debut. In 1911 these three organizations merged to become the National League of Urban Conditions Among Negroes (later abbreviated to National Urban League), espousing the theme that the Blackamerican needs "not alms but opportunity—opportunity to work at the job for which the Negro [is] best fitted, with equal pay for equal work, and equal opportunity for advancement." This has remained the league's controlling philosophy, and jobs for Blacks has received its major program emphasis, although other services are frequently made available.

The league today maintains branches in most states. Its executive offices, like those of the NAACP, are in New York City. Along with screening, training, and selling of black labor, most local affiliates offer a multitude of other services. They may operate day nurseries and baby clinics, promote health weeks, find homes for wayward girls, provide individual testing and counseling services, serve as clearinghouses for information about Blacks, or advise government or municipal agencies on matters affecting the black community. But the primary concern of every local Urban League is to find jobs, more jobs, and better jobs for black citizens.

Like the NAACP, the National Urban League has been criticized by members of both races as being "too radical" or "too conservative," depending largely upon the perspective of the critic. During the early 1960s the leadership of the Urban League fell to Whitney Young, Jr., former dean of the Atlanta University School of Social Work. In ten years of effective salesmanship, Dr. Young managed to sell his organization to some of America's most distinguished corporation executives. They supported him with jobs *and* money. As a result, the League took on a distinctively new image. It became a multimillion-dollar enterprise, run like the corporations which supported it. Doors began to open for able Blacks in areas of employment never before available to them. But for all that, the League image for the black rank-and-file remained that of a distant, elitist, black-run appendage to the white establishment. Although he frequently appeared at "black togetherness" meetings and identified himself with some of the causes and issues espoused by some of the more militant organizations, Mr. Young was never able to sell himself or his organization to the black masses. In a most tragic accident, the young executive was drowned while swimming in the surf in Nigeria in 1970. He was succeeded in office by Vernon L. Jordan, a young lawyer from Atlanta who had been head of the Voter Registration Project in the early sixties, and later, Executive Director of the United Negro College Fund.

It is probably fair to say that each local league moves as rapidly as local conditions warrant. Sometimes it moves slightly in advance of the community it has undertaken to serve, but it never moves so far ahead as to isolate itself and its program from the good will and financial support of its interracial supporters. In contrast to the NAACP, the National Urban League pioneers without being adventurous, and the type of interracial rapport it seeks to establish could hardly be accomplished in any other way.

## Anti-Segregation Organizations

As Gunnar Myrdal has suggested, no single organization can be effective alone in combating racial prejudice, for no single organization can work simultaneously through speed and gradualness, through assertiveness and compromise. A variety of specialized groups concentrating on limited and particular problems is far more successful than any multifaceted, monolithic organization could be—far more capable of exciting the imagination and eliciting the support of major segments of the general population.

For this reason, a number of black, or black-oriented, antisegregation organizations have come into being or become prominent since 1954, when the Supreme Court rejected the "separate but equal" doctrine for public schools. Perhaps the most famous of these groups is the Montgomery Improvement Association, organized in 1955 by Dr. Martin Luther King and his associates in Montgomery, Alabama. The MIA grew out of a protest against segregated seating on the Montgomery city buses. It eventually won the support of most of the fifty thousand Blacks in that city and thousands of people of every race throughout the world. For more than a year, the black people of Montgomery walked to their jobs, to school, and to church, rather than submit any longer to the indignities and abuse of segregated seating on public buses. Eventually, segregation on the buses was outlawed, as it has been in many another city since. Dr. King moved to Atlanta to continue his work as president of the then new organization, the Southern Christian Leadership Conference, which stresses nonviolent action as a technique for effecting social change. The whole world was thrilled by Dr. King's long, nonviolent crusade against racial injustice, in recognition of which he received the Nobel Peace Prize in 1964. Dr. King met his death at the hands of an assassin in April of 1968, in Memphis, Tennessee. He had gone there to help black sanitation workers in their efforts to gain more equitable pay. The leadership of SCLC then fell to the Reverend Ralph Abernathy, a long-time associate of Dr. King. As it turned out, by the time Dr. Abernathy was fairly well in control of the forces which had rallied to Dr. King with such fervor and enthusiasm, the mood of the country had changed and new styles and techniques of leadership were indicated. SCLC was never again a potent force in social change.

For a number of years, the Atlanta-based Southern Regional Council has worked quietly behind the scenes to keep open the channels of communication between Blacks and whites in the South. The biracial council does not consider itself a "race-relations" organization in the strictest sense of that word; it works toward equal opportunities for both races as a means to a higher standard of well-being for all men. The council operates in twelve Southern states. It compiles data and statistics, provides information on racial frictions and interracial achievements, and strives to reduce conflict while producing equality of opportunity. Its several agencies are professionally staffed with social scientists and experts in human relations.

The student sit-in movement introduced more direct action, though it pledged itself to techniques of nonviolence. This movement began as a spontaneous rejection of segregation on February 1, 1960, when four black students who had been shopping at a Woolworth store in Greensboro, North Carolina, sat down at the lunch counter and requested service. They were refused but continued to wait patiently—a gesture that fired the popular imagination and was quickly imitated elsewhere. In Atlanta, the sit-ins crystallized into a structured organization, and the colleges of the Atlanta University Center became rallying points for black and white "sit-inners" from all over America. Even the Ku Klux Klan failed to daunt their spirit.[30]

Numerous other direct-action groups found action in the turbulent sixties. Some were strictly local and *ad hoc.* Others like the Congress of Racial Equality antedated the great crusade for desegregation. A few survived it. As the racial crisis deepens and anything less than parity becomes less and less tolerable, new leaders and new movements will doubtless arise and spend themselves in the fight against bigotry. The fear and intimidation of yesterday have given way to the incaution born of rage and the courage born of long-suffering in a righteous cause. This generation of black youth is not afraid. They are committed to change *now,* in their lifetime. They have tried nonviolence. Now they say "by any means necessary." They may not have the means, necessary or otherwise. That will be their tragedy. And America's.

## IV. THE BLACK MUSLIM MOVEMENT

The Black Muslims have no exact parallels among other black protest groups in America. The Muslim Nation of Islam is often compared with the Garvey movement, from which, indeed, some of its fundamental concepts are borrowed. In its commitment to racial uplift and to the unification of black peoples, for example, the echo of Garveyism is loud and distinct. On the other hand, the flamboyance and bombast of the Garvey movement, while potentially present in such Muslim organizations as the Fruit of Islam, is muted or undeveloped. The Black

Muslims have no order of nobility, no diplomatic corps. There are no Deputy Potentates, High Commissioners General, no Motor Corps, Flying Corps, Chaplain General, or Star-and-Crescent Nurses. In theory at least, Muhammad is the only "ranking" Muslim, and the resplendent uniforms and public "turn-outs" which were so much a part of the Universal Negro Improvement Association do not figure significantly in Black Islam.

But like Garvey, Elijah Muhammad does recognize the inevitable relationship between economic self-sufficiency and sociopolitical power. Indeed, what Garvey glimpsed in principle, Muhammad either understands in depth or has surrounded himself with men who do, for he has made the basic economic principles of the capitalist system work successfully for his Nation at the level of small business enterprises and small-time agriculture. The Muslim shops, bakeries, farms, and small factories seem to flourish in an age of conglomerates and big corporations. What is more, they utilize black labor—trained in advance for the projected needs of the Nation.

Like the NAACP the Muslims are frequently before the courts—but only on behalf of their own membership. They want justice and fair play, but unlike the NAACP, they do not really expect the courts to give it to them through the normal processes of American jurisprudence, because the white man is by nature incapable of justice toward Blacks. *By nature he is a devil.* Hence, the white man's justice will always be less than just because he cannot conceive of justice for people who are not white. The Muslims, then, do not really want the white man's justice. Instead, they say they want separation from the white man so they may live under their own laws and administer justice to themselves according to the teachings of Islam. Because the Muslims are highly litigious—repairing to the courts on the slightest infringement of their rights as individuals or as a religious group, a paradox seems apparent. It is explained by the oft-repeated assertion that "the Muslims live under the law. Islam *is* submission." "Though the white man can never give us justice," says Muhammad, "so long as we must live under his law we want all that law can give us; and we will still be short-changed." Hence, the Muslims appear to believe in the efficacy of the white man's law without believing in its justice—a pragmatic adjustment to political reality as they perceive it.

In apparent conflict with this *modus vivendi* is the *lex talionis*, the law of Allah, which requires every Muslim believer to exact "an eye for an eye and a tooth for a tooth." The Black Panthers and others who go about openly armed are expressing their anticipation of inevitable (or perhaps continuous) confrontation with the white establishment. The Muslims admit the same expectation of conflict but are prepared to meet it without arms. For the Panthers and other radical groups, the source of corruption which breeds the confrontation is "the system," or "the establishment." Hence, the problem is a political one which can be resolved by displacing the existing system with a more perfect one. For the Muslims, the root of the problem is theological rather than political. The imperfections of the white man's system are but the imperfections of the individual, the race, the religion—writ large on the pages of human intercourse. When every man is observing his proper religion (all black men are by nature Muslims), then every nation will be in its own territory (the white man's home is in Europe), and there will be peace. Short of the ideal, the best possible arrangement is some sort of *detente* permitting a civilized coexistence. Under such an arrangement, life must go on, but it must reflect the Muslim's understanding of Allah's will not only for today, but for tomorrow as well. Hence, the Muslims see no necessary conflict between "submission" to temporary "legal authority" and "retaliation" as required by the *lex talionis.* Civil authority ends where Muslim law begins. A case in point was the assault on the Harlem Mosque by a team of New York policemen allegedly answering a call for help from a detective thought to have been inside the Mosque. [31] Since the presence of weapons in the mosque is prohibited, and the presence of whites is restricted, the Muslim response was predictable. When the shooting was over, one officer had been killed and several others wounded. The Muslims in the Mosque were reported "unarmed" by the press. The black community was outraged, and the threat of a riot hung over New York City for several days.

The Urban League slogan, "Not Charity but a Chance," could be adopted by the Muslims without change, but the Muslims would be quick to point out, as they have on occasion, that the Urban League begs for a chance from the white man, while they want black people to create their own chances. None of the Muslim enterprises is funded by such agencies of the federal government as the Small Business Administration, or by private loans from white institutions, the Muslims say. [32] "Charity," declares Muhammad, "begins at home. We have built on the nickels and dimes of my followers. But we have not even scratched the surface of what black people can do when they learn to come together and go for self. We could become a mighty nation overnight." The ABCs of Elijah's Islam are disarmingly simple: Know yourself and your kind; protect yourself and your kind; do for yourself and your kind. It is a pragmatic philosophy born of the common black experience in the ghettos of America, and while it is susceptible to extreme chauvinism, it was undoubtedly functional for the times and the circumstances which gave it birth. The degree to which it has remained functional and attractive would seem to be a commentary on the rate as well as the degree of change in the options for meaningful black survival in America.

The theological basis of the Muslim social doctrine reflects in part the extraordinary degree of their alienation from the American mainstream. The contemporary preoccupation of black Christians with "black theology" and "black religion" suggests a deepening sense of estrangement throughout the whole black community, and the increasing acceptability of the notion of separate identity and its implied differentiated destiny. The Black Muslims and the black Christians alike reject the white Christian's age-old presumption of superiority, and "black theology," Christian *or* Muslim, is in part a response to the Blackamerican's interpretation of the way the white American Christian perceives reality and orders his system of values. Black Muslims and black Christians are painfully aware that the characteristic posture of whites toward Blacks has been the presumption of white-*over*-black with its derivative train of discomfitures for Blacks.

Religion deals with ultimates, and the Muslim willingness to locate the white man's racial proclivities in the *nature* of the individual rather than in his behavior, or in the institutions through which those proclivities may be expressed, is an attempt to settle once and for all the question of when the white man will get over his racial hang-ups. The answer implied is "Never!" Since it is his "nature," "the white man can no more treat you like a brother," Malcolm X once said, "than a bulldog can sit down with a rabbit and have tea." The Christian advocates of black religion have not gone that far. From the black Christian perspective, the white man may be degraded and corrupt but he is never completely beyond the pale of grace. His weakness is the weakness common to all men, though differently expressed. The Muslim's simplistic view obviates the question of "why" the white man's weakness is consistently expressed as the hatred of black people and dismisses the options for change or negotiation. The Muslim movement proceeds on the assumption that since the white man's perfidy derives from a peculiar defect in his nature, his hatred of Blacks (and his opposition to Allah) are finalized for all time. He is a literal "devil" and will always behave as such. His every "good" is an aspect of his larger strategy of evil. Hence, the Nation of Islam must be ever wary of the white man's tricknology, but must get on with the fulfillment of its own destiny. Allah and history are believed to be on Islam's side, and the strategies of the civil rights organizations, of the militant reformers and others, are all doomed to failure because they misconceive the nature of the problem.

## V. THE DEEPER CAUSE

"Minorities," Gordon Allport has written with wisdom and insight, "are damned if they seek assimilation, damned if they don't. . . . What is needed is freedom for both assimilation and pluralism to occur according to the needs and desires of the minority group itself."[33]

The Blackamerican has chosen to be both "Black" and "American." It is a deliberate, self-conscious choice with due consideration to the reality of the options available, as well as to the full meaning of the choice. His energies have been marshaled to achieve this goal. He does not want segregation or separation; he wants only to be an American citizen, with the rights and privileges of every other citizen. He is not shaken in this determination, even though he is receiving no significant support from any powerful factor of the white community. His prolonged and baffling failure to secure his rights does, however, leave him prey to frustration and anxiety.

There is general agreement among Blackamericans that the white man has failed to demonstrate any real capacity for genuine brotherhood and justice. There is a widespread belief that the white man will *never* of his own accord accept nonwhites as his equals in status and opportunity, in America or elsewhere. There is a broad conviction that—as the Muslims insist—the white man has deliberately "written the black people out of history," refusing to recognize the Black Man's contribution to the human enterprise, and most especially, to the development of America. Blacks are bitterly aware of the lack of recognition, official or otherwise, given to their extensive, and sometimes critical, participation in the shaping of history in America. They know that the history of America is in significant instances the history of Blackamericans. They know too, that any future America may have is inevitably intertwined with the future of Blackamericans—and vice versa. They are weary of waiting for the white man to learn what they have known so long.

Of the twenty-five to thirty million Blacks in this country, not many are prepared to repudiate the Christian faith as the Muslims demand, but there is a significant if silent reservoir of sympathy for the Muslims' racial doctrines and an increasing hostility for the white man. Acceptance of Elijah Muhammad in the black community has been far from universal, yet his influence in changing black self-concepts and fostering black pride among the masses has been unmatched by any individual since Marcus Garvey. The Black Muslims were the vanguard of the new black ethnicity. They were the first to accept their blackness and turn it into an asset. The world around us is in cataclysm. It is hard to wait until tomorrow for what everyone else has today, especially in an age when tomorrow may never arrive. The Black Muslim Movement represents one attempt to break out of this bondage of discrimination and despair, which threatens the peace and casts a dark shadow over the happiness and prosperity of all America.

Some Americans may believe with Harry Ashmore that "the Muslims are not themselves going anywhere."[34] Many others take comfort in a belief that the Movement has reached the zenith of its membership and influence. Perhaps it has. But the Muslims are embarrassing to both the white and the black communities, for they call attention to a situation so irrational and so ugly that neither side wants to face it squarely. It is therefore to be expected that many people wish the Muslims would simply fold their tents and go away, and that they will try to hex them away by refusing to admit that they really exist.

But the Muslims do exist. They do attract the support of the black masses in the ghetto and of an increasing number of intellectuals who have given up in disgust and despair. And they will continue to expand as long as institutionalized racism is permitted to flourish in America. True, the Movement in its present form may be crushed by an embarrassed and apprehensive citizenry. It can be stopped today by "white backlash" or "law and order" initiatives. However, in shattering the Movement we shall not eliminate the tension and the need which created and catapulted it to its present momentum. Out of the ashes of the Black Muslims, another "black" specter will inevitably rise to challenge us. We can destroy the Muslim organization as the visible symbol of our deeper sickness, but that will hardly make us well. Nor will it dispel the rising dissatisfaction with the way things are, and the deepening conviction that this is not the way things have to be.

# Notes

*Preface*

1. See Erdmann D. Beynon, "The Voodoo Cult Among Negro Migrants in Detroit," *The American Journal of Sociology,* XLIII, No. 6 (May 1938), 894.

*Introduction*

1. " 'Resource scarcity' is a condition in which the supply of desired objects (or states of affairs) is limited so that parties may not have *all* they want of anything." " 'Position scarcity' is a condition in which . . . a role cannot be simultaneously occupied or performed by two or more actors, and different prescribed behavior cannot be carried out simultaneously." Raymond W. Mack and Richard C. Snyder, "The Analysis of Social Conflict–Toward an Overview and Synthesis," *Conflict Resolution,* 1, No. 2 (1957), 218.

2. See St. Clair Drake, "Some Observations on Interethnic Conflict as One Type of Intergroup Conflict," op. cit., p. 162.

3. See Melville J. Herskovits, *The Myth of the Negro Past* (Boston: Beacon Press, 1941), pp. 86-109.

4. I.e., American Negroes.

5. "Armageddon" is Greek transliteration from Hebrew "Har-Magedon."

6. *Muhammad Speaks,* July 31, 1962.

7. For an excellent interpretation of the American creed see Arnold Rose, *The Negro in America* (Boston: Beacon Press, 1957), pp. 1 ff.

*Chapter 1*

1. Mike Wallace and Louis Lomax, "The Hate that Hate Produced," *Newsbeat.* New York: WNTA-TV, July 10, 1959. This excerpt is from the unpublished typescript of the television documentary.

2. The author of *The Trial* is Louis X, a talented and versatile young Bostonian. Before joining the Muslims, Louis (whose Christian name was Gene Walcott) had been a popular calypso singer and musician, and had attended college in North Carolina. He is now Minister of the Boston Temple of Islam. He and his family were previously Episcopalians; his wife is a former Roman Catholic.

3. A companion piece, also by Louis X, is *Orgena,* which seems to be "A Negro" spelled backwards. *Orgena* satirizes "Americanized" Negroes in such stereotyped roles as dope addicts, alcoholics, flashily dressed businessmen, educators,

and the "400 set." This is what the white man has made of them since "kidnapping them from their ancient cultures three hundred years ago." Near the end of the play, the Muslim faith and the teachings of Elijah Muhammad restore to the Black Man the traditional dignity and intelligence he once enjoyed in his own great civilization. *Orgena* and *The Trial* are usually staged on a single bill.

4. Malcolm X, "The Truth About the Black Muslims." An address at the Boston University School of Theology, May 24, 1960. Italics supplied.

5. *Time*, August 10, 1959.

6. The *Washington Post*, October 17, 1971.

7. The *New York Times*, January 16, 1972.

8. *Muhammad Speaks*, January 28, 1972.

9. From a series of street interviews by the author.

10. Nat Hentoff, *The Reporter*, August 4, 1960, p. 40.

11. Arnold J. Toynbee, *A Study of History* (2d ed.; London: Oxford University Press, 1935), I, 224.

12. W. Lloyd Warner and Leo Srole, *The Social Systems of American Ethnic Groups* (New Haven: Yale University Press, 1945), p. 285.

13. Mike Wallace and Lou Lomax. "The Hate that Hate Produced," *Newsbeat.* New York: WNTA-TV, July 10, 1959. [Typescript of a television documentary.]

14. See George E. Simpson, "Recent Political Developments in Race Relations," *The Phylon,* Second Quarter (Summer 1958), p. 209. Cf. Liston Pope, *The Kingdom Beyond Caste* (New York: Friendship Press, 1957), pp. 64-68.

15. The rejoicing at the Supreme Court's overturning of legalized segregation in American schools was not quite universal. Says Liston Pope, "Even the Afrikans-language press in the Union of South Africa gave extensive attention to it, while generally denying that the situation in the Union permitted movement in any similar direction." Op. cit., p. 11.

16. "Every part of the United States comes under federal executive orders that forbid discrimination on *some* jobs. Fifteen states have laws against discrimination on *most* jobs. Thirty-seven cities, many of them outside these fifteen states, have city ordinances against discrimination on *most* jobs." Quoted from *Your Rights Under State and Local Fair Employment Practice Laws* (American Federation of Labor and Congress of Industrial Organizations Publication No. 23 [Washington: 1956]), p. 2.

17. See William Peters, *The Southern Temper* (New York: Doubleday & Co., 1959), pp. 225-227. Quoting from the *Harvard Business Review* (1957), Peters points out *inter alia* that "The median income of all United States Negro families is 56 percent of the income of white families—$2,410 a year as opposed to $4,339. In the South, where conditions are worse, the median income of Negro families is only about 49 percent of what white families take in." See also Mr. Peters' discussion on the dearth of Negroes in federal employment in the South, pp. 241-266. In spite of federal safeguards against discrimination, Peters finds that ". . . with rare exceptions, Negroes are not employed above the level of janitorial and labor services by federal agencies in the South." Cf. the *New York Times,* November 16, 1959, p. 1: "A Presidential committee has made what it considers 'significant breakthroughs' in obtaining skilled jobs for Negroes in the South. . . . Instead of asking contractors for a generalized and practically unenforceable commitment not to discriminate, the committee is now seeking a specific promise to hire Negroes for new jobs immediately. . . . The committee's new policy has also

had results in Border and Northern areas where Negroes had had a hard time breaking out of menial factory work. . . . [But] no one on the committee suggests that these [cited] cases are enough to make a fundamental change in job opportunities for large numbers of Negroes."

18. See *Ebony,* September 1960.

19. For several years, the reported number of lynchings has declined. However, the infamous lynching of Emmett Till, a Negro boy visiting in Mississippi in 1955, and the lynching of Mack Parker, another Negro in Mississippi, in April 1959, have again focused international attention upon the continuing tenuousness of civil security for Negroes in parts of this country. The Federal Bureau of Investigation, called into the Parker case at the request of the Mississippi governor, spent $80,000 in an extended investigation of the lynching. The U.S. Attorney General described the case as "one of the most complete investigations I've ever seen conducted." The FBI report was turned over to a Mississippi grand jury, which declined to call a single FBI witness and adjourned without returning any indictment whatever. See the *New York Times,* November 18, 1959, p. 1. Many Negroes consider the Parker lynching to be little more than "official murder." Parker was left in an unguarded, small-town jail under circumstances which seemed to invite his abduction and murder. However, killings in this category are often at the hands of the arresting or detention officials themselves, who find it necessary to shoot their unarmed prisoners "in self-defense" or "to prevent escape." See Peters, *The Southern Temper,* pp. 214-218, for a description of a double "self-defense" killing by a Southern sheriff.

20. "The campaign of the whites for 'white supremacy' has, on the whole, been successful. That is, the Negro has been put and kept in a subordinate status. The actual story of the Negro since slavery is the story of this attitude in practice." Abram Kardiner and Lionel Ovesey, *The Mark of Oppression* (New York: W.W. Norton & Co., 1951), p. 61.

21. The *Christian Science Monitor* (Boston), January 27, 1960, p.4.

22. Ibid.

23. E.D. Beynon, "The Voodoo Cult Among Negro Migrants in Detroit," *The American Journal of Sociology,* XLIII (July, 1937–May, 1938), 896. Nadim Makdisi, editor of the Voice of America's Arabic service, points out that the second largest Moslem community in America is concentrated in the Detroit-Dearborn area.

24. Beynon, op. cit., p. 895. From an interview with Sister Denke Majied, formerly Mrs. Lawrence Adams.

25. Ibid.

26. Ibid., p 895.

27. Ibid, p. 896. From an interview with Brother Challar Sharrieff.

28. Ibid. From an interview with Sister Carrie Mohammad.

29. Ibid.

30. Ibid., p. 897.

31. *The New Crusader* (Chicago), August 15, 1959, p. 1.

32. Beynon, op. cit., p. 899.

33. Ibid., p. 902

34. Ibid., p. 901.

35. Ibid., p. 897.

36. Ibid., p. 904.

37. "The Truth about the Black Muslims." An address at the Boston University School of Theology, May 24, 1960.

38. *New York Courier,* August 6, 1960.

39. See Beynon, op. cit., p. 897.

40. Ibid., p. 898.

41. Temples or missions have also been reported in Cuba, Hawaii, and Jamaica, but the report is unconfirmed.

42. As indicated, this sampling may not be a completely reliable index. In the first place, it is too small, and the ecological distribution of the respondents (Atlanta, 34; Chicago, 111; Boston 183; New York, 133) does not present an adequate relation to the distribution of the Muslim membership. Secondly, the sampling was done piecemeal over an extended period; and since names or other positive identification could not be used, it is possible that some persons responded more than once.

43. Beynon (op. cit., 898), asserts that "practically none of them [the Muslims] had been in the North prior to the collapse of the Marcus Garvey movement." But there are certainly a number of ex-Garveyites in the movement today, perhaps as many as 10,000-15,000.

44. Beynon, op. cit., p. 905.

45. Ibid.

46. Ibid.

47. Ibid.

48. E. Franklin Frazier, *Black Bourgeoisie* (Glencoe, Ill.: The Free Press, 1957), p. 120.

49. The *Chicago Sun,* October 24, 1942.

50. From a series of interviews with Muslim leaders in Chicago and New York.

51. *Color and Conscience* (New York: Harper and Brothers, 1946), p. 191.

52. Malcolm X, "The Truth About the Black Muslims" (*Supra 37*).

53. Malcolm X at Boston University Human Relations Center, February 15, 1960.

54. James Hicks, editor of the New York *Amsterdam News* and a close observer of the movement, says: "They have high regard for their women and fight like hell for each other." *The Reporter*, August 4, 1960, p. 39.

55. Malcolm X at Boston University Human Relations Center, February 15, 1960.

56. *Muhammad Speaks,* October 29, 1971.


Chapter 2

1. Edmund D. Cronon, *Black Moses* (Madison: The University of Wisconsin Press, 1955), p. 66.

2. Arnold Rose, *The Negro in America* (Boston: Beacon Press, 1948), pp. 17-18.

3. Ibid., p. 16.

4. Ibid., pp. 11-12.

5. E. Franklin Frazier, *The Negro in the United States* (New York: The Macmillan Co., 1949), p. 88. Quoting Lionel Kennedy and Thomas Parker, *An Official Report of the Trials of Sundry Negroes Charged with an Attempt to Raise an Insurrection in the State of South Carolina.*

6. W. Lloyd Warner and Leo Srole, *The Social Systems of American Ethnic Groups* (New Haven: Yale University Press, 1945), p. 295.

7. Abram Kardiner and Lionel Ovesey, *The Mark of Oppression* (New York:

W.W. Norton & Co., 1951), p. 39. But see a somewhat broader concept of ethnocentrism in Brewton Berry, *Race and Ethnic Relations* (Houghton, 1951), p. 77. Says Berry, "The ethnic group is a human group bound together by ties of cultural homogeneity.... Above all, there is a consciousness of kind, a we-feeling. The ethnic group may even regard itself as a race, but the fact of such common descent is of much less importance than the *assumption* that there is a blood relationship, and the myths of the group develop to substantiate such an assumption."

8. For discussion on race, see the following: Ethel Alpenfels, *Sense and Nonsense About Race* (New York: Friendship Press, 1957); Ruth Benedict, *Race: Science and Politics* (New York: Viking Press, 1950); Franz Boas, *Anthropology and Modern Life* (New York: W.W. Norton & Co., 1928); J. Deniker, *The Races of Man* (London: Walter Scott Publishers, 1913); Oscar Handlin, *Race and Nationality in American Life* (New York: Doubleday & Co., 1957); F.H. Hankins, *The Racial Basis of Civilization* (New York: Alfred Knopf, 1926); Ben J. Marais, *Colour, the Unsolved Problem of the West* (Capetown: Howard B. Timmins, 1952); George E. Simpson and J. Milton Yinger, *Racial and Cultural Minorities in the United States,* 1st ed. rev. (New York: Harper and Brothers, 1958); W. Ashley Montague, *Man's Most Dangerous Myth* (New York: Columbia University Press, 1942); Gordon Allport, *The Nature of Prejudice* (New York: Doubleday, 1958).

9. "A 'stock' may be defined as the descendants of a large group of people who once lived in the same geographical area and shared certain physical traits that are inherited. These traits set them apart from other groups who have other combinations of physical characteristics." Alpenfels, *Sense and Nonsense About Race,* p. 19.

10. See Gunnar Myrdal, "Race and Ancestry," *An American Dilemma* (New York: Harper & Bros., 1944), pp. 113-136. See also John Hope Franklin, *From Slavery to Freedom* (New York: Alfred A. Knopf, 1956); E. Franklin Frazier, *Negro in the U.S.,* n6.

11. W.E.B. Du Bois, "Three Centuries of Discrimination." *The Crisis,* LIV (December 1947), 362-363. Cf. Melville J. Herskovits: "The word 'Negro,' as employed in the United States has no biological meaning.... a social definition takes precedence over the biological reality." *Man and His Works* (New York: Alfred A. Knopf, 1950), p. 144.

12. Melvin Conant, *Race Issues on the World Scene* (Honolulu: University of Hawaii Press, 1955), p. 119.

13. See Michael Clark's comprehensive article on the "Rise in Racial Extremism," the *New York Times,* January 25, 1960, p. 1.

*Chapter 3*

1. Drew was born in 1866. For a description of his movement, see Arthur H. Fauset, "Moorish Science Temple of America" in J. Milton Yinger, *Religion, Society, and the Individual* (New York: The Macmillan Co., 1957), pp. 498-507; or see E. Franklin Frazier, *The Negro in the U.S.,* pp. 358-359.

2. For an enlightening discussion of this nineteenth-century doctrine, recently resurrected by some American Christians, see Everett Tilson, *Segregation and the Bible* (Nashville: The Abingdon Press, 1958), pp. 23-26.

3. Arthur H. Fauset. Quoted in Yinger, *Religion, Society, and the Individual,* p. 498.

4. Yinger, op. cit., p. 500.

5. Ibid., p. 504.

6. Ibid.

7. Dr. George W. Bagnall in a discourse entitled, "The Madness of Marcus Garvey," quoted in Edmund Cronon, *Black Moses* (Madison: University of Wisconsin Press, 1948), p. 107. Cronon's book is probably the best recent study of the Garvey Movement.

8. J. Saunders Redding, *They Came in Chains* (Philadelphia: J.B. Lippincott Co., 1950), p. 261.

9. John Hope Franklin, *From Slavery to Freedom* (New York: Alfred A. Knopf, 1956), p. 472.

10. Ibid., pp. 473-474.

11. Ibid., p. 471.

12. Cronon, *Black Moses*, p. 16.

13. Ibid., p. 17.

14. Redding, *They Came in Chains*, p. 259.

15. Cronon, *Black Moses*, p. 41.

16. Garvey's understanding of the American caste system was probably faulty. In his native Jamaica, the mulattoes formed a more or less distinct class between the whites and the unmixed blacks. In America, a Negro is commonly identified as anyone having any Negro ancestry whatever; and all Negroes of whatever color are relegated to a common caste.

17. Cronon, op. cit., p. 44.

18. Ibid., p. 47.

19. Ibid.

20. Quoted in ibid., p. 65.

21. Ibid., p. 67.

22. Ibid., p. 70.

23. Ibid., p. 185.

24. Ibid., p. 187.

25. Ibid., p. 184.

26. Ibid., pp. 124-125.

27. Elmer T. Clark, *The Small Sects in America* (New York: Abingdon Press, 1949), p. 172.

28. Cronon, op. cit., p. 178.

29. Ibid., p. 179.

30. Ibid., pp. 129-132.

31. See E. Franklin Frazier, *Black Bourgeoisie* (Glencoe, Ill.: The Free Press, 1957), p. 123. These Negroes "who were acquiring middle-class status," Frazier says, "did not only regard his program as fantastic, but they did not want to associate with his illiterate poor black followers, especially since West Indians were prominent in the movement." See also, J. Saunders Redding, op. cit., pp. 260-261.

32. See John Hope Franklin, op. cit., p. 482.

33. Frazier, op. cit., p. 260.

34. Cronon, op. cit., pp. 113 ff.

35. Ibid., p. 111.

36. Ibid.

## Chapter 4

1. The basic doctrines of the Muslims are laid down in a booklet written by

Muhammad and called *The Supreme Wisdom*. This is the primary source book for all that is peculiar to the Muslims and for Muhammad's teachings as they appear in the black press.

2. Malcolm X at the Boston University Human Relations Center, February 15, 1960.

3. *Supreme Wisdom* (2d ed.), pp. 6-7.

4. Ibid., p. 17.

5. Ibid.

6. Ibid., p. 19.

7. Ibid., p. 21.

8. Ibid., p. 27.

9. Ibid.

10. "Mr. Muhammad Speaks," *Pittsburgh Courier*, August 15, 1959.

11. Malcolm X at Boston University Human Relations Center, February 15, 1960.

12. Ibid.

13. *Supreme Wisdom* (2d ed.), p. 33.

14. From a typescript of "The Hate that Hate Produced," a television documentary on the rise of black racism by Mike Wallace and Louis Lomax. *Newsbeat* (New York: WNTA–TV, July 10, 1959).

15. *Muhammad Speaks*, February 11, 1972.

16. "The Hate that Hate Produced," op. cit.

17. "Mr. Muhammad Speaks," *Pittsburgh Courier*, June 16, 1959. Unless otherwise noted, all excerpts from "Mr. Muhammad Speaks" appeared in his column by that title in the *Pittsburgh Courier*.

18. Ibid., May 2, 1959.

19. Ibid.

20. *Supreme Wisdom* (2d ed.), p. 39.

21. Ibid., p. 33.

22. Malcolm X on *Newsbeat*.

23. *Supreme Wisdon*, p. 38.

24. "Mr. Muhammad Speaks," July 4, 1959.

25. Ibid., December 13, 1958.

26. Ibid., July 18, 1959.

27. "Mr. Muhammad Speaks," December 13, 1958.

28. *Supreme Wisdom*, p. 12.

29. Ibid., p. 13.

30. Ibid.

31. Ibid.

32. Ibid., p. 28.

33. Ibid., p. 36.

34. "Mr. Muhammad Speaks," January 17, 1959.

35. Ibid., August 9, 1958.

36. From an interview with Malcolm X.

37. "Mr. Muhammad Speaks," August 22, 1959.

38. Len Holt, "Norfolk News Beat," *Afro-American*, August 13, 1960.

39. See *The Supreme Wisdom*, pp. 21 and 42.

40. Ibid., p. 22.

41. Malcolm X at Boston University Human Relations Center, February 15, 1960.

42. Eric Hoffer, *The True Believer* (New York: New American Library, 1951), pp. 55-56.

43. "Mr. Muhammad Speaks," August 9, 1958.

44. From an interview with Elijah Muhammad, March 4, 1959.

45. *Los Angeles Herald-Dispatch,* February 6, 1958.

46. Ibid., January 16, 1960.

47. Ibid., January 30, 1960.

48. *Muhammad Speaks,* October 29, 1971.

49. *Los Angeles Herald-Dispatch,* February 7, 1959.

50. Ibid., August 8, 1959.

51. Ibid., February 20, 1960.

52. Ibid.

53. *Muhammad Speaks,* February 11, 1972.

54. *Pittsburgh Courier,* August 15, 1959, quoting *U.S. News and World Report* of August 3, 1959.

55. "Mr. Muhammad Speaks," August 9, 1958.

56. *Los Angeles Herald-Dispatch,* January 30, 1960.

57. *Afro-American,* February 20, 1960.

58. Malcolm X on *The Jerry Williams Show,* Boston: Radio Station WMEX, April 2, 1960. From a taped transcription. Italics supplied.

59. Beynon, op. cit., pp. 905-906.

60. Ibid.

61. "Mr. Muhammad Speaks," August 16, 1958.

62. Beynon, op. cit., p. 905.

63. *Los Angeles Herald-Dispatch,* January 16, 1960.

64. *Muhammad Speaks,* November 12, 1971.

65. Ibid., December 10, 1971.

66. *The Islamic News,* July 6, 1959.

67. *Chicago Daily Defender,* March 5, 1960. In a radio interview over Boston's station WMEX on April 2, 1960, Malcolm X called for "nine or ten states."

68. "Mr. Muhammad Speaks," *Los Angeles Herald-Dispatch,* July 16, 1960.

69. "Mr. Muhammad Speaks," *Pittsburgh Courier,* August 2, 1958.

70. Ibid., October 11, 1958.

71. At the Boston University Human Relations Center, February 15, 1960.

72. "Mr. Muhammad Speaks," August 2, 1958.

73. Ibid., May 3, 1958.

74. Ibid., September 6, 1958.

*Chapter 5*

1. See Richard T. La Piere, *Collective Behavior* (New York: McGraw-Hill Book Co., 1938), pp. 504-510. La Piere describes a mass movement as a spatial movement of a considerable portion of the social population to some new, promised land. A movement built around some person or idea (which need not involve spatial relocation) is termed a "messianic movement." The messianic movement is built around a "miracle man" or a "miracle cure" or upon the idea of a "political messiah." "The messianic movement [is] . . . a collective flight from reality . . . following a new form of leadership which will bring health, wealth or happiness. The movement beings with the idea that some person . . . is a messiah who has come to deliver the faithful from whatever it is that ails them."

2. I am indebted to Eric Hoffer, *The True Believer* (New York: New American Library, 1951), for many of the concepts discussed in this and the following sections.

3. Hoffer, pp. 52-53.

4. Ibid., pp. 105-106.

5. Ibid., p. 107.

6. Ibid., p. 104. Hoffer quotes John Morley, *Notes on Politics and History* (New York: Macmillan Company, 1914), pp. 69-70.

7. Ibid., p. 18.

8. Ibid., pp. 85-86.

9. Ibid., p. 86.

10. Ibid., pp. 93-94.

11. *Muhammad Speaks,* January 28, 1972.

12. "The Hate that Hate Produced," *Newsbeat* (New York: WNTA-TV, July 10–17, 1959).

13. *Time,* August 10, 1959.

14. James N. Rhea, *Providence Bulletin,* August 6, 1959.

15. From an interview with Malcolm X.

16. See "Mr. Muhammad Speaks," *The Reader's Digest,* March 1960.

17. From a series of Muslim interviews.

18. See, for example, Arna Bontemps, *Story of the Negro* (New York: Alfred A. Knopf, 1958).

19. From an interview with Minister Louis X.—The Muslim philosophy is limited, and the temple lectures are, without exception, rephrasings of statements already made in printed materials, interviews, or public lectures. For the sake of documentary accuracy, the quotations in this section are drawn from these other sources; but in content and range they faithfully represent the typical—one might almost say, the universal—temple lecture.

20. From an interview with Malcolm X.

21. "Mr. Muhammad Speaks," September 20, 1958.

22. "Mr. Muhammad Speaks," June 6, 1959.

23. Ibid., April 18, 1959.

24. Ibid., May 2, 1959.

25. Ibid.

26. *Supreme Wisdom* (2d ed.), p. 19.

27. Ibid.

28. From a series of interviews with Muslims.

29. Bernard Cushmeer, *This Is the One* (Phoenix, Arizona: Truth Publications, 1970), p. 85.

30. *Supreme Wisdom,* p. 51.

31. A translation by Maulana Muhammad Ali and one by Allama Yusuf Ali are approved for the followers of Elijah Muhammad. Beynon says of Fard that he "used only the Arabic text which he translated and explained to the believers ... [thereby making them] completely dependent upon his interpretation." However, Fard gave his followers texts he himself prepared which were memorized by all converts. (P. 900.)

32. *Los Angeles Herald-Dispatch,* February 20, 1960.

33. Oakland, Los Angeles, San Diego, Detroit, Chicago, Cincinnati, New York, Youngstown, Washington, Atlanta, Newark, Philadelphia, Baltimore, and Miami.

34. *Muhammad Speaks,* November 28, 1969.

35. Beynon, op. cit., p. 903.
36. *Detroit Free Press,* August 14, 1959.
37. Ibid.
38. The *New York Times,* August 25, 1970.
39. The 1971 *Yearbook* of the University of Islam No. 2, p. 10.
40. Ibid., p. 8.
41. Ibid., p. 10.
42. "Mr. Muhammad Speaks," May, 1960.
43. *Los Angeles Herald-Dispatch,* July 16, 1960.
44. Ibid., February 13, 1960.
45. Ibid.
46. Ibid., January 9, 1960.
47. Ibid., July 30, 1960.
48. Ibid., January 9, 1960.


*Chapter 6*

1. *New York Amsterdam News,* July 30, 1960. Reprinted from *The Saturday Review.*
2. An address: "The Truth About the Black Muslims," May 24, 1960.
3. *Denver Post,* August 13, 1959.
4. Malcolm X at Boston University Human Relations Center, February 15, 1960.
5. See *Pittsburgh Courier,* July 19, 1958. Cf. *New York Amsterdam News,* July 12, 1958.
6. Cushmeer, op. cit., p. 26.
7. See *Time,* August 10, 1959.
8. Survey by the author; the results will be published later in an appropriate journal. A small percentage of business and professional men had clients or customers whom they knew to be Muslims. A very small percentage had Muslim friends. None had visited a Muslim temple.
9. *Sepia,* November, 1959, p. 22.
10. Vol. I, No. 1, 1959, pp. 20-21.
11. *Pittsburgh Courier,* September 12, 1959.
12. Ibid., October 24, 1959.
13. *New York Amsterdam News,* March 5, 1960.
14. *The New Crusader,* August 1, 15, 22, 29; September 5, 19, 26; November 28 (all 1959).
15. Ibid., August 29, 1959.
16. Statement issued on August 5, 1959.
17. Quoted in *Pittsburgh Courier,* September 5, 1959.
18. *Chicago Daily Defender,* October 3, 1959.
19. *Los Angeles Herald-Dispatch,* January 30, 1960.
20. Ibid., January 16, 1960.
21. Ibid.
22. *New Jersey Herald News,* January 2, 1960.
23. The *New York Times,* January 25, 1960.
24. Excerpt from a letter to the author, dated February 19, 1960.
25. *Columbus* (Ohio) *Dispatch,* August 10, 1959.
26. *Time,* August 10, 1959.
27. *Los Angeles Herald-Dispatch,* January 9, 1960.

28. Ibid.

29. Malcolm X at Boston University Human Relations Center, February 15, 1960.

30. Ibid.

31. *New York Courier,* July 22, 1960.

32. Elijah Muhammad, *Message to the Blackman* (Chicago: Temple No. 2, 1965), pp. 240-242.

33. *Los Angeles Herald-Dispatch,* March 5, 1960.

34. *New York Amsterdam News,* July 16, 1960.

35. *Indianapolis Times,* August 10, 1959.

36. *Los Angeles Herald-Dispatch,* June 5, 1958.

37. *New York Amsterdam News,* April 26, 1958.

38. The churches involved were St. John's Congregational, Bethel AME, and the Third Baptist Church. Police decided that there had been no breach of the peace, and no arrests were made. The *Springfield Daily News,* February 2, 1959.

39. *Chicago's American,* February 23, 1960.

40. *Pittsburgh Courier,* April 26, 1958.

41. *Muhammad Speaks,* April 4, 1969.

42. The *New York Times,* January 25, 1960.

43. *Pittsburgh Courier,* March 3, 1958.

44. Observed personally by the author.

45. *Sepia,* November, 1959.

46. *Muhammad Speaks,* November 26, 1971.

47. From an interview with Malcolm X.

48. *Detroit Jewish News,* August 21, 1959.

49. *Currents,* No. 2, February 1972.

50. *Muhammad Speaks,* February 4, 1972,

51. Ibid., October 22, 1971.

52. Ibid., February 4, 1972.

53. *The Muslim World,* Vol. L, No. 1, January 1960.

54. The (Westchester, New York) *Observer,* April 19, 1958. See also *The Moslem World and the U.S.A.* August, September, 1956.

55. *Muhammad Speaks,* April 4, 1969.

56. *New York Amsterdam News,* April 4, 1958.

57. Ibid., May 3, 1958.

58. Malcolm X at Boston University Human Relations Center, February 15, 1960.

59. Ibid.

60. "The Truth About the Black Muslims," an address by Malcolm X.

61. Ibid.

62. *Time,* August 10, 1959, p. 25.

63. The *Christian Science Monitor,* May 16, 1960.

64. Ibid., August 29, 1959.

65. The *Denver Post,* August 13, 1959.

66. *Providence Bulletin,* August 6, 1959.

67. The *Boston Herald,* February 8, 1960.

68. The *Detroit Free Press,* August 14, 1959.

69. *The Reporter,* August 4, 1960, p. 40.

70. The *Boston Globe,* May 12, 1960.

71. Cushmeer, op. cit., pp. 39-40.
72. Ibid., p. 95.
73. Ibid., p. 90.


*Chapter 7*

1. *Muhammad Speaks,* December 25, 1970.
2. 1950 population, 4,480.
3. Beynon, op. cit., p. 903.
4. Elijah Muhammad, *The Supreme Wisdom: Solution to the So-called Ne-groes' Problem* (2d ed.; Chicago: The University of Islam, 1957), p. 15. This booklet first appeared as "Volume I" in 1955 or 1956. The initial volume was revised and somewhat systematized in a "First Edition" printed in February 1957. An identical "Second Edition" was printed in April 1957.
5. "Mr. Muhammad Speaks," May 1960.
6. *Supreme Wisdom,* p. 43.
7. Nat Hentoff, "Elijah in the Wilderness," *The Reporter,* August 4, 1960.
8. *Muhammad Speaks,* November 7, 1969.
9. *Supreme Wisdom* (2d ed.), p. 21.
10. *The Islamic News,* July 6, 1959.
11. Ibid.
12. "Mr. Muhammad Speaks," May 1960.
13. September 22, 1942, p. 9.
14. Ibid.
15. The *Chicago Sun,* October 24, 1942.
16. Malcolm explained that since all Black Men are from the tribe of Shabazz, his "Muslim" name is theoretically available to any member of the sect.
17. Alex Haley, *Reader's Digest,* March 1960.
18. *Sepia,* November 1959, p. 26.
19. Nat Hentoff,"Elijah in the Wilderness," op. cit., p. 39.
20. Ibid.
21. From unpublished notes by Alex Haley.
22. The *New York Times,* December 2, 1963.
23. *Muhammad Speaks,* May 28, 1971.
24. Ibid., June 5, 1971.
25. Ibid., February 11, 1972.
26. The *New York Times,* January 21, 1972.
27. *Newsweek,* January 31, 1972.
28. *Muhammad Speaks,* November 12, 1971.
29. Ibid., November 12, 1971.
30. Ibid., January 28, 1972.
31. Ibid., November 26, 1971.
32. Ibid., January 28, 1972.
33. Beynon, op. cit., p. 902.
34. *Muhammad Speaks,* April 4, 1969.
35. Ibid., February 4, 1972.
36. Beynon, op. cit., p. 903.
37. *Chicago's American,* January 18, 1958, and February 22, 1960.
38. The *Pittsburgh Courier,* January 18, 1958.

39. *Los Angeles Herald-Dispatch,* February 18, 1960.

40. Ibid.

41. *Chicago's American,* February 23, 1960.

42. *Los Angeles Herald-Dispatch,* February 18, 1960.

43. Ibid.

44. Ibid., February 20, 1960.

45. Ibid., February 18, 1960.

*Chapter 8*

1. Polygamy and snake-handling are common examples. Also, the courts will usually enforce the education of children up to age sixteen, and they have uniformly overridden religious objections to hospital care and such medical attention as blood transfusions, while prohibiting religious "healers" from claiming professional status.

2. See *New York Amsterdam News,* November 7, 1959.

3. *Muhammad Speaks,* October 17, 1969.

4. Ibid., February 4, 1972.

5. Ibid.

6. Ibid.

7. Ibid., February 11, 1972.

8. Ibid., October 29, 1971.

9. Cf. Hadley Contril, *The Psychology of Social Movements* (New York: John Wiley & Sons, Inc., 1941, pp. 169-210.

10. Emile Durkheim, *The Elementary Forms of Religious Life,* trans. by Joseph Ward Swain (Glencoe, Ill.: The Free Press, 1947), p. 24.

11. Ibid., p. 36.

12. Ibid., p. 37. Cf. J. Milton Yinger, *Religion, Society, and the Individual* (New York: The Macmillan Company, 1957), p. 14.

13. See Durkheim, op. cit., p. 47.

14. Ernst Troeltsch, *The Social Teaching of the Christian Churches,* trans. by Olive Wyon (London: George Allen & Unwin Ltd., 1931), 331.

15. H. Richard Niebuhr, *The Social Sources of Denominationalism* (New York: Henry Holt & Company, 1929), pp. 65-67. Cited in Yinger, *Religion, Society, and the Individual,* p. 151.

16. Yinger modifies Troeltsch's dichotomy of church and sect into a six-fold typology: universal church, ecclesia, denomination, established sect, sect, and cult. The first five are merely subdivisions of Troeltsch's categories and are not substantively significant in evaluating the Black Muslim Movement.

17. J. Milton Yinger, *Religion in the Struggle for Power* (Durham: Duke University Press, 1946), p. 22.

18. Yinger, *Religion, Society, and the Individual,* p. 155.

19. Ibid.

20. Ibid., p. 154.

21. See Elmer T. Clark, *The Small Sects in America* (New York: Abingdon Press, 1949), p. 14.

22. See also "The Legalistic or Objectivist Sects," ibid., pp. 23-24.

23. *Supreme Wisdom,* p. 4. See also the Introduction to *The Supreme Wisdom,* in which a Pakistani Moslem defends Muhammad's brand of Islam as appropriate for racial circumstances in this country.

24. For a discussion of this Moslem "heresy," see Charles S. Braden, "Moslem Missions in America," *Religion in Life,* Summer, 1959.

25. Wilfred Cantwell Smith, *Modern Islam in India* (London: Victor Gollancz Ltd., 1946), p. 299.

26. Braden, op. cit., *supra.*

27. There follows a lengthy description of the ritual and ceremony incident to entering the Holy City and of the Kaaba, or Black Stone. *Los Angeles Herald-Dispatch,* January 30, 1960.

28. Ibid., January 2, 1960.

29. *The Islamic News,* July 6, 1959.

30. *Los Angeles Herald-Dispatch,* February 2, 1958.

31. *Pittsburgh Courier,* April 15, 1958.

32. Ibid., August 15, 1959.

33. Ibid.

34. *Los Angeles Herald-Dispatch,* February 20, 1960.

## Chapter 9

1. Arnold and Caroline Rose, *America Divided* (New York: Alfred A. Knopf, 1948), p. 218.

2. *New York Courier,* August 20, 1960.

3. Arnold and Caroline Rose, op. cit., p. 219.

4. See Carl Wittke, *We Who Built America* (New York: Prentice Hall, 1939), for a systematic cataloguing of various national groups in the United States, their newspapers and societies.

5. Arnold and Caroline Rose, op. cit., p. 233.

6. Ibid.

7. Ibid., p. 234.

8. Paul A. Walter, Jr., *Race and Culture Relations* (New York: McGraw-Hill Book Co., Inc., 1952), p. 325.

9. Ibid., p. 338.

10. Ibid., p. 328.

11. E. Franklin Frazier, *Black Bourgeoisie,* op. cit., p. 87.

12. Mays and Nicholson, *The Negro's Church.* Quoted in Simpson and Yinger, *Racial and Cultural Minorities in the United States,* op. cit., p. 583.

13. "Relative Route to Absolute," *Time,* January 18, 1960, p. 48. Cf. Liston Pope, *The Kingdom Beyond Caste* (New York: Friendship Press, 1957), p. 117.

14. Arnold M. Rose, *The Negro's Morale* (Minneapolis: The University of Minnesota Press, 1949), p. 98.

15. Simpson and Yinger, *Racial and Cultural Minorities in the United States,* p. 582.

16. Frazier, *Black Bourgeoisie,* op. cit., p. 88.

17. Simpson and Yinger, op. cit.

18. Alpha Phi Alpha, 27,000; Kappa Alpha Psi, 20,000; Omega Psi Phi, 20,000; Phi Beta Sigma, 11,605; Alpha Kappa Alpha, 20,000; Delta Sigma Theta, 21,000. Harry Hansen (ed.), *The World Almanac* (New York: *New York World Telegram,* 1960), pp. 489-490. Figures for Zeta Phi Beta and Sigma Gamma Rho were not included in the data offered by this source. The writer offers 15,000 as a minimum estimate based on information from members of these sororities.

19. Frazier, *The Negro in the United States,* p. 382.

20. Ibid.

21. Black power is undefined in the sense that no substantial agreement exists on what it is. Long after the term was popularized, Carmichael and Charles Hamilton defined it as "a call for black people in this country to unite, to recognize their heritage, to build a sense of community . . . to define their own goals." Stokely Carmichael and Charles V. Hamilton, *Black Power: The Politics of Liberation in America* (New York: Random House, 1968), p. 44.

22. See C. Eric Lincoln, "Anxiety, Fear and Integration," *Phylon: Journal of Race and Culture,* September 1960.

23. Whether assimilation presupposed amalgamation is, I believe, purely academic. Amalgamation is a biological phenomenon, and in the United States it is also a well-documented social fact. Further, amalgamation is cognizant of neither "integration" nor "assimilation"; it is oblivious of both.

24. W.L. Warner and P.S. Lunt, *Status System of a Modern Community* (New Haven: Yale University Press, 1942), pp. 285-286.

25. J. Saunders Redding, *They Came in Chains* (New York: J.B. Lippincott, 1950), p. 225.

26. National Council of Churches, *Information Service,* February 23, 1957, quoting the *Independent,* p. 2.

27. Redding, op. cit., p. 255.

28. Interview with the Reverend Mr. McDaniel.

29. Redding, op. cit., p. 229.

30. See C. Eric Lincoln, "The Strategy of a Sit-In," *The Reporter,* January 6, 1961, pp. 20-23.

31. *Muhammad Speaks,* April 14, 1972.

32. In April of 1972, the Muslims announced a three-million-dollar loan from the government of Libya.

33. *The Nature of Prejudice,* pp. 233-234.

34. The *Boston Globe,* May 12, 1960.

# Index